Investigative Methods

ART BUCKWALTER

BUTTERWORTH PUBLISHERS
Boston • London
Sydney • Wellington • Durban • Toronto

Library of Congress Cataloging in Publication Data

Buckwalter, Art.
    Investigative methods.
    Bibliography: p.
    Includes index.
    1. Detectives.   2. Criminal investigation — Methodology.   I. Title.
HV8085.B83   1983   363.2'5   83-13509
ISBN 0-409-95078-5

Butterworth Publishers
80 Montvale Avenue
Stoneham, MA 02180

10 9 8 7 6 5 4 3

Printed in the United States of America

Contents

Preface

During my tenure as Director of an academy for private investigators, it was my privilege to be in daily contact with career investigators and to learn from them the practical principles of the profession. The need to create a seventy-syllabus course in the Fundamentals of Professional Investigation for the academy led to extensive personal research in public and law libraries to enhance teaching of basic techniques and methods.

Shortly after completion of this course, which became the basis for the academy's successful training of investigators, I was asked to publish my findings in book form for the benefit of those entering any field of private investigation, and as a reference work for those already in service. Obviously, the wide range of material covered by the course could never be contained in one book; that would require a number of volumes comprising a small reference library. My work at the academy, however, precluded the undertaking of such a project.

Since leaving the academy I have devoted more time to research in this field and to writing about the world of the private investigator. The four volumes on investigation, of which this is one, are the result. These volumes in no way reproduce any of the courses previously written. They are more in the nature of an instructional text or source of information. They concentrate on fundamental methods, techniques, and procedures used by investigators in their ceaseless quest to discover the truth about matters under investigation.

Fundamental legal and professional principles are inherent in investigation. The techniques reviewed in these volumes covering both civil and criminal investigations are dealt with from the viewpoint of private investigators and their potential for contributing to the cause of right and justice. Varied means are considered by which investigators obtain the relevant, evidential facts to present to clients or before a court of law or other tribunal. Adequate knowledge of professional techniques is essential to effective investigation.

Mark Twain once facetiously observed: "Adam was the only man who, when he had said a good thing, knew that nobody had said it before him." Any writer owes a debt of gratitude to the wisdom imparted by those who have gone before and by his contemporaries. I am indebted to a host of writers and investigators in many disciplines—many of whom are quoted and referenced in these volumes—for the insights and information they have provided to enhance the educational value of this work.

The reader may find some new ideas along with restatement of tested techniques and clarification of other methods. The author's main objective is to provide a practical—and one hopes interesting—guide to the fundamental techniques of the art and science of investigation. The material has been gleaned from my own observations, from my association with private investigators and discussion with them of techniques and procedures, and from many hours of research into works that deal directly or indirectly with the methods and strategies of this intriguing profession. It is hoped that these volumes on investigation may prove valuable to those who seek to pursue the highest ethical and professional achievements of a career in private investigation as well as to all those whose interest is not career-oriented.

To my wife, Doreen, I am indebted for the typing of the final copy of the manuscript for the publishers, and for her valued assistance in proofreading. In addition to her full-time employment as an executive secretary, she has given long hours to this task. Illustrations appearing in two of the volumes in the series were drawn by Patty McGrath and Lew Harrisson of Los Angeles.

As I sit at my typewriter in my office on the ninth floor of a Wilshire Boulevard office building in Los Angeles, and occasionally pause to look out over a vast area of this city, I am painfully reminded of the increasing crime, fraud, brutality, and inhumanity of man to man that hovers like a curse over the great cities of our nation, and even casts its sinister shadow over rural areas. Evil and pathetic forces ever threaten to blot out the sunshine of human rights, human liberties, human happiness, and even human lives. Surely as these increasing shadows grow, so also will grow the demand for professionally trained and qualified practicing investigators who will help preserve our justice, our security, and our liberties.

Introduction

To enable the reader to put this volume of the series on investigation in proper perspective, a very brief preview of the contents of four books is in order.

One book delves into the private investigator's world with a look at the many facets of investigation and its methodology. It deals with both human and paper sources of information, and the principles and problems of investigative observation, description, and identification.

Another book in the series highlights investigators' search for evidence. What is evidence? Where is it found? What are the criteria of its admissibility? The volume deals with the competence and credibility of witnesses; the importance of the words and signatures of evidential, questioned, and forged documents; and the numerous kinds of physical evidence. The recording and reporting of evidence and the photographing of all visual evidence are all considered, along with practical guidelines to be followed in implementing these important investigative procedures.

The techniques for interviewing witnesses and others, interrogating suspects, taking written or recorded statements from interviewees, and confessions from suspects are all discussed in a third book. The most successful investigators are those who learn how to excel in the fine art of interviewing.

Finally, a fourth title deals with surveillance and undercover operations. Techniques for both foot and automobile surveillance are diagrammed and illustrated. The chapter on undercover operatives and their methods is followed by a discussion of undercover investigations of internal theft operations.

Every chapter in every volume contains practical guidelines for a particular investigative procedure. The four books cover the primary methods whereby investigators obtain, record, and present relevant information essential to the successful completion of assignments.

The reader of this series of books journeys progressively through the investigators' world of procedures and strategies used to obtain the necessary information from other persons and from their own efforts and observations. We wish each reader a pleasant and rewarding journey.

I. THE WORLD OF THE PRIVATE INVESTIGATOR

Chapter 1

The Scope of Professional Investigation

"Investigation is nothing more or less than a search for the truth."
—George B. Mettler[1]

"You start with a client who knows or suspects that a civil or criminal offense has been committed. You finish by proving that someone is either guilty or innocent. In between you use certain very similar techniques and technologies — and, of course, your head."
—Tom Ponzi[2]

In the early days of detective work, England's Scotland Yard sent out some of its senior police officials in plain clothes to enable them to mingle incognito with the crowd in an effort to more readily detect criminal offenders. The outcry in the public press was so formidable that the word "detective" early became a dirty word. Plainclothed policemen were denounced as spies to be shunned and hindered.

Results, however, soon proved the wisdom of secret detective methods. Efficient plainclothed operatives quickly demonstrated the value of the unrecognized sleuth in surveillance and undercover operations and in their ability to track down offenders. Their success brought honored distinction to plainclothes police detectives.

Their counterparts in the private sector are private investigators who belong to a "breed" of privately supported investigators who serve clients who have been wronged by civil offenses or brutalized by criminal acts. They also serve in numerous other investigations resulting from clients' personal and business needs.

HISTORY

Private investigation in the United States had a remarkable beginning. It all started with a man of unusual ability. It is doubtful if anyone could have foreseen that Allan Pinkerton, a man from Glasgow who began his work in America making and repairing barrels, was to become America's first private detective and an internationally famous sleuth.

Allan Pinkerton's uncanny ability to detect and rightly interpret signs of criminal activity became known when he discovered the hideout of a gang of counterfeiters and helped the local Dundee, Illinois, sheriff capture them. The sheriff had such great respect for Pinkerton's ability to track down evidence that he swore the Scotsman in as his deputy. Pinkerton performed his duties so well that it wasn't long before the sheriff of Cook County called him to Chicago to become a member of his staff.[3] Those were the days before Chicago had a regular police force.

Pinkerton's devotion to duty led to his appointment as a special agent for the United States Post Office Department to investigate mail fraud, extortion, and blackmail. Later, when Chicago did establish a regular police department, Pinkerton was asked to join the force as its first and only detective. With total commitment, he wholeheartedly threw himself and his unusual talents into his dual role as lawman and investigator.

In 1850 Pinkerton resigned from the Chicago Police Department to become a private investigator. He founded Pinkerton's National Detective Agency, which under his capable direction wrote an incredible saga of early American investigative achievement, secret service, criminal apprehension, and industrial protection. His was the only private investigation agency in Chicago and apparently, in the United States, and was probably one of the first organized anywhere in the world.

Private investigators have been called a breed all their own. They truly do play a unique investigative role in our ever expanding world of personal, business, civil, and criminal investigations. Their roles change along with the changes in our modern urbanized society and the increasing problems created by great concentrations of people with widely divergent social and economic levels and varied affiliations.

More and more the investigative world focuses on the ethical and professional responsibilities of private investigators. The demand for uncompromising integrity and unquestioned capability grows continually in our modern world. Today the plainclothes police detectives and the private investigators are increasingly important as a front-line defense against rapidly multiplying civil wrongs and criminal offenses.

MODERN AGENCIES

Thousands of private investigation agencies of varied size and services
are scattered across America. Some of them are very efficient; others leave
much to be desired. Some agencies employ many investigators; others only a
few. Some highly professional private investigators work alone, but most work
for someone else. The entrepreneurs among them venture to establish their
own agencies.

Some agencies and their operatives cover a whole gamut of investigations,
or attempt to do so. Others specialize in certain types of investigations. A recent directory of agencies comprising member offices of the California Association of Licensed Investigators (CALI) indicated a wide variety in the specialties
offered by member offices ranging all the way from the one-specialty offices
to those that listed nineteen separate areas of investigation.

The *CALI Membership Directory* listed specialty codes representing forty-
four types of professional services offered by their member firms. Forty-two
of the 370-plus member offices identified their services with those forty-four
specialties. CALI members represent a select but comparatively small percentage of the total number of licensed investigators registered in the state of California, which in 1980 exceeded 2,400. This spectrum provides a wide range of
energies and images, from countless small agencies to the giant agencies of the
profession. Territorially, their operations may be limited or not, being confined
to certain locales or covering wide areas. The size and expertise of an agency
usually determines the types and quantities of investigations it undertakes.

One-Specialty Private Investigators

Some private investigators offer their services in only one specialty and
seek to excel in it. An example of the one-specialty private investigator is the
missing persons expert, Anthony (Tony) Joseph Pellicano of Los Angeles. By
concentrating his efforts, Pellicano has developed remarkable expertise in
locating the missing.

Pellicano, who also goes by the name Tony Fortune, had his baptism into
his missing persons career as a "skip tracer" for a Chicago department store,
tracking down customers who had moved away without paying their bills. His
talent for locating these individuals inspired him to launch out as a private investigator specializing in missing persons. He perfected his art and came to be
recognized as one of the outstanding "people finders" in the nation.[4]

Norman Perle of Los Angeles is another example of a one-specialty investigation service. His specialty is "debugging"—sweeping offices, boardrooms,
and other premises in search of hidden microphones and electronic listening
devices. Electronics investigators check for telephone and boardroom "bugs"

and for all forms of clandestine listening equipment. They perform a valuable service as a countermeasure against illegal commercial and industrial audio surveillance and the attempts of competitors to steal secret information. Specialists in this field are frequently called on by corporate clients to sweep executive offices and boardrooms in search of hidden microphones and wiretaps, a common necessity in the war against industrial espionage.

When necessary, one-man operatives solicit assistance from other private investigators, particularly on cases that call for investigation some distance from their home base.

Multispecialty Agencies

The pendulum swings from the one-specialty investigator through the small agencies that may specialize in several areas of investigation, to the large multispecialty firms. One agency advertising in the Yellow Pages of the Los Angeles Telephone Directory lists the following investigative services available on a local, national, or international scale:

- Air crash investigation
- All criminal and civil cases
- Arson
- Attorney service
- Bodyguards
- Dishonest employees
- Domestic affairs
- Handwriting comparisons
- Industrial espionage
- Interrogations
- Laboratory examinations
- Limousine service
- Locating assets
- Locating individuals
- Malpractice
- Maritime issues
- Photography
- Polygraphic examinations
- Surveillance
- Traffic accident investigation
- Uniformed guards

Several private investigation firms with display ads in the same directory list from fifteen to twenty-five, or more, types of investigative services. Some firms advertise general classifications of investigative services such as "Domestic–Industrial–Civil–Criminal." Another firm of professional investigators lists twenty-six types of services:]

- Antitrust
- Computer security
- Embezzlement
- Environmental impact
- Executive protection
- Explosions
- Fingerprinting
- Fire and safety
- Forgery
- Handwriting comparison
- Hostages, kidnapping
- Insurance claims
- Inventory shortages
- Loss prevention
- Medical malpractice
- Missing persons
- Narcotics problems
- Organized crime
- Patents, trademarks
- Personal background
- Polygraphs
- Questionable documents
- Safety inspections
- Undercover
- Wills and estates
- Witnesses located

The reader in any large city can pick up local Yellow Pages, and by checking the advertisements listed under "Investigators" can get a fair idea of the types of services offered by local agencies. A number of well-established firms have valuable connections that enable them to pursue their investigations on an international scale.

The Jay J. Armes agency, The Investigators, according to Armes's business card, handles "inventory shortages, industrial undercover work, counterindustrial espionage, shadowing, photography, employee background, extortion, forgery and fraud, missing persons, heirs and witnesses, embezzlement and theft, domestic relations, personal injury, hotel and store detection work, bodyguard and special police assignments, plant and building protection, debugging phones and offices, and closed-circuit television installation."[5]

THE SCOPE OF PRIVATE INVESTIGATOR ACTIVITIES

It has been said that private investigators can be hired by almost anyone to investigate almost anything. That statement approaches the truth, but it needs to be qualified.

First, the expertise of an individual, or the size and expertise of an agency, will largely determine the scope of that private investigator's — or that agency's — investigative services.

Second, ethical private investigators will never accept an assignment from anyone who wishes to use the information obtained for illegal or criminal purposes. There are, of course, unscrupulous investigators who are trained by, and work for, sordid and criminal elements, but they function outside of the ethical profession and are banished from its social favor and fellowship.

Third, one has to look at all the talents and varieties of professional expertise found within the total spectrum of private-sector operatives to understand the wealth of available services implied in the above assertion.

Licensed investigators are not the only employers of investigative personnel. Attorney groups, insurance companies, and other financial enterprises either have their own investigators or contract with private investigation firms on an assignment basis. Some American industrial complexes employ their own undercover operatives.

Considering the number of agencies and their many investigative and security services, the work of private investigators covers the full range of civil, criminal, personal, and business investigations. In their totality they provide a remarkable number of investigative services.

Investigators for Government Agencies

A number of government agencies on federal, state, county, and city levels employ investigators and offer a variety of investigative careers. Regulatory agencies employ investigators to check on compliance and to investigate violations. The FBI and the Drug Enforcement Administration are federal investigative agencies in the field of law enforcement. Their assignment is to solve major crimes and investigate suspected criminal operations that come under their respective jurisdictions.

Investigators directly employed by government agencies and by American industry are not considered to be private investigators since their services are generally not available to other clients. Moreover, government agencies function in the public domain rather than in the private sector. The potential employers of investigators, however, include both the public and private sectors. They indicate the vast scope of investigative functions operating in our modern social, legal, governmental, and business life. But it is the private investigator who remains the investigative phenomenon of the private sector.

Fictitious Private Investigators of the Movies and TV

Contemporary private investigators are a far cry from the unregulated, unreal "private eyes" of cinema and television, with their flare for the spectacular and their ability to conjure up any private investigation misconception that will bolster the plot. Real private investigators are not the romantic, dashing heroes of fiction, embroiled in shooting matches, fist-fights, and acts of violence, sex, and intrigue. They quietly, patiently, persistently, and often laboriously track down evidence to find the missing pieces to fit together the jigsaw puzzle of clues, leads, interviews, impressions, documents, objects, and whatever to solve investigation problems. They are confronted with a considerable amount of routine investigations to offset the excitement of the unusual or the challenge of a difficult assignment. Action and excitement are a part of their life, but the greater part is just plain intelligent hard work.

Contrary to filmed stories, most private investigators have never been shot at in their lives. In fact, the majority of them are unarmed, they carry no concealed weapons. Private investigators use their heads rather than guns. Their forte is know-how, not the ability to shoot it out with a thug or his bodyguard.

Their most lethal instrument is the camera with which private investigators document evidence. With deadly accuracy, photographs and movie film can expose fraudulent claims and identify persons, documents, impressions, and objects.

There are, of course, exceptions. Investigators who accept dangerous assignments, particularly those who are involved in criminal investigations and those who have created enemies in the performance of their duties, carry concealed weapons on securing a permit to do so.

Some private investigators are experts with firearms. Jay J. Armes, for example, is a crack shot with such weapons. He practices every day, shooting from "standing, kneeling, running, falling and prone positions,"[6] in simulated real life situations. Armes has a private underground concrete bunker, computerized and excellently equipped, in which to practice so that he will be able to defend himself against any surprise attack. But Armes knows that a gun is only to be used in extreme danger. His advice is well worth remembering:

The man I admire is the one who carries a gun but uses his head instead. You'll get out of more tight corners using your head than you ever will using a gun.[7]

Those private investigators who are expert in the use of firearms seldom have need to use them, even in criminal investigations. The majority of assignments are of such a nature that a weapon is neither needed nor advisable.

CLASSIFICATION OF INVESTIGATIONS

The world of investigation is one of great diversity and considerable dimensions. In an attempt to simplify the broad spectrum of activities, we have classified investigations under four general headings: civil, criminal, personal, and industrial.

Investigations may be concerned with civil litigations, criminal prosecutions and defense, or with personal individual or business matters that do not involve adjudication in either the civil or criminal courts, such as business background and credit investigations and the search for missing persons who are not wanted persons.

Violations of law that come under investigation involve either civil wrongs and civil litigation, or alleged crimes and consequent criminal prosecution and defense. Two kinds of offenses occur: private wrongs and public crimes. Two kinds of law are involved: civil and criminal.

It is important to understand the general scope of the civil law as it applies to the personal and business activities of our modern society. This will help us to deal intelligently with the principles of civil investigation and to recognize the difference between civil wrongs and criminal offenses.

The Civil Law—Human Rights and Obligations

Functioning as they do in the private sector, private investigators are often concerned with the private rights and obligations of the citizenry in their personal, domestic, business, and other relationships. Rights and obligations are the legal basis for civil litigations.

According to Jeremy Bentham, author of *The Theory of Legislation:*

> Rights and obligations, though distinct and opposite in their nature, are simultaneous in their origin, and inseparable in their existence. In the nature of things, the law cannot grant a benefit to one without imposing, at the same time, some burden upon another; or, in other words, it is not possible to create a right in favor of one, except by creating a corresponding obligation imposed upon another.[8]

A person's right to ownership of property, for example, imposes on all others an obligation not to seize that property or any portion thereof, or any of the produce provided by that property. The rights granted in any business contract, title, or possession impose corresponding obligations on the other parties to the contract, to the one who conveys the title and all who are obliged to recognize those rights of possession.

The law that has jurisdiction with respect to the rights and obligations of its citizenry is the civil law, sometimes called the common law. It is the law that exercises control in society, the law of human rights and obligations.

Civil law appears to many people to be the least interesting branch of legislation, and civil investigations to be routine. Actually, however, civil law deals with nearly everything in human interrelationships that is most precious to all of us — domestic issues, security, property, business transactions, and protection of our individual rights.

In civil investigations private investigators deal with the rights and obligations of individuals in their private dealings with one another whenever a private offense, violation of a right, or failure to fulfill a legal obligation occurs. The same is true of the dealings between business firms operating within the private sector.

CIVIL CODES. The civil codes of all states cover a wide range of domestic and business relationships, with emphasis on protection of private rights, personal relationships, and recovery of damages for private wrongs. Investigators have access to the civil laws of their respective states in law libraries. While it is up to an attorney to apply the law to the investigative findings of the private investigator when a case goes to court, the investigator is at an advantage when he understands the basic applications of the civil code to a case. Although civil codes naturally vary somewhat, they all basically cover the common ground of rights and obligations.

The civil code of the State of California, for example, is divided into four divisions. The first relates to persons ("persons" means "a natural person, partnership, joint venture, corporation, or other entity"[9]); the second to property; the third to obligations; and the fourth to general provisions.

Civil law legislates in such matters as livelihood, equality, security, privacy, and inalienable rights. The law, for example, confers on individuals the right to personal security (physical and mental), to private relationships (domestic and business), to ownership and security of property (real, personal, and business), to protection of personal honor, and to receive state aid in the event of dire material need. All such rights, including many others not listed here, create their corresponding obligations. To violate any legal right granted by the civil law is a civil offense.

Civil law, therefore, may be described as the legal order of a politically organized civilized society. It embraces those divisions of municipal law that deal with:

1. The exposition, enforcement, and protection of private rights
2. Prevention and redress of private wrongs
3. Recovery of damages, penalties, or forfeitures for an invasion of such rights
4. The social control of society, and the legal settlement of social and business disputes and conflicts that occur therein

In a sense civil law is a law of private protection since it functions in the domain of human relationships between individual private citizens and between private businesses. It seeks to protect persons in their personal and business rights and relationships, in their rights legally to guard their properties and enforce their contracts. It holds them liable for violations of the rights of others, and provides remedies at law for those whose rights have been violated. Civil law is the law of redress. It also regulates the enforcement of legal claims.

Civil law, in contrast to criminal law, governs all the legally recognized relationships of citizens to each other except those criminal activities that are subject to the punishment of offenders by the state as stipulated in the penal code.

Within the wide range of civil law, private investigations are more likely to occur within three broad areas:

1. Contracts—legal contractual obligations
2. Equity—equity and property rights and obligations
3. Torts—personal injuries, both physical and emotional

THE LAW OF TORTS.   In *Denny* v. *State,* the court defined a tort as "any wrong, not consisting in mere breach of contract, for which the law undertakes to give to the injured party some appropriate remedy against the wrongdoer."[10]

The law of torts, or tort law, is basically that part of the civil law that deals with matters of personal injury. Robert H. Sulnick notes that: "Tort law is a broad comprehensive body of law which redresses both physical and emotional personal injuries. The types of conduct over which it has jurisdiction include careless conduct, assaultive conduct, defamatory conduct, and unavoidable injurious conduct."[11]

A tort is a civil wrong that violates a civil right and results in injury to the person or property of another. It presupposes antisocial conduct that in some specific manner violates "a duty imposed on individuals by the state" for the "welfare of society."[12]

The duty to respect the rights of others must be imposed by law to protect society from the "wrongful acts of its members"; violations of legally recognized duties or obligations that result in some form of injury to another or to his legal rights are torts.[13]

According to the California Civil Code, "Every person is bound, without contract, to abstain from injuring the person or property of another, or infringing upon any of his rights."[14]

A basic principle of tort law set forth in the Civil Code states: "Besides the personal rights mentioned or recognized in the Government Code, every person has, subject to the qualifications and restrictions provided by law, the right of protection from bodily restraint or harm, from personal insult, from defamation, and from injury to his personal relations."[15]

Tort law deals with (1) intentional harm to persons, land, and chattels; (2) negligence and resulting harm or injury to person or property; and (3) liability, deceit, libel, slander, wrongful litigation, and interference with a person's domestic or business relationships.

According to *Forrest Cool Law Review. Torts,* "Human beings are generally liable for three forms of misconduct:

1. Voluntary interference with the rights of another. . . .
2. Careless interference with the rights of another. . . .
3. High-probability interference with the rights of another. . . ."[16]

Voluntary interference with another's right is intentional, that is, it is willed or planned activity. Intentional invasion of rights is neither accidental nor negligent. It is consummated knowingly or by mistake, but in either case it constitutes volitional conduct.

Careless invasions of another's rights are negligent invasions resulting from conduct deemed to be unreasonably dangerous to the individual's rights, person, or property.

High-probability interference is a form of liability without fault resulting from inherently dangerous conduct. The preferable legal title for this third situation is usually strict liability. The legal doctrine of strict liability simply implies that "one must suffer the consequences regardless of intention of negligence" when one performs any act that is inherently dangerous to other persons. This includes any activity that "experience shows, often results in injury."[17] The strict liability doctrine applies if indeed such an injury does occur and exists in fact.

The *Forrest Cool Law Review. Torts* lists the following basic rights that must be protected against tortious conduct:

1. Personal security (physical and mental)
2. Property security
3. Security in reputation
4. Privacy
5. Security in certain social relations (marriage)
6. Security in contracts
7. Security in business[18]

As a general rule, all persons are liable for torts when they violate a civil duty or civil right that injures another's person, property, or relationships, for which violation the courts provide a remedy at law for the victim, and for which violation the courts will entertain an action for damages.

Two types of duties are recognized by tort law: (1) contractual duties that are voluntarily assumed by the individual and (2) those imposed by the state on its citizenry for the welfare of all.

A tort is a private wrongful act for which the law provides compensation or damages. A tort feaser is one who commits such an act. An action in tort entitles the injured party to compensation from the tort feaser without subjecting the wrongdoer to punishment by the state. When two or more persons conspire in a common purpose resulting in injury to another's person or property, they are known as joint tort feasers.

Torts may result from intentional acts or from negligent or inherently dangerous conduct. In a brief look at various types of torts, we draw heavily on that volume of the *Forrest Cool Law Review — Torts.*

Intentional torts include, for example, trespass, conversion, seduction, and deceit. Trespass involves "direct and immediate injury to the plaintiff's person or to his corporeal property by the wrongful act of the defendant."[19] Trespass is always a direct physical act.

Conversion implies "an unauthorized assumption and exercise of the right of ownership inconsistent with the real owner's right of possession."[20] Seduction is the illegal obtaining of sexual intercourse by making false promises. Deceit implies the "false representation of a material fact," which results in damage to a plaintiff who relied on that false representation.[21]

There are numerous other related intentional torts such as defamation, slander, publicizing private matters, interference with contracts, suits by next of kin for wrongful deaths, intentional infliction of emotional disturbances, and malicious prosecution.

With respect to negligent conduct, the law justly requires that its subjects respect the implicit duty to exercise care when involved in any activity that also involves a risk of harm to others. Negligent conduct, as well as willful conduct, can injure and damage. When that duty is breached, one fails to act as a "reasonably prudent man."

According to the *Forrest Cool Law Review — Torts,* the courts have defined actionable negligence as "neglect of the use of ordinary care or skill towards a person to whom the defendant owes the duty of observing care and skill, by which neglect the plaintiff, without contributory negligence on his part, has suffered injury to his person or property."[22]

A TORT VIOLATES LEGAL DUTY. The following comment from B.E. Witkin is to the point: "A tort, whether intentional or negligent, involves a violation of a *legal duty,* imposed by statute, contract, or otherwise, owed by the defendant to the person injured."[23]

A duty, a violation of duty, and an injury must all exist to constitute a tort:

TORTS

1. A duty the defendant owes the plaintiff must exist
2. A violation or breach of that duty must have been committed by the defendant
3. An injury must occur to the plaintiff's person, property, or relationships as a result of the defendant's breach of duty

The violation must be the proximate cause of the injury. Proximate cause may be interpreted as near, close, or direct: near as distinguished from far; close as distinguished from remote; and direct as distinguished from indirect.[24]

Actionable negligence may arise, for example, if the occupier of a specified premises fails to keep those premises in a reasonably safe condition, and an injury to another person results from that failure. Or it may arise in the case of a manufacturer who is liable to a consumer for a proximately caused injury resulting from a defective or contaminated product. Negligence by statutory violation exists when regulatory statutes are ignored such as driving an automobile without a driver's license. Statutory liability may exist when specific requirements such as are found in worker's compensation laws are disregarded.

Strict liability torts involve culpability in such matters as (1) vehicular and equipment accidents; (2) accidents occurring on premises due to faulty construction; (3) the escape of dangerous substances such as deadly gas; (4) injuries resulting from the keeping of dangerous animals; and (5) engaging in inherently dangerous activities such as blasting operations.

A condition of liability without fault exists where the resulting harm to another's person or property, or both, is not intentional and not due to the defendant's failure to exercise reasonable care, but is dangerously inherent in the conduct itself, so much so that anyone who so acts is held liable for any damage caused by such action.

The above paragraphs cover some of the rights and obligations of citizens under the civil law. They give an indication of the many possible causes for civil action and therefore of the possible scope of civil investigations. Civil law, civil litigations, and civil investigations always have to do with that which is purely civil.

TORTS AND CRIMES.   Torts are private wrongs. Crimes are public offenses. Civil laws deal with the definition of rights and obligations in a free society and the settlement of private disputes by litigation. Criminal laws deal with the definition of crimes, the stipulations of punishments, and the prosecution and defense of a criminal suspect.

Crimes are positive acts (or negative omissions) that violate the criminal law as set forth in statutes of the penal code. The word penal has the connotation of punishment or penalty, and is used to describe the statutes of the criminal law that define crimes and their punishment.

Crimes are public offenses against the state or the peoples of the state. They are punishable by the state as the protector of the people. On conviction, a criminal perpetrator is punished by imprisonment or fine, or both, and sometimes even by death.

A tort feaser is not punished by the state. When the court finds for the plaintiff, the state does require the tort feaser to make restitution for his breach of the plaintiff's rights.

Civil investigations probe private wrongs. Criminal investigations probe public offenses arising out of prohibited criminal acts (or criminal omissions) that are punishable by law. Federal and state criminal or penal codes prohibit the various species of crime defined in their statutes and establish punishment for the guilty parties.

Civil law governs the private settling of disputes by means of adjudication in the civil courts. It aims at elimination of force and implementation of procedural justice in rendering judgment based on the facts of the case and the presentation of evidence made by parties to the dispute. Such adjudication, in harmony with the rules of justice, has been hailed as one of the great achievements of civilization over the vengeance retribution of ancient times.

Table 1-1. Some basic differences between crimes and torts

Crimes	*Torts*
Criminal offenses	Civil offenses
Public offenses	Private offenses
Prosecutor: the people	Plaintiff: the victim
Objective: punishment of guilt	Objective: redress for injury,
Fines: accrue to people's	etc.
treasury	Damages awarded: accrue as
Out-of-court settlements: few	compensation to victim
permitted	Out-of-court settlements: in ma-
Contributory negligence: no	jority of cases
defense	Contributory negligence: good
Appeal: usually the prosecution	defense
cannot appeal	Appeal: either party may appeal

Blalock notes, "Human prejudices and errors permeate lawsuits," and "An erroneous verdict may be reversed on appeal by either party in a civil case, but the process is lengthy, expensive, and uncertain."[25] These troublesome factors tend to increase the numbers of out-of-court settlements. Many civil litigations center around the amount of money involved and determination of financial settlements.

PHYSICAL PAIN AND MENTAL SUFFERING. A sizable portion of civil cases involves personal injury damages to person, property, or personal relationships. Pain and suffering constitute a legal concept for which the law provides redress, and can be translated into large sums for settlements. Whitkin observes that the civil law that protects against injury provides that "The plaintiff is entitled to damages for physical pain and for mental suffering which result from or accompany the physical injury."[26]

Tort law, the "judicially developed system for awarding damages to the injured,"[27] is very much alive in America today. Its vitality is revealed in the many judicial awards made to citizens who have been injured by personal, business, or institutional malfunctioning of one kind or another. It is the law of recourse for injured citizens.

CIVIL REMEDIES. Civil remedies at law are primarily in the form of monetary compensation. They include (1) monetary redress (reparation); (2) injunctive remedies; and (3) possible punitive damages. The redress functions of civil law are designed to set right civil abuses by making amends for them. They restore and repay by providing redress in the form of monetary damages to reimburse for financial losses.

Injunctive remedies, or relief, granted by a court require a party either to do or to forbear doing certain acts. Injunctions may prohibit a person from doing what ought not to be done, or may require one to do what ought to be done. Injunctive relief may be awarded in lieu of or in addition to damages. To disobey an injunction is a form of contempt of court and can send the offending party to jail.[28]

Punitive damages are a form of financial punishment under civil law. They are assessed when it is deemed necessary to provide a financial deterrent against any repetition by the defendant of similar wrongs. As punishment penalties, punitive damages may far exceed in amount the financial loss or redress damages allowed.

Based on the preponderance of the evidence, a judgment rendered against a defendant in civil litigation may be in the form of any of the three types of remedies referred to above. It may include both redress damages and injunctive relief: granting a specified sum of money to the plaintiff and issuing a court order to the defendant prohibiting or requiring the performance of certain acts; or the judgment could involve all three remedies by adding punitive damages as well. The stigma of having the court legally find him in the wrong can be very distressing to the offending party.

Law-abiding citizens look to the civil law for protection against the wrongs that might be committed against them. It is their recourse when they have been unjustly victimized, when either property or person has been injured, or they have been deprived of any legal right.

CIVIL TERMS DEFINED. The word civil embraces the whole body of citizens of a free political society, as well as their legally recognized domestic, social, business, and other interrelationships with each other. It pertains to the government of law-abiding citizens of the state, relating in particular to the private rights and obligations of individuals, and any legal proceedings pertaining thereto.

Civil action is the presentation of an issue for trial instigated by one party against another party for (1) the enforcement or protection of a right, or (2) the redress or prevention of a wrong. Civil action implies adversary parties: a plaintiff (the party who initiates a personal action or suit) and a defendant (the party who is required by law to answer to an action or suit). Civil action involves both a complaint and a denial with respect to an issue at law.

A civil wrong (or civil offense) is a violation of civil law, civil right, or civil obligation. Such violations are wrongs or offenses, but not crimes, even though they could occur during the commission of a crime. They are private wrongs perpetrated in the private sector. They may result from intent, negligence, or accident.

Civil rights refer primarily to the rights guaranteed by the amendments to the Constitution of the United States of America. Secondarily, they include all rights recognized by civil statutes. The term is frequently used today to designate the legal rights of minority groups. The right to privacy, the right against self-incrimination, the right of one taken into custody to have the benefit of the presence of counsel, and the right against unreasonable search and seizure are all basic rights with which private investigators should be familiar, and which are amplified subsequently. Even a brief reference to the rights and obligations of the citizens of a free society opens wide vistas of potential investigative situations that may arise in their personal, business, and social relationships.

Civil obligations are created by civil rights. Wherever rights exist the obligation to honor them also exists. Civil obligations may be in the form of civil duties or of civil charges to be fulfilled or complied with. Returning to our former illustration, the ownership of a parcel of productive land creates the obligation on the part of all others to honor the right of ownership and not to take to themselves any of the produce of the land without negotiating with the owner for the purchase of such produce.

A civil suit is a comprehensive term that applies to any proceeding in a court of justice by means of which a plaintiff pursues any claim of redress, demand of right, or other remedy provided in the civil law courts. Civil suits generally include all cases at law and in equity that cannot be classified as criminal.

CIVIL LITIGATIONS.   Civil litigations, or suits at law, arise from personal injuries, intended or accidental; from the voluntary or careless interference with the rights of another; from the illegal or fraudulent conversion of property rights; from the failure to perform contractual obligations; and from any number of civil wrongs perpetrated against individuals in the social and business worlds. A just court will exact retribution on behalf of a defrauded or injured person. Civil law seeks to distribute the rights and obligations of its citizens with equal justice.

Many of the civil cases in which private investigators are involved will doubtless be settled out of court, primarily through conciliation. Litigation under civil law continues to function as a judicial means for settling disputes within the private sector, however, and as a result, private investigators will often be called on to testify relative to the findings of personal investigations of the matter before the court and any relevant evidence that has been obtained pertaining thereto.

ESSENTIAL ELEMENTS FOR CIVIL ACTION.   As all experienced private investigators are aware, there are four essential elements for a good cause of action in a civil court:

1.   The existence of the plaintiff's legal right in the matter
2.   The corresponding legal duty of the defendant
3.   A violation of that duty by the defendant
4.   A consequential injury or damage to the plaintiff

The legal right is a right invested in a person, and for which the law provides a remedy in the event of its violation or infringement.

Here is where the basic axioms of civil law come into play:

- No one should suffer by the act of another.
- For every wrong there is a remedy.
- It is the legislative policy of the state to provide a remedy for every legal wrong.[29]

It is when a violation of legal duty by the defendant results in some damage or injury to the plaintiff that the law grants the plaintiff the right of redress. Thus civil law becomes the law for all citizens.

Civil Investigations

In civil investigations, private investigators are concerned with the private rights and obligations of individuals in their dealings with one another. When rights or obligations or their denial or abuse result in civil litigation (suits at law), private investigator's services are often solicited to help ferret out relevant evidence.

Private investigators on civil assignment seek true evidence pertaining to the civil matters in dispute or subject to litigation. If the matter goes to court, they search for the true facts on which the attorney can base a case.

Since the civil law covers such a wide field of social and business relationships — of human rights and obligations — the field of investigation can vary tremendously. In all civil investigations private investigators should recognize that an agreeable out-of-court settlement is often more satisfactory to the litigants than is a favorable in-court decision for one of them.

TYPES OF CIVIL INVESTIGATIONS. The list of areas of civil investigations that follows is not exhaustive. It does account for numerous noncriminal investigations, both those that may involve litigation and those, which by their very nature, would not usually be brought to civil trial. A similar list of typical criminal investigations follows later in this chapter.

Civil, personal, and business investigations include:

- Accidents (vehicular, industrial, constructional, domestic)
- Adjusting (settlements)
- Aircraft accidents
- Antitrust activity
- Assault and battery (torts as well as crimes)
- Asset location searches (to satisfy judgment or debt)
- Background (preemployment, high position, potential partner, etc.)
- Breach of contract
- Condemnation and zoning (private lands for public use)
- Consulting
- Conversion (wrongful dominion over another person's property)
- Defamation
- Detection of electronic eavesdropping (debugging telephones, offices)
- Domestic relations (child custody, divorce settlements, etc.)
- Employees (loyalty, leakage, pilferage, dissidents, organizers)
- False imprisonment
- Feasibility
- Fingerprinting (ID)
- Fire cause
- Fraud and deceit torts
- Industrial counterespionage
- Injunction suits
- Insurance claims

- Invasion of privacy
- Investigative accountant
- Investigations (miscellaneous)
- Inventory shortages and shrinkage
- Legal matters (case and trial preparation)
- Libel and slander
- Locating and interviewing witnesses
- Loss
- Malicious prosecution
- Malpractice
- Marine investigations
- Marketable titles
- Mergers and acquisitions
- Misappropriation of another's work, labor, title, literary property, etc.
- Missing heirs
- Missing persons (runaways, disappearances, debtors, witnesses, etc.)
- Negligence
- Personal injury
- Patent infringements
- Photocopy services
- Photography (documentation of evidence, sub rosa photography)
- Polygraph examinations
- Probate (last wills and testaments)
- Process service
- Products liability
- Property and equity issues
- Psychological stress evaluation
- Public records searches (vital statistics, debts, assets, titles, etc.)
- Questioned documents
- Repossessions
- Security surveys (assets, personnel and property protection; crime prevention)
- Suicide
- Surveillance (shadowing, tailing, stakeouts)
- Trespass torts
- Tort violations of rights and obligations
- Trial preparation
- Undercover operations
- Unfair competition (protection of trade marks, trade names, trade secrets)
- Witnesses (interviewing, taking statements from, providing protection for)
- Worker's compensation cases

No list can possibly cover all potentialities. Constantly new situations and complexities develop, calling for special investigative assignments. One of the realities for investigators is the persistence of variable factors that make every case and every career different. These variables of personalities and situations can never be standardized. They spring from the nature of the human heart and mind and from the conflicts and complexities of our modern life.

The above list does, however, offer insights into the broad scope of civil investigations. Specific cases, of course, may include matters not referred to, such as fraudulent conveyances of titles to property, the withholding of chattels belonging to another, problems in buyer's and seller's contracts, and many others. Most firms would not attempt to undertake all types of investigations. Some of the more highly departmentalized and sophisticated agencies, on the other hand, are very versatile and can meet most investigative demands.

Personal and Business Investigations

Frequently, private investigators are involved in assignments that are purely private matters occurring in normal social and business relationships such as background investigations, security surveys, credit investigations, and a sizeable percentage of missing persons cases. (Both categories of personal investigations and assignments involving the business world call for the services of a private investigator.)

Credit investigations are a normal part of many business transactions. Before large sums of money are lent, credit investigations are run on the borrowers. Before several people merge their interests in a large business venture, credit and background investigations determine the practicality of the venture.

Background investigations are conducted for preemployment purposes, or to learn more about a person who is being considered for promotion or high position in business, industry, or government. A business executive may wish a background check on a potential partner. One who is about to marry, or a parent of the person, may want the benefit of such an investigation of the potential spouse.

Probating a will may call for an investigator to locate missing heirs. In the event the will is contested, private investigators may be called on to find evidence for or against the testamentary capacity (the sound and disposing mind) of the testator. Was the testator mentally competent? Was he free from undue influence by the beneficiaries? Did he understand who the natural heirs were? Did he know the extent of his properties and assets?

In probate investigations, private investigators contact and interview the witnesses to the will. They also interview those who have had personal acquaintance with the private and business life of the testator, and who can testify to his or her mental alertness and capacity.

In any investigation involving condemnation and zoning procedures, private investigators will need to understand the principle of eminent domain — the right of a government entity to take over private property for its use. The Fifth Amendment requires that just compensation be made to the owner of the property. Moreover, the Fourteenth Amendment's due process clause requires that no one may be deprived of life, liberty, or property without due process of law.

If the owner of the property in question should resist the condemnation proceedings and the government's intended action to take over the property, the matter must be decided in court and the property owner awarded an equitable amount. Investigators will frequently be involved in helping to establish the fair market value of the property as determined by the price it would bring in the open market.

Locating missing persons is a common private investigator assignment. A person may be missing either intentionally or unintentionally. Missing persons may be wanted or merely lost. They may be rootless individuals or people with marital difficulties who just turn up missing; they may be petty larceny criminals; they may be on the run from obligations they cannot meet. Missing persons could be mentally or physically ill, or be the victims of foul play. Even when they are not wanted by the law or by their creditors, they may certainly be wanted by their loved ones.

These types of personal and business investigations clearly establish the fact that it is not necessary for a civil or criminal law to be broken before an investigation is called for. Many investigations are conducted as part of the regular social and business needs of our time.

Criminal Law — Crimes and Punishments

Criminal law relates to crimes and their punishment. Criminal law is wholly statutory, that is, no act or omission is punishable as a crime unless it has been prohibited by a statute of the state's penal code. The nature of crimes, as well as the specific species of crimes, are stated in the penal or criminal code, along with the punishment for their violation.

Section 15 of the California Penal Code, for example, offers the following definition:

> A crime or public offense is an act committed or omitted in violation of a law forbidding or commanding it, and to which is annexed, upon conviction, either of the following punishments:

1. Death;
2. Imprisonment;
3. Fine;
4. Removal from office; or,
5. Disqualification to hold and enjoy any office of honor, or profit in this state.

A crime is simply any act or omission forbidden by law that violates any statute of the penal code, and which, on his conviction, subjects the criminal to the punishment stipulated in the code. The elements of each crime vary according to the nature of the crime, and are described in the pertinent statute(s).

Crimes are divided into three separate classifications; (1) felonies, (2) misdemeanors, and (3) infractions (petty offenses). Felonies are serious crimes punishable by death or by imprisonment in state prison. All other crimes are misdemeanors, except minor ones that are classified as infractions, violations, or petty offenses and are not punishable by imprisonment.

CORPUS DELICTI ELEMENTS OF A CRIME. "Every crime consists of a group of elements laid down by the statute or law defining the offense and every one of these elements must exist or the statute is not violated. This group of essential elements is known as the 'corpus delicti,' the body or elements of the crime."[30]

The term corpus delicti always refers to the specified elements of a crime and not to the body of a deceased victim, as is often mistakenly assumed. Nor is the identity of the perpetrator part of the corpus delicti. The penal code's definitions of crimes clearly lists these elements. Every element must be established before there can be a conviction. Consequently, criminal investigation seeks to establish all the elements of any crime under investigation.

Legislators are responsible for criminal law. McCaghy defines criminal law as "a set of rules legislated by the state in the name of society, and enforced by the state through the threat and application of punishment."[31]

Crimes are considered to be harmful to society as a whole and therefore punishable by the state. The state employs the governmental powers that apprehend, judge, and punish the criminal (with the exception of the jury and attorneys for the defense). The police, prosecutors, and judges who interpret the law and impose sentences, together with the entire criminal justice personnel, are involved in the application of the criminal laws in the punishment of offenders. Unfortunately, too many criminals escape the punishment for their crimes.

It is important to note that in punishing the criminal, the state acts for society, and not to reimburse the victim or his relatives. Criminal law is a law of punishment, not of restitution. A victim, however, may resort to the civil courts and sue the offender to recover loss. The criminal offender, therefore, may face criminal prosecution and later, civil litigation. Several states have passed laws granting some financial assistance from state funds as compensation to victims of crimes for economic losses resulting from death or injury.

No crime exists without a law prohibiting it and precisely stating its component elements, and the punishment to be meted out in the event of its perpetration. Criminal statutes provide minimum and maximum penalties for each crime. The judges in sentencing act between these limits as the states allow discretion to do so and as offenders' situations warrant.

The constitutional provisions of the Fifth and Fourteenth Amendments are very important in criminal proceedings against suspects. They provide that no person shall be deprived of liberty or property without due process of law.

Matters pertaining to court procedure are considered elsewhere. It should be noted that merely the intent to commit a crime is not punishable. The criminal act or omission must occur. Crime is a union of intent and act. Whenever a criminal act is knowingly done, the law implies it was done with intent. In the case of some crimes, however, intent is an essential element of the corpus delicti, since they are crimes only when committed with specific intent.

Defendants are entitled to a fair and speedy public trial by an impartial jury. They are usually represented by counsel. They have the right to produce witnesses to testify in their own behalf, and to be confronted with the witnesses who testify against them. They have the right not to incriminate themselves.

Criminal Investigations

Weston and Wells define criminal investigation as "a lawful search for people and things useful in reconstructing the circumstances of an illegal act or omission and the mental state accompanying it."[32] All investigations search for truth. Criminal investigations seek the truth about the elements and perpetrators of crimes. This is primarily a function of the police, although sometimes they will call in able private investigators to assist in an extended investigation, or in tracking down the evidence in a yet unsolved crime. The rising crime rate challenges private investigators as well as law-enforcement officers. Private investigators are also called in to assist defense attorneys by conducting investigations on behalf of the defendants. In unsolved crimes, a private investigator or private investigation agency may be asked to track down perpetrators or to go in search of the stolen property. Victims of crimes frequently employ the services of a private investigator.

FOUR BASIC OBJECTIVES. The basic objectives of criminal investigation are:

1. To establish the fact that a criminal offense has been committed. In identifying the elements of the offense (the factors that make up the components of the crime), investigators often find clues and leads

that reveal the offender's modus operandi (mode of operating) and provide starting points for the investigation.

2. To detect and identify the offender. Identification of the offender is essential to the solution of the crime. An arrest warrant must provide either the name or an adequate description by which the accused can be recognized and identified with reasonable certainty. The name of the suspect(s) may be unknown, or a suspect may be arrested under an alias. Repeat offenders may be arrested under different aliases.

3. To locate and arrest the suspect(s). Apprehension of a suspect is basically the first step in the prosecution of the accused. According to the United States Constitution, all suspects have a right to be present at their own criminal trial to face their accusers.

   Before criminal suspects can be arrested they must be located. Very few are apprehended in the actual act of committing a crime. To make an arrest is to take into custody in a manner authorized by law. This is usually handled by the police.

4. To produce the evidence against the offender. This phase of criminal investigation involves obtaining and developing evidence sufficient to secure a conviction in a criminal court proceeding. Evidence must establish guilt beyond a reasonable doubt to sustain such conviction. Moreover, this proof must be established by legally admissible evidence.

CITIZEN'S ARREST. An investigator as a private citizen can make a citizen's arrest (1) when a public offense has been committed or attempted in his presence; (2) when a person has committed a felony, even though it was not committed in the investigator's presence; or (3) when a felony has in fact been committed and the investigator has reasonable cause to believe the person he is arresting has committed it. Private investigators generally have no additional powers of arrest beyond those of any citizen.

Whenever private investigators, security officers, or private persons make an arrest, the person arrested must be turned over to a peace officer (a policeman) or a magistrate without delay. It requires the cooperation of a police officer to make the arrest effective.

The reasonable cause element of the citizen's arrest must be strictly adhered to; mere suspicion will not suffice. There must be reasonable grounds for believing that the person being arrested is the guilty party. There must also be a factual basis for the arrest; that is, the crime must have been committed, and private investigators should be in possession of facts that focus directly on the suspect. Precaution should be taken to avoid arresting the wrong party, as an investigator can be held liable for an unreasonable detention. As long as there were reasonable grounds — grounds on which any reasonable person would have acted — the private investigators would be allowed to make a mistake in the identity of a suspect provided a felony had been committed and those reasonable grounds made the arrestee a suspect.

There is a difference between the arrests executed by law-enforcement officers and those made by private investigators. Law-enforcement officers are subject to basic constitutional limitations and must not deny the arrestee's civil or constitutional rights. They must not obtain evidence by unconstitutional methods. Before conducting a custodial interrogation of an arrested person, they must read the suspect his rights, commonly known as the *Miranda* warnings, which include the suspect's right to remain silent and right to counsel, including an attorney appointed by the state if he cannot afford his own.

In most jurisdictions, citizen's arrests have not been made subject to these constitutional limitations unless the citizen has been deputized by a law-enforcement officer or other authority. Such arrests performed by a private person as authorized by state statutes do not fall within governmental law-enforcement action. It is advisable for private investigators who make citizen's arrests to leave interrogation of the subjects to the police. The private investigators usually are not obligated to warn suspects of their rights, but they must operate within the limits of the law.

It is incumbent on all private investigators, therefore, to know the laws of their state in the matter of citizen's arrests. What are their arresting powers and limitations? Moreover, most agencies have established policies pertaining to citizen's arrests that they expect their staff private investigators to adhere to. Some agencies discourage such arrests, others require private investigators to call for a law-enforcement officer to make the arrest in most instances. Some restrict citizen's arrests to situations in which there is no immediate opportunity to call the police.

NO UNREASONABLE USE OF FORCE. Citizen's arrests are privileged by law. The conduct of the arresting private investigator is important. While some degree of force may be necessary to consummate the arrest, at no time should it exceed that which is reasonably necessary. In most jurisdictions, deadly force can only be used to protect life, to prevent a felony, or to arrest for a felony whenever that felony would jeopardize the life of another human being. It can never be used to prevent a misdemeanor or to arrest for a misdemeanor.

Agencies should be conversant relative to the measure of force that may be used in effecting arrests within their jurisdictions. These privileges vary, and wise private investigators will know their limitations as set forth in the statutes, or as adhered to in the common law practices of their area of operations. Experienced private investigators are aware that a citizen's arrest power is limited, that there are legal pitfalls that must be avoided, and that a working knowledge of relevant laws is essential.

The term apprehension is generally applied only to criminal cases, and the word arrest refers to both civil and criminal cases. The law requires a person being legally arrested to submit peaceably, but suspects may not be aware of that fact. Suspects may be subjected to such restraint as is reasonable, but, as in citizen's arrests, no amount of force can be resorted to in excess of that necessary to make the arrest. The use of excessive force can subject the arresting person to a criminal charge of assault and battery or to a civil lawsuit.

A warrant for the arrest of a defendant is a writ issued by a magistrate, justice, or other competent authority. It is addressed to a law-enforcement officer — sheriff, constable, or other officer — requiring him to arrest the person named or described therein and to bring the arrestee before the magistrate or court to be examined relative to the crime he is alleged to have committed.

As a general rule, either a police officer or a private citizen can make an arrest without a warrant in cases of felony situations noted above. As soon as possible after the arrest, the arrested person should be taken without unnecessary delay to a committing officer to be charged and to have bail set.

B. E. Whitkin states, "Either a police officer or a private person may arrest for an offense committed in his presence at the time of the offense, or within a reasonable time thereafter, or upon fresh and immediate pursuit of the offender."[33] Consequently, private investigators in immediate pursuit of a criminal suspect would have the right to arrest him according to California law.

Situations can arise in which the police are called but are unable to make an arrest because the offense was previously committed and not in their presence. Citizen private investigators can then make the arrest, and the officers will follow it up by taking the suspect into custody.

PARTIAL LIST OF POTENTIAL CRIMINAL INVESTIGATIONS. The list that follows makes no attempt to survey the whole gamut of known criminal offenses. It does pinpoint key areas of criminal activity that may call for considerable investigation, such as:

- Arson (fire cause)
- Blackmail
- Bomb threats and criminal explosives
- Burglary
- Conspiracy to commit crime
- Criminal defense
- Criminal evidence
- Embezzlement
- Extortion
- Fencing (receiving stolen goods)
- Forgery
- Fraud
- Graft

- Hijacking
- Homicides (murder and manslaughter)
- Insurance fraud
- Internal theft
- Kidnapping
- Land frauds
- Motor vehicle theft
- Narcotics, drugs
- Organized crime
- Rape
- Shoplifting
- Swindles (confidence scams)
- Theft (personal, commercial, and industrial)
- Terrorism
- White-collar crime (business, computer, corporate, workplace)

SKYROCKETING CRIME. The tremendous upsurge in crime in recent years places an increasing burden on law-enforcement agencies throughout America. Entrenched criminal organizations add to the problem. Many police departments find it impossible to investigate adequately every crime of significance. This is a matter of deep concern in many communities.

Greenwood, Chaiken, and Petersilia in *The Criminal Investigation Process* comment on how little actual investigation time police can spend on many reported felonies because they are swamped by the increasing incidence of crime. As a result, only major felonies are invariably investigated and most minor crimes are not.

In an analysis of the computer-readable case assignment file maintained by the police department of a midwestern city, the authors found that "less than half of all reported crimes receive any serious attention by an investigator, and the great majority of cases that are actively investigated receive less than one day's attention"; many felony cases "did not receive as much as a half-hour's attention from an investigator."[34]

The extent to which this problem plagues our cities is not fully known. As crime problems intensify, qualified private investigators may be more frequently enlisted as investigative adjuncts to undermanned law enforcement agencies. The emphasis here is on qualified private investigators. Only those who are ready to cope with the criminal challenge can be employed with maximum results.

COMBATING THE IDOLATRY OF CRIMINAL HEROES. The visual media unfortunately tend to create a romanticized picture of infamous criminals and their devastating acts. Movies exalt the perpetrators of crimes to hero roles and exploit to the hilt the publicity of real life criminals who stab, shoot, steal, rape, and murder. As Mettler reminds us, the investigator cannot afford to ignore this unfortunate tendency to "glorify violence and immorality."[35]

Margaret Hyde calls our attention to the fact that a tattoo on the arm of Richard Speck, murderer of eight student nurses in Chicago, bore the self-incriminating message: "Born to raise Hell."[36] Far too many rapists and murderers are apparently bent on the same course, with little or no concern for the lives of their hapless victims.

Society cannot afford to let those who flaunt their crimes before a shocked world get away with it. The war against crime can never be abandoned. It calls for the combined efforts of the police, the detective, and the investigator. It calls for a court system that is more sensitive to the plight of the victims and more determined to put the perpetrators of crime where they belong. Qualified private investigators engaged in criminal investigations should play an increasingly significant role in achieving these ends.

Crimes against Commerce and Industry

Richard Akin says, "Private investigators fill a meaningful and useful function in crimes against commerce."[37] Crimes against industry and business, since they are perpetrated against a private enterprise, are in a sense private crimes. Industries frequently turn to private investigator agencies for help in solving problems of internal theft and industrial espionage and sabotage.

Losses from inventories in retail establishments are primarily due to employee theft, and secondarily to shoplifting and errors in accounting. Losses due to embezzlement and pilferage exceed those due to burglary and robbery. Most crime-related losses in all business are due to internal theft.

Crimes that violate trust are not so readily detected as are street crimes. Extended investigations may be needed to establish the facts of embezzlement, falsification of company records, and theft of computer data. Other areas of industrial crime include occupational graft, restraint of trade, crimes against the consumer, and other abuses of power, in all of which criminal ties can be factors.

The author sees an increasing role for dedicated and qualified private investigators in helping to cope with the criminal element. Those who specialize in criminal investigation are the civilian commandos who war against the violations of trust and against the violent elements that incessantly and insanely decimate our society.

INTERTEL. One agency that specializes in criminal investigations is International Intelligence, Incorporated (Intertel). The firm was founded in 1970 by a veteran of Naval Intelligence, the National Security Agency, and a graduate of Georgetown University Law School — Robert Dolan Peloquin.

According to George O'Toole, Peloquin launched his enterprise with a formidable team of experienced investigators from the FBI and other government agencies. The charter members of Intertel were actually brought together during Peloquin's tenure in the Justice Department. Just four years after they went into service together, Peloquin described their effort as the "first organized strike force against crime operating in the private sector." Intertel also functions as a management consultant firm on organized crime, advising its business clients on "how to keep the Mafia out."[38]

Investigation and Security Agencies

There remains one more aspect of the investigator's world to consider briefly, namely, the close association of the private investigation industry with the security industry.

Many private investigation agencies are also security agencies, but firms that offer both services are really two entities operating under the same general management. Investigators and security personnel provide separate and distinct services, each trained to serve in their respective fields.

Private security may well be the fastest growing industry in America. It is a multibillion-dollar-a-year business. In many large cities, the number of functioning security personnel considerably exceeds the number of police and law-enforcement people. Residences and commercial and industrial businesses seek the services of security people and the installation of security systems. The services range from private guards and patrols to alarm and control systems that are increasingly sophisticated. The uniformed guard is familiar in the commercial, financial, and industrial world. Many large industrial complexes, institutions, and commercial houses employ their own in-house security personnel and others contract with private agencies for their services.

PROTECTION SERVICES PROVIDED BY PRIVATE SECURITY AGENCIES. A variety of protection services is provided by security agencies:

- Bodyguards and escorts
- Burglar alarms
- Closed-circuit TV installations
- Communication centers and controls
- Guard dogs
- Industrial security surveys
- Limousine services
- Security patrols
- Surveillance cameras
- Uniformed guards

To Allan Pinkerton goes the credit for having also pioneered the modern security protection services. In the early days of his own private investigation agency, he organized his armed guard and patrol services under the name: Pinkerton's Protective Patrol. There is thus a very early precedent for the close affiliation of private security with private investigation.

There is, of course, a decided difference between the plainclothed private investigation detective and the uniformed security guard or patrol officer. The private investigator is in the business of gathering intelligence, information, and evidence. The uniformed guard's role is to give private protection. Both are essential to the preservation and protection of the rights of our citizenry.

The startling upsurge in crime in recent years has proved to be a financial bonanza to the security business. Commerce and industry have greatly increased their reliance on security services and equipment. Homes, businesses, and important personages all need to be protected. The rank and file of our citizens find a growing need for protection devices of one sort or another. Security agencies accordingly provide a variety of personnel, alarm, and surveillance services for their commercial, industrial, and individual clients. In short, security is a paramount need of our modern world.

WHAT LIES AHEAD?

This chapter provides only a glimpse of the legal and investigative environments in which the private investigator works. In the following chapters we will see methodologies, techniques, and strategies employed in probing the avenues of evidence, and we will learn more about private investigators and how they operate.

NOTES

1. Mettler, G. B. *Criminal investigation* (Boston: Holbrook Press, 1977), 23.

2. von Block, B. W. *Super-detective. The many lives of Tom Ponzi, Europe's master investigator* (Chicago: Playboy Press, 1972), 111.

3. Rowan, R. W. *The Pinkertons, a detective dynasty.* (Boston: Little, Brown, 1931), 24-5.

4. O'Toole, G. *The private sector. Private spies, rent-a-cops, and the police-industrial complex.* (New York: W. W. Norton & Co., 1978), 105-8.

5. Nolan, F. *Jay J. Armes, investigator.* (New York: Macmillan Publishing Co., 1976), 38.

6. Ibid., 45.

7. Ibid., 47.

8. Bentham, J. *The theory of legislation.* (Dobbs Ferry, N.Y.: Oceana Publications, 1975), 57.

9. Deering's California codes. *Code of civil procedure.* Vol. 1102–1230, section 1203.51. (San Francisco: Bancroft-Whitney Co., 1981), 262.

10. *Denny* v. *State* (1899) 123 C. 316, 323, 55, P. 1000.

11. Sulnick, R. H. *Civil litigation and the police.* (Springfield, Ill.: Charles C Thomas Publisher, 1976), 7.

12. *Forrest Cool law review — Torts,* rev. ed. (Forrest Cool Publications, 1966), 1. See also pp. 9–12.

13. Ibid., 1.

14. Deering's California codes. *Civil code.* Vol. 1625–1724. Part 3: Obligations imposed by law. No. 1708, Abstinence from injury. (San Francisco: Bancroft-Whitney Co., 1971), 469.

15. Deering's California codes. *Civil code.* Vol. 1–706. Part 2: Personal rights. No. 43, General personal rights. (San Francisco: Bancroft-Whitney Co., 1971), 167, 168.

16. *Forrest Cool law review — Torts,* 2.

17. Ibid., 2.

18. Ibid., 9, 10.

19. Ibid., 43.

20. Ibid., 53.

21. Ibid., 56.

22. Ibid., 19.

23. Witkin, B. E. *Summary of California law.* Vol. 4, *Torts.* (San Francisco: Bancroft-Whitney Co., 1974), 2306.

24. *Forrest Cool law review — Torts,* 21.

25. Blalock, J. *Civil liability of law enforcement officers.* (Springfield, Ill.: Charles C Thomas Publisher, 1974), 8.

26. Witkin, B. E. *Summary of California law. Torts,* 3171, 3172.

27. Blalock, J. *Civil liability of law enforcement officers,* 9.

28. Sulnick, R. H. *Civil litigation and the police,* 89.

29. Deering's California codes. *Civil code.* Vol. 3509–end. Part 4: Maxims of jurisprudence. Vols. 3520, 3523. (San Francisco: Bancroft-Whitney Co., 1972), 37, 42, 43.

30. Fricke, C. W., and A. L. Alarcon. *California criminal law.* (Los Angeles: Legal Book Corp., 1977), 21.

31. McCaghy, C. H. *Crime in American society.* (New York: Macmillan Publishing Co., 1980), 13.

32. Weston, P. B. and K. M. Wells, *Criminal investigation.* (Englewood Cliffs, N.J.: Prentice-Hall, 1980), 3.

33. Witkin, B. E. *Summary of California law — Torts,* 2508.

34. Greenwood, P. W.; J. M. Chaiken; and J. Petersilia. *The criminal investigation process.* (Lexington, Mass.: D. C. Heath & Co., 1977), 229.

35. Mettler, G. B. *Criminal investigation,* 23.

36. Hyde, M. O. *Crime and justice in our time.* (New York: Franklin Watts, 1980), 9.

37. Akin, R. H. *The private investigator's basic manual.* (Springfield, Ill.: Charles C Thomas Publisher, 1976), 7.

38. O'Toole, G. *The private sector,* 105–8.

Chapter 2

The Successful Investigator

"I believe the true road to preeminent success in any line is to make yourself master of that line."

— Andrew Carnegie[1]

"Success is made largely by yourself. It does not come ready-built. It is a commodity hand-tailored to your personal needs and only *your* efforts can make it come true."

— J.V. Cerney[2]

Success is a lifetime journey. It is the total achievement of a career of integrity and service. It is not some destination, a place to move into and close the door. Allan Pinkerton has left on record his assessment of the seven qualities necessary for a successful private detective:

> The detective must possess certain qualifications of prudence, secrecy, inventiveness, persistency, personal courage, and, above all other things, honesty; while he must add to these the same quality of reaching out and becoming possessed of that almost boundless information which will permit of the immediate and effective application of his detective talent in whatever degree that may be possessed.[3]

Pinkerton's qualifications for effective private investigation service include three other essentials: the temperament to respect confidentiality and secrecy, the resourcefulness to invent strategies to adapt to persons and circumstances, and the capacity to become informed, including skill in obtaining relevant information from others.

Various combinations of characteristics have been used to describe the successful investigator, such as intelligence, persistence, and resourcefulness combined with experience and common sense. The best private investigators radiate integrity and reliability; they inspire believability. Their confident, businesslike, and friendly approach creates the atmosphere of professional skill.

Ideally, private investigators have personalities that attract and motivate people. Cerney calls magnetic personalities "powerhouses of persuasion."[4] A sincere, convincing, and considerate personality is a pleasant, forceful personality. Another characteristic of successful private investigators is their motivation to serve others.

Some basic skills are also essential for increasing the private investigators' potential performance and influence. Other capabilities also help to enhance their performance. This chapter deals with the areas of personal abilities that have proved effective.

Personality and development of one's capabilities should have high priority in every field of activity where success depends primarily on one's ability to deal effectively with people. There are seven essential people-oriented abilities that can help investigators handle people-oriented problems inherent in the profession.

PEOPLE-ORIENTED ABILITIES

The investigator's career is totally people oriented. Investigation is concerned, directly and indirectly, with and about people. Thus private investigators need to feel at home with them, understand, motivate, and communicate with them.

Investigators take statements from witnesses, insurance beneficiaries, victims of fraud or other crimes, litigants, and sometimes from suspects. They have to glean information from contacts and informants. Thus it is essential for private investigators to know how to contact people and how to obtain the necessary information from them. They must be able to communicate kindly and positively with all kinds of people under many varied circumstances. The seven key abilities discussed below enhance effectiveness in this area.

Dealing Effectively with People

"The art of dealing with people is the foremost secret of successful men."[5] With these words, Dr. Paul Parker focused on the primary qualification of successful private investigators. The key to success is knowing or learning how to deal effectively with people. Private investigators communicate with all kinds of people who have all kinds of problems and all kinds of attitudes. Even when private investigators work alone and secretly, they are dealing with people. Some persons are willing and eager to help investigators; others are just as eager and anxious to hinder them.

ATTITUDE. Attitude is a state of mind affecting behavior and conduct; indicating opinion or purpose; and suggesting thought, feeling, or action. Attitude can express itself consciously or subconsciously. Investigators may be aware or unaware of the effects of their attitudes on others.

Take an interview situation, for example. The feeling, mood, or attitude of private investigators toward the interviewee is a primary factor contributing toward the success or failure of the interview. It is, in fact, more important than the attitude of the interviewee. Granted, however, attitude will vary according to the types of personalities and circumstances involved. Sometimes the ability to maintain a communicative attitude will be put to the test by the disreputable, deceitful, or criminal nature of the subject.

In every person-to-person relationship, the investigator's attitude is what the other person sees most — even more than his facial features or the clothes he wears. Attitude includes one's bearing, feelings, mood, mental reaction to the other person, and the message radiated to the other person. The attitude the private investigator radiates is the attitude the subject must respond to. It will, to a considerable degree, influence the other person's attitude toward him. The private investigator's attitude toward others affects their attitude toward him.

If the subject's attitude is initially cold or even hostile there is some hope that the right attitude of the private investigator will change that hostility to cooperation. But if the attitude of the private investigator is cold or hostile to the subject, there is little or no hope for a successful interview or interrogation.

People have an uncanny ability to sense how we feel toward them. Our attitudes toward people in general and toward specific persons in particular radiate from us to them. People immediately sense whether someone is friendly or hostile, sincere or hypocritical, or somewhere in between. This is a crucial factor for investigators to consider, because they must radiate an attitude that will lead others to cooperate, trust, and confide in them.

SHOWING INTEREST IN OTHERS. Showing a genuine interest in the other person is a vital key to effective human relationships. The key word here for successful investigators is genuine. Feigned interest is easily detected and insincerity exposes itself.

When private investigators show an interest in one with whom they wish to communicate, that person will usually respond with at least some degree of interest in both the investigator and in his investigation. Even an initial interest born of curiosity is helpful. Those private investigators who are liked, respected, and trusted will have no problem in winning the cooperation of others. The secret is for each private investigator to be the kind of person others will want to deal with.

The old pros among investigators have learned how to show interest in others, and how to deal with the varied emotions, rationalizations, prejudices, excuses, motivations, and reasonings of willing and unwilling witnesses, victims, litigants, suspects, and others. This expertise comes only in time. Unfortunately, too many have fallen by the way because they have never learned how to be interested in their fellow men and women.

BUILDING GOOD HUMAN RELATIONS.   Private investigation thrives on good human relations. Investigators work with humanity in all walks of life, and none can perform professionally without the ability to create good interrelations. Every act, event, or situation that calls for an investigation, as well as the investigation itself, can only be explained in human terms. People are involved from start to finish — by their acts, their statements, their injuries, their resources, their torts, their crimes, and their investigations. It takes a considerable amount of good human relations to encompass all of these. Sincere, friendly interest in other people and their welfare, combined with integrity, honesty, and dependability lay the groundwork for successful human relations.

Showing Concern for Others

Concern relates to interest in and feeling for another person and that person's welfare. It is revealed in expressions and attitudes of respect, deference, regard, understanding, sympathy, and consideration.

The sympathetic and understanding approach has been known to break down many barriers to communication and disarm opposition. A recent study of the art of persuasion has been made with specific reference to sympathetic identification with the subject's predicament. It was found that sympathy enhanced the ability to persuade lawbreakers to confess their crimes. Some criminals respond to those who can sympathize with them and understand them. People in any predicament surely respond more readily to sympathy than to censure.

The key factor in the sympathetic, understanding approach is the ability to put oneself in another's place and to understand a situation from another's viewpoint. By showing such empathy we strike a responsive cord in the other person. It should be easy to recognize the definite and positive influence such empathy has on the outcome of an interview or interrogation.

EMPATHY.   Empathy is the ability to feel with another person and have that person sense that you feel with him. It puts a person in another's shoes and offers the warmth of an understanding, open mind. Being able to feel with others makes it possible to interact successfully with them. It breaks down the separating conflict between the "I feeling" and the "You feeling" by creating the "We feeling."

Empathy does not demand agreement or imply that one condones another's actions. It does not require similar opinions or conclusions. But it does require consideration and respect for other persons, if not for their ideas.

For private investigators, empathy also means not being judgmental. Their sole interest is in finding the truth while showing concern for each person's welfare—witnesses, litigants, victims, and suspects—without allowing their personal feelings to interfere with their objectivity. Empathy is the outreach of the open mind and tends to open up the mind of the interviewee toward private investigators and the investigation. Respect, consideration, and understanding generate power to swing open the mental doors of a closed mind.

OUTREACH

Establishing Rapport with Strangers

The word rapport comes from the French language. It implies reciprocal relationships of harmony, accord, conformity, or affinity. It is the common ground of sympathetic relationship between two persons. There are obviously many degrees of rapport, all the way from a workable basis for communication to the strongest affinity. Rapport designates that element of reciprocal understanding that is the common ground for communication.

Establishing rapport is the first step in every interview. Sometimes it is readily achieved, other times investigators must put forth a real outgoing effort to establish rapport with the subject.

Following a courteous and friendly greeting, private investigators should look for a common ground or common interest with the subject. The subject's interests are the key to creating the accord that will unlock the doors of information. Once this bridge is built and combined with the investigator's empathy, the result will be like twin keys to twin locks that open up the flow of information.

One should never try to conduct an interview without first creating that essential receptivity. The higher the degree of rapport, the more satisfactory the interview will be to both parties. Obviously, this will vary considerably with different subjects. Some subjects are hardly capable of reaching rapport; the investigator must always take the initiative. Without some kind of accord private investigators cannot win the cooperation of the subject. It is an art to be able to establish rapport with a total stranger in the first meeting with that person—and to do so within a few moments.

Fortunately for the investigators, there are many people who are willing to disclose any information they may have in the interests of truth and justice. There is, however, a tendency on the part of others to avoid becoming involved. The private investigators with tolerance toward all seek to meet every person on his or her own level, and to establish whatever rapport is necessary to secure cooperation. In most cases they will be successful if they courteously and persistently probe for the information.

Adapting to Differing Personalities and Circumstances

People who are adaptable are capable of making suitable adjustments to fit different personalities and of altering strategy to cope with changing circumstances. Such adaptability is fundamental to a successful private investigation career. Investigators must adapt to accommodate different people. Tact and ingenuity may be taxed to the limit to enable investigators to communicate with difficult people. A sudden change in a situation may force modification of approach, method, or technique to meet different attitudes, altered conditions, surprise, and unexpected moves or reactions of subjects or interviewees.

Assignments will often require private investigators to communicate with people whose lifestyles and ideas are not the same as theirs. To obtain the desired information they will need to adapt to these lifestyles, personalities, and characters. In doing so, they will quickly discover that different persons have different perspectives toward investigative situations and will react differently to the same happening, tort, or crime. Some tell us that to be a private investigator a person needs to be broad-minded, cool-headed, warm-hearted, thick-skinned, totally adjustable, and both insult-proof and shock-proof.

Adaptability does not mean compromise, however. Effective private investigators adapt without sacrificing principle, human rights, justice, or fair play; and without compromising the purpose of an interview. Professional private investigators constantly strive to be equally effective with people at all levels of life.

Adaptability achieves its maximum potential when it bridges seemingly incompatable personality differences. It is always a source of satisfaction to obtain information from difficult people. Not only are investigators individuals, but each case, whether civil or criminal, has its own peculiar characteristics. No two cases are exact replicas of each other; no two investigations are identical in all aspects. The nature, circumstances, and personalities of each case, even when similar to others in some ways, tend to differ to a greater or lesser degree. The human relations bridge is adaptability, and investigators will need to cross that bridge on every assignment that involves contact with other people.

Communicating Effectively

Communication is the channel through which information flows, and information is the heart of investigation. All successful private investigators are effective at communicating with other persons and at getting others to communicate with them. They communicate in the field with all kinds of interviewees, contacts, and informants, and, of course, their clients. They communicate in the office, the courtroom, and wherever and whenever else they seek to obtain or impart information. Interviews, interrogations, consultations, and negotiations all call for communication verbally and, later, through written reports. Therefore, private investigators' communications must be clear, accurate, and easily understood, whether they are spoken or written.

There are four basic objectives that should always be considered in any interview, interrogation, consultation, or other type of communication.

1. Private investigators must be able to communicate on the other person's own level and to make known just what is wanted from that person. In interviewing, that would be the disclosure of whatever relevant information the interviewee has.
2. Private investigators must be sure that they are clearly and accurately understood by the interviewee (or person).
3. Private investigators must get the interviewee (or other party) to communicate with them. In the case of an investigative interview, the interviewee must clearly make known just what he knows about the matter.
4. Private investigators must be sure that they clearly and accurately understand what the interviewee is saying.

Interviewing is not the place for big words, complicated statements, and long confusing questions. Often investigators must speak so simply that a child can understand and intelligently respond. Everything they say and every question they ask should be clearly understood by the interviewee, with explanations and clarification as necessary. They listen carefully to make sure they correctly understand both what the interviewee is saying and what he means to say. If there is any question about the subject's statements, investigators clarify each point so that they can report it accurately and clearly. Only in this way can investigators determine the evidential substance of the testimony.

BELIEVABILITY. Before an interviewee really confides in a private investigator, he seeks for some basis to believe in the investigator's sincerity and trustworthiness. He needs to believe that the investigator not only has a right to the information, but can be depended on to make use of the information fairly, legally, and accurately. Believability is an essential element of communication.

Investigators are responsible for initiating and consummating effective communication, and for creating believability, confidence, and trust in the minds of interviewees. Investigators who are believable usually win the cooperation of their subjects. People do not trust those they cannot believe.

A witness who cooperates relies on the investigator's fidelity, adherence to duty and to the legal obligations of his profession. A witness also counts on the investigator's loyalty to his sources of information. That means protecting those sources as necessary to assure their safety whenever they incur danger through their cooperation. A witness also trusts private investigators to report accurately what they have been told. No witness wants his information misinterpreted. Before information can be accurately reported it must be accurately understood. Anybody who helps and cooperates in an investigation is going to place confidence and trust in the investigator. So also do clients, contacts, informers, and others who assist in digging up evidence. No sane private investigator will ever betray this trust.

Believability is the foundation of confidence and trust. Subjects who believe in an investigator's fair dealings and trustworthiness cooperate willingly. Without believability private investigators are lost. With total strangers, believability must be created quickly by investigator's attitudes, manners, and methods of approach. The more quickly an interviewee's confidence and trust are won, the more effectively can the investigator set the stage for a good interview.

CLARITY AND ACCURACY. Clarity and accuracy are the primary essentials of intercommunication between interviewer and interviewee. All private investigators must be able to communicate clearly and accurately in every face-to-face interview. They must also be able to help the interviewee disclose all his information as clearly, completely, and accurately as possible. Private investigators ask specific questions to clarify details, and even more precise questions to ascertain the accuracy of the interviewee's information. Does the interviewee mean to say what the private investigators think he said, or did he mean something else?

HOW GOOD ARE THE PRIVATE INVESTIGATORS' QUESTIONS? When interviewing, efficiency is judged by investigators' questions, not by subjects' answers. How finely tuned are the questions to investigative needs and communication problems of a specific interview? How skillfully can questions be used to probe for facts and details? Have the questions secured all the information the interviewee has?

The private investigators who want clear and accurate answers must ask clear and accurate questions. Interviewees must understand the questions before they can reply with understanding. Both the ability to listen accurately and to question clearly and effectively to draw out all known facts are among the most vital skills in the whole field of investigation. These abilities are given more attention in a separate volume that deals with the art of interviewing.

The interview reveals the impact of the investigator's personality on the subject. A kindly persuasive personality combined with investigative expertise and courteous consideration can make the giving of information a reasonably pleasant experience for the interviewee, even when unpleasant matters must be discussed.

Persuading People

Investigators frequently have to persuade a reluctant subject to cooperate with their investigative efforts. They need to be able to change the subject's viewpoint and persuade him to react in a different way than he is inclined to react.

The art of persuasion is the ability to overcome barriers to communication erected by the internal and external influences that affect the subject's position. One's thoughts, feelings, attitudes, responses, and actions are stimulated by the outer world and by the inner world. When the outer world threatens in any way, it influences a person's judgment and the position he feels obliged to take.

Prudent private investigators are aware of this dual influence and understand how it affects a subject's responses to questions. Thus they are not dismayed by any initial reactions those influences may cause. To the extent the occasion may require, they probe for the real reasons behind an interviewee's reluctance to disclose what he or she knows.

Assume a private investigator is confronted with a reluctant interviewee who for some inner or outer reason(s), or both, hesitates or is afraid to disclose what he knows. At first, the private investigator usually has no idea what conflicts or compulsions impel the subject to react in a certain manner. He is not aware of all the inner and outer stimuli that may be making all sorts of demands on the subject. But all these influences have some bearing, consciously or unconsciously, on the response to the interviewer.

Such situations call for tact and consideration. One does not bully a reluctant interviewee into submission. Effective private investigators seek to draw the interviewee's fears, anxieties, animosities, or compulsions out into the open where they can be dealt with intelligently, considerately, and positively.

GETTING A RELUCTANT SUBJECT TO TALK. Whenever a subject manifests initial reluctance to disclose information, the private investigator should not hesitate to ask why the subject feels as he does. Courteous, concerned questions encourage a subject to talk about his problems. This in turn may make the subject aware of the weakness of his position and lead him to abandon it.

The private investigator should also be alert to the fact that the subject may not go directly to the heart of the problem with his first replies. Some conversational detective work may be necessary to get at the real reasons for the reluctance. It is very important at this stage not to allow the subject to take over the interview. The investigator must keep control at all times while he attempts to get the subject to lay his problems or fears on the table.

It is generally good strategy to get the subject to talk about his reluctance, hostility, or fears until he reaches a point of inconsistency, which tends to create self-doubt as to the validity of his position. The private investigator can help point out this inconsistency. When a reluctant interviewee actually exposes his own inconsistency, he is more amenable to the private investigator's persuasion to cooperate. In this way he helps the investigator break down his own reluctance or hostility.

The private investigator should also be aware that he may initially be a part of the subject's anxieties, and will need to allay those fears. A subject whose feelings are a barrier to communication should be encouraged to talk out his feelings and reveal their source and extent. How strong is the fear or anxiety? From what source does it come? How valid is it? When a subject becomes aware of the private investigator's interest in his concerns, he becomes more receptive to the assurances that can allay them. Fear that remains inside continues to create anxiety. Fear that is brought out into the open and freely talked about becomes less threatening and repressive. It then becomes easier for the investigator to help the subject look at his problem from a more constructive viewpoint. By doing so he removes the barrier and opens the door to information. In addition, the subject's ego is strengthened when the investigator replaces his self-doubt with willingness to communicate and disclose important information. This is the interview-conditioning atmosphere created by the persuasive ability of the private investigator.

No experienced private investigators labor under the illusion that theirs is the only impact affecting the subject at the moment, particularly if the subject is a victim or a suspect. There are usually many personal factors influencing what the subject will do or say; he is not just waiting for private investigators to come along and interview him.

IMPLANTING THE SPIRIT OF WILLINGNESS. Most cooperative witnesses are glad to communicate even before they are approached, but when the desired response is not shortly forthcoming, the private investigator's first task is to create a willingness to cooperate in the mind of the interviewee.

Tactful persuasion is the art required to instill willingness in another person's mind, or to strengthen a favorable response that is weakly beginning to emerge. The objective is to establish first a mood of receptivity to the process of communication, and then willingness to disclose known information.

Investigators often find it necessary to help the subject free his mind of personal distractions or concerns so he can focus his attention on the recall matters pertaining to the interview. Barriers created by inner preoccupations may need to be broken down. The private investigator may have to build up the subject's ego to help him maintain his self-image while cooperating with the investigation.

Influencing another by persuasion is not a matter of outside pressure; it is an inside job. Therefore the private investigator first must put forth an effort to become a part of the other person's world. He seeks for that "we interaction" that puts them both on the same side in the search for the truth. With experience, the private investigator soon detects whether or not the interviewee or contact is favorably inclined toward disclosing all he knows. If the subject is favorable the interview is soon under way. If not, the private investigator indicates his respect for the other person's viewpoint, and if there is any part of it on which he can agree, he tells him so, but continues to point out the importance of the subject's contribution to the search for truth. It is a matter of sensitivity created by empathy, and courteous consideration of others that leads to communicative rapport.

Persuasion is not the forceful bending of another's will or a matter of powerful argument or authoritative voice. It is the ability to influence the mind of another by understanding as well as logic, by sympathy as well as common sense, and by concern as well as conviction. It always includes the private investigator's friendly interest in his subject, and in his concerns as well as in his information. Thus persuasion is not pounding into the subject from the outside, but rather that skillful art of getting him to reach for the idea from the inside.

COPING WITH THE SUBJECT'S EMOTIONS. Emotions frequently erect a barrier to communication in that they tend to "give out" rather than "take in." Sometimes private investigators will need to let a subject explode and blow off his emotional steam before they can engage him in reasonable conversation, particularly if he is a suspect or accomplice, or a close friend or relative of one. But while the investigator allows the subject to give vent to his feelings, he must never lose control of the interview or allow the situation to get out of hand. Within limits determined by the investigator, the interviewee releases his emotional reactions. This calls for the private investigator's understanding, not condemnation. Explosions do not last forever; they are usually over in a few moments at the most and followed by a period of relative calm. The subject having discharged his pent-up feelings is more receptive, and the interview has a chance to succeed.

Problem interviews are another test of the investigator's patience. Patience, however, combined with a conscious effort to adjust to the subject's feelings, emotions, and concerns can often achieve a cooperative meeting of the minds and willingness on the part of the subject to disclose the desired information. It is often possible to create a good feeling within a subject who initially disclosed only bad feelings.

PRIVATE INVESTIGATORS' SELF-CONTROL. Self-control is an essential quality for investigators. They will often need to control their own emotions while making allowance for those of others. Above all, private investigators must keep from losing their tempers. By concentrating on the subject, they help to keep their emotions in control.

All private investigators may have reason to be angry at times, but that anger should be kept under control. The moment they explode in anger, they lose control not only of themselves but of the interview or interrogation. Anger defeats them and their objective and sabotages investigative communications. Professional private investigators know how to keep their emotions under control—especially the wrong kinds of emotions.

RELATING TO THE SUBJECT'S PERSONAL CONCERNS.   The private investigator's persuasion and reassurance take on significance only as they relate specifically to a subject's personal concerns. Persuasion to cooperate, when such persuasion is necessary, begins with the investigator's own adaptation to the interests, fears, and concerns of his subject.

By first considering a reluctant subject's viewpoints, the investigator shows his interest in and concern for the subject. The interviewee may be worried about what he knows, about the consequences of disclosing that information, or even about the consequences of not disclosing it. Who will be hurt by the information he has to give? How many people will be affected by it? How will he become involved? What risk will he take? While the investigator must be careful not to allow the interviewee to take over the interview, he nonetheless must be ready to consider the interviewee's rational concerns.

Perhaps the information the interviewee has to disclose pertains to a crime, and he or some member of his family has been warned or threatened if he tells what he knows. The situation becomes complicated by the subject's increased fear. Obviously strong reassurance from the investigator is a must, and dispelling the subject's fears and anxieties becomes a key element in investigative persuasion.

CLUES TO THE SUBJECT'S CHANGING ATTITUDE.   A subject's tone of voice is an inevitable indicator of his inner feelings and attitudes. Any softening or warming of the voice tone indicates that resistance is yielding to private investigators' persuasion. Another clue to growing receptivity is when the subject asks questions about what the investigators want from him, or about the personal consequences of disclosing or not disclosing information. This is especially true when questions are asked in a reflective rather than belligerent manner. Questions are a sign of increased receptivity, while statements or assertions are not necessarily so.

Any self-doubt a subject may express regarding his reluctance, non-cooperation, or hostility is a receptive breakthrough. In cases where establishing rapport takes longer, private investigators may have to probe for weakness in the subject's position. They should tactfully concentrate on it until the subject is aware of the weakness and begins to question its merit.

The ability to persuade is vital to private investigators. They are not armed with the legal power to make people talk, but must persuade their subjects to do so. This is why it is so important that private investigators radiate a genuine and persuasive personality.

The Ability to Make Friends

Abraham Lincoln reportedly once gave advice to the effect that one who wished to win another man to his cause must first convince that person that he was his sincere friend. Friendliness and the ability to make friends are priceless keys to success in any people-oriented business in that they make others feel appreciated and secure.

Making new friends is a lifelong practice for professional investigators. No investigator ever had too many friends. Their business, law-enforcement, and professional friends, including other private investigators, are the greatest assets. Friends represent an extension of influence and are channels of private investigators' goodwill. Many are key contacts who can provide vital information or advice.

"True friends," according to Wolfgang Lotz, are a "rare commodity . . . worth their weight in diamonds." In *A Handbook for Spies* he reminds those contemplating becoming spies, "Your capacity for friendship may save your life one day."[6] In private investigation it is also true that a capacity for friendship may save an investigator's career when some key contact built on genuine friendship proves decisive in the solution of a very difficult case.

The ability to make friends begins with the investigator's interest in other people and their welfare. As Charles Gow once said, "You can make more friends in two months by becoming interested in other people than you can in two years by trying to get other people interested in you."[7] Investigators must be able to line up their personalities with those of other persons and mesh mental gears with them. The empathy shown by service to others is the surest motivational identification with other people and their concerns.

PERSONALITY TRAITS TO DEVELOP

There are so many good traits that can enhance the professional abilities of private investigators. Determination is one important factor. "The surest way not to fail," advises Sheridan, "is to determine to succeed."[8] All successful private investigators share this characteristic. Consider again the decisive role determination played in the investigative careers of Pinkerton and William J. Burns. It is said of Burns that "his skill very probably was a rare and highly perfected form of common sense, combined with dogged perseverence . . . ."[9]

Key Qualities

Every word in the list below could be commented on at length if space would permit. The list is not exhaustive, but it does contain excellent personal qualities to be coveted and cultivated for effective service. Each quality is followed by descriptive comments to elucidate its significance:

- Affable—easy to speak to, amiable, good natured
- Agreeable—pleasing to the mind or senses; pleasant

- Alert — ready and quick to understand or act; aware
- Believable — one whom other persons can believe and trust
- Broad-minded — tolerant and considerate of others' views
- Calm — able to control emotions; free from agitation and excitement
- Courageous — dauntlessly able to meet difficulties and danger
- Common sense — down-to-earth good judgment
- Courteous — shows courtesy and respect to everyone
- Curious — habitually inquisitive, anxious to learn, prying
- Dependable — worthy of being depended on; reliable and trustworthy
- Determined — resolute, decisive, able to see an investigation through to its finish
- Empathic — able to put oneself in another's place and feel with him
- Energetic — possesses an active drive; performs with energy and reserve strength
- Enthusiastic — inspired with living; ardent and alive; comes alive with interest
- Faithful — firm in adherence to promises, contracts, and keeping one's word; worthy of confidence
- Gentle — refined in manners, of a gentle rather than harsh nature; has a soothing, respectful influence on others
- Honest — has integrity; truthful, frank, and straightforward in conduct or speech; free from fraud, honorable
- Humble — unassuming but efficient; not aggressively and assertively proud
- Impartial — unbiased, equitable, free from favoritism, fair
- Ingenious — possessed of inventive ingenuity, shrewd, capable of creating a clever and effective solution to an investigative problem
- Just — equitable and impartial in action and judgment
- Kind — deals kindly with others; has a considerate nature
- Law-abiding — conforms to or lives in accordance with law
- Level-headed — has sound judgment, balanced reasoning
- Likeable — is liked for attractive nature and qualities
- Motivated — has inner qualities that impel to action
- Natural — free from artificiality or pretense
- Objective — able to concentrate on facts and external aspects of investigation without focusing on subjective feelings
- Observant — takes careful notice; blessed with keen powers of observation
- Patient — capable of calm waiting and forbearance under provocation; undaunted by obstacles and delays
- Perceptive — discerning, aware; has alert senses
- Persistent — tenacious, dogged, able to see the problem through

- Persevering—steadfast in a pursuit or undertaking, persisting in spite of counterinfluences
- Prudent—capable of directing and conducting self wisely and judiciously; discreet, sensible, reasonable, and skillful in the application of capabilities
- Remembers well—capable of recollection and recall
- Responsible—accountable, reliable; able to answer for own conduct and obligations and to assume trust
- Resourceful—able to fall back on other sources or strategies when the usual means are not effective; has reserve abilities and alternative resources
- Self-confident—self-reliant and self-determined, able to rely on and have confidence in own efforts and skills
- Self-controlled—in command of self, acts, and emotions; self-disciplined, self-possessed; has self-mastery
- Sincere—is what he appears to be; genuine, real, unfeigned, wholehearted; free from hypocrisy or simulation
- Sagacious—has keen sense perceptions; discerning in judging men, motives, and means; shrewdly penetrating and far sighted
- Sociable—of a nature to be companionable with others; friendly, able to have pleasant social relations
- Thinker—is capable of deliberate and deductive reasoning; able to reflect on and analyze information received and evidence examined
- Thorough—able to carry things through to completion; painstaking, exact, and careful about details
- Tolerant—tolerates practices, habits, and beliefs that differ from his own; treats those who differ with consideration
- Understanding—capable of comprehending and discerning true interpretations; has reasoned judgment and rational discernment
- Versatile—has many aptitudes, especially the ability readily to accommodate changing attitudes, circumstances, and situations that require change in tactics or positions
- Vigilant—alertly watchful
- Vigorous—strong, robust, full of physical strength; has the vitality to endure
- Warm-hearted—cordial and sympathetic; has feelings for the welfare of fellow beings
- Well-spoken—has ability to speak with propriety under all circumstances

Ability and personality develop as we set specific goals to make desirable traits and capabilities part of our nature and talents. It is not merely what we have been, even what we now are, but rather what we may yet become that really counts. By conscious practice and experience these personality desirables become inherent in our lives and our interpersonal relationships.

NOTES

1. Montapert, A. A. *Distilled wisdom.* (Englewood Cliffs, N.J.: Prentice-Hall, 1964), 315.

2. Cerney, J. V. *How to develop a million dollar personality.* (West Nyack, N.Y.: Parker Publishing Co., 1964), 16.

3. Pinkerton, A. *Criminal reminiscences and detective sketches.* (New York: G. W. Carleton & Co, 1897. Reprint. New York: Garrett Press, 1969), 283.

4. Cerney, J. V. *How to develop a million dollar personality,* 14.

5. Montapert, A. A. *Distilled wisdom,* 273.

6. Lotz, W. *A handbook for spies.* (New York: Harper & Row, 1980), 13.

7. Montapert, A. A. *Distilled wisdom,* 164.

8. Ibid., 146.

9. Caesar, G. *Incredible detective. The biography of William J. Burns.* (Englewood Cliffs, N.J.: Prentice-Hall, 1968), 19.

Chapter 3
Methodology of Investigation

"Investigations, regardless of type or ultimate purpose, involve the task of gathering and evaluating information."
— The Training Key[1]

"The agent has to adapt his m.o. [method of operation] to his own personality and to the circumstances of a given situation. Besides a variety of technical skills that he has to master in every detail, all he can be taught are the basic principles of the profession. His success or failure will depend on how he applies them."
—Wolfgang Lotz[2]

The quotation by Wolfgang Lotz, taken from his work *A Handbook for Spies,* is equally applicable to agents of private investigation. The mastery of the techniques of investigation is essential to their high-quality performance. But it is how the techniques are adapted to the personalities of the operatives and to the people and circumstances of investigations that determine their practicality. Investigative principles must be tactfully applied to persons, events, situations, conditions, and circumstances. Having said this, we come back to the initial necessity of understanding the methodology of investigation. One must know of the method before one can attempt to apply it or improve on it in actual experience.

Methodology is the branch of logic that deals with the principles of procedure—it is the science of method, the basis on which skilled performance is built. Although the methodology that discloses verifiable, effective procedures and principles of investigation together with the knowledge of proved operational methods may be called a science, it is not an exact science because all these principles have to be adapted to an endless variety of persons and circumstances.

Private investigators deal with what Jay J. Armes calls the "infinitely variable factors" of the "human heart and mind," and because they are so variable, private investigators should not "try standardizing the approach to either."[3] Investigators constantly need to adapt themselves and their methods to different personalities and situations. Beginners, however, must begin with known, proved methods of investigation. Experience will teach them how to fine-tune and refine these methods to increase their effectiveness in dealing with all kinds of people. They are well advised to study and practice the observation, gathering, and classification of facts as demonstrated in the know-how of the successful pioneers and professionals who have left us a heritage of knowledge, method, and experience upon which we can build our own individual investigative skills and expertise.

It would take many volumes to cover the entire field of investigation. Its incredible scope defies any attempt to confine it. In this work we hope to provide the reader with some basic methods and techniques that are essential to effective performance. Each of the four volumes deals with methodology, describing the techniques and strategies of investigation and skills of performance.

There are fifteen key words that define private investigators' essential activities. Other important definitions are considered in the other books, but the following paragraphs give a preview of principal activities of the private investigation career.

SEVEN I'S OF INVESTIGATION

This section introduces aspects of investigation to assure an awareness of their importance to the private investigation career. Throughout all the volumes we will be reminded continually of the key role they play in successful investigation.

Information

Information must be considered as the lifeblood of investigation. Investigation is primarily the gathering of evidential information. Private investigators are literally sponges who absorb all available information from every possible source—human, documentary, and material.

Evidential information is the bottom line. What are the facts? What is the truth of the matter? Facts alone provide evidence, and they must be

Facts - Happened
Acts + Actions

obtained, recorded, verified, evaluated, and reported by whatever legal investigative techniques necessary—researching records, interviewing people, collecting physical evidence, conducting surveillance, sub rosa photography, going undercover. To be evidential, information must also be factual and relevant to the issues of the case.

Investigative information must be factual and accurate. A fact has really happened or is actually the case. Acts and actions are facts. Fantasies are not. Private investigators search for the truth known by observation as they deal with personalities, circumstances, conditions, identifications, and happenings of one sort or another. Factual evidential information is their stock in trade. Every private investigator will do well to always keep in mind the basic maxim of the profession, namely, that "an investigator is no better than his information."

Interviewing

- interviewing Primary way to recieve info

Interviewing is the primary "how" of obtaining information. Most of the information private investigators gather over the years will come from other people, who by virtue of their proximity to, involvement in, or awareness of the situation or event, or their relationship with the parties involved, have personal or exclusive knowledge of relevant facts. The investigative process involves interviewing these individuals. Therefore there is nothing more important to an investigator than the ability to interview people successfully.

All private investigators should master the art of face-to-face communication. It is vital to be able to conduct a conversation with the purpose of stimulating a free flow of evidential information. The art of interviewing actually involves four basic capabilities:

imp

1. To motivate the other person to talk and tell all he or she knows about the subject of the investigation
2. To listen attentively and perceptively to all the factual information disclosed
3. To ask clear, concise, pertinent questions to draw out the answers that will clarify all relevant details
4. To obtain signed written statements of fact from interviewees

Personal interviews play such a vital role in the information-gathering process that all private investigators should make mastering the art of interviewing one of the first career objectives. The more effective they become in interviewing, the more their services will be in demand.

Interrogation

To interrogate is to examine or probe by asking questions. The word implies a formal questioning or inquiry that is more exacting than an interview. It is usually the procedure for questioning uncooperative or hostile persons.

Carroll R. Hormachea, in his *Sourcebook in Criminalistics,* makes this observation:

> A distinction is made between interviewing and interrogation. While both have much in common, the essential difference is perhaps best suggested by the words: antipathy, uncooperativeness, hostility. Thus victims and eyewitnesses are interviewed; suspects and criminals are interrogated.[4]

The attitude of the subject largely determines whether he will be interviewed or interrogated. The specific intent of the questioning is also a factor. If the subject is very reluctant to discuss the matter, he is not likely voluntarily to disclose much information unless private investigators can succeed in breaking down that reluctance and motivating him to adapt a more cooperative attitude. Interrogators must be both astute and persuasive to get a reluctant subject to disclose the desired information.

The authors of *Principles of Investigation* comment on the problems of interrogation:

> The investigator has to work within, around, and in spite of the resentment and resistance of the person being interrogated, and this requires more than communication skills alone. Interrogation is a creative process which calls upon insight, sensitivity, a wide background of knowledge, innovation, logic, a grasp of facts, and an understanding of human nature.[5]

Kenney and More acknowledge that some techniques prove to be more effective than others. Most interrogations of suspects, particularly of those in custody, are conducted by police officers or detectives. Private investigators commonly use the interrogation process when dealing with a reluctant, uncooperative, or hostile witness, or other person who will not voluntarily disclose information.

When law-enforcement officers conduct custodial interrogations of a suspect held in custody or who has been apprehended, they are obligated to advise the subject of his basic rights—the right to counsel and to remain silent (commonly known as the *Miranda* rights, from the 1966 Supreme Court decision in *Miranda* v. *Arizona*).

Identification

Investigators are often called on to establish the identity of persons, documents, or material objects of evidence. Persons and things are identified by accurate descriptions. For persons this includes appearance, facial features, characteristic movements, and marks such as scars or birthmarks. Clothing, laundry marks, fibers, hairs, fingerprints, palmprints, and the like may also help to identify a person. Appliances, machines, or equipment may be identified by serial numbers. A tire impression may identify both the car and the manufacturer who made the tire. A shoe impression can identify the person who wears the shoe. Tool marks or impressions may identify the instrument that made them. All of these items that identify vary according to the person or object involved and the circumstances of the case. It is exceedingly important to identify the right suspect and not to subject an innocent person to the rigors and often tragic consequences of a trial.

Correct identification is also important in missing persons and surveillance assignments. Private skip tracers must have positive identification with which to recognize a person. It is also obviously important that a person who is to be placed under surveillance be clearly identified so that private investigators will not observe the wrong individual. Likewise, stolen goods must be identifiable in order to be returned to their rightful owner.

The task of the forensic pathologist in laboratory analysis of items of evidence, such as fingerprints, transfer evidence, document alterations, and the like is primarily one of identification.

Intercommunication

Intercommunication is the two-way exchange that takes place during investigative interviews or interrogations. It is also an important part of all conversations with contacts, informants, complainants, victims, clients, and fellow investigators.

The term intercommunication combines the word "communication," which means to impart or convey information, and the prefix "inter," which means among, between, or together. "Togetherness" increases the satisfaction and effectiveness of communications between two people and among larger groups.

Two skills are required for successful intercommunication: the ability to communicate effectively with another person, and the ability to get that other person to communicate. These abilities are more readily implemented in interviews than they are in interrogations, although the intercommunication process is always at work, to a greater or lesser degree, in every information-obtaining interview or interrogation. The intercommunication of investigative conversations is realized when the spirit of cooperation is established in a mutual desire to find the truth of the matter under discussion.

It is the responsibility of private investigators tactfully and courteously to establish this conversational exchange between both parties so that together they can focus their attention on the available evidential information. The principles of the art of intercommunication are discussed in the volume on interviews and interrogations.

Inspection

To inspect is to take a close and critical view of something. The term inspector has a variety of applications. The title Building Inspector is a typical example of its application to official examinations.

Scotland Yard detectives are called Inspectors, implying their duty and responsibility to examine closely and critically all items of observed or uncovered evidence; to conduct detective inspections of reported criminal scenes and activities; and carefully to inspect any situations or evidences disclosed by such investigations. In the United States, Inspector is a title given to a police official in charge of several precincts, who ranks below a superintendent.

For private investigators, the term applies primarily to close examination of any form of evidence uncovered in the pursuit of facts. It may be the inspection of a scene of an industrial accident, for example, or a vehicle, document, footprint, tire impression, tool mark, or other object or substance of physical evidence. Nothing should escape the private investigators' keen observation and scrutiny. When inspecting all tangible objects of potential evidence, great care should be taken to preserve the evidence intact without injury, contamination, or damage in any way.

Investigative scrutiny calls for close examination. It includes the inspection of the entire area of any event under investigation. It may involve the minute examination of some physical clue—a mark, a number, a fiber, a hair, a strange impression. It may call for the inspection of specific premises, vehicles, machines, tools, equipment, furniture, clothes, shoes, documents, records, or any other object of evidence—large or small, massive or minute, movable or permanent.

Scientific inspection is a primary task of the forensic scientist. It embraces all the techniques of the criminal lab where all kinds of items of evidence are subjected to the closest scrutiny and analysis. From investigator to lab technician, inspection plays an important role in determining evidential value.

Intelligence

Intelligence is a word with many applications. It deals with a most outstanding phenomenon—the perceptiveness, sagacity, and capabilities of the intelligent human mind. It also refers to secretly obtained and verified information such as is gathered by the Secret Service, the CIA, or by private investigators in sensitive investigations.

A Hoover commission task force, in a 1955 survey of the national intelligence community, arrived at the following definition: "Intelligence deals with all the things which should be known in advance of initiating a course of action."[6]

In *The Intelligence Establishment,* Ransom notes that "Nothing is more crucial in the making of national decisions than the relationship between intelligence and policy, or, in a broader sense, between knowledge and action."[7]

We use the term intelligence to designate the secret information imparted to private investigators during the course of sensitive investigations. This information may come from informers, relatives, business associates, or from other members of the same association, union, syndicate, or other groups. Intelligence applies to information that has been evaluated, analyzed, verified, and proved to be significantly accurate, and can therefore serve as the basis for intelligent and just action. In investigation, intelligence is synonymous with verified secret information.

According to Ransom, Admiral William F. Raborn, Director of Central Intelligence from 1964 to 1966, defined the word thus:

> Intelligence, as we use the term, refers to information which has been carefully evaluated as to its accuracy and significance. The difference between "information" and "intelligence" is the important process of evaluating the accuracy and assessing the significance in terms of national security.[8]

Translating the above into private investigator applications, we note that intelligence involves not only information, but accuracy and significance. The more accurate and significant the facts obtained, the greater the intelligence status of the investigation. One can readily see how, for example, verified intelligence reports or "counterintelligence" would aid in combating industrial espionage. Counterintelligence efforts are often launched to nullify the activities of secret agents who operate among the workshops, laboratories, and research centers of the industrial complexes of our nation.

Generally, the word intelligence is applied to the work of the Secret Service and the Central Intelligence Agency (CIA), and similar organizations in other countries of the world. But these agencies do not have a monopoly on intelligence operations. Private investigators often function as intelligence agents for industrial or individual clients. They may, for example, obtain the secret information that will enable a client to take appropriate action to protect himself against any individual or corporate danger that may threaten him or his company.

One of the lessons the nation's intelligence community was taught in World War II also holds significant meaning for private investigators. In *The Craft of Intelligence,* Allen Dulles quotes then President Truman as follows:

> The war taught us this lesson—that we had to collect intelligence in a manner that would make the information available where it was needed and when it was

wanted, in an intelligent and understandable form. If it is not intelligent and understandable, it is useless.[9]

These words underline two basic essentials: the matter of meeting intelligence deadlines, and the imperative need for all intelligence information to be understandable.

Before leaving the subject of intelligence, we come back to its application to the human mind. Of all the tools private investigators use in this profession, the most important is the mind. Intelligence is intuitive, resourceful, awake, alert, and aware. It is tactful and understanding. It knows how to deal with unexpected situations and uncooperative persons. It motivates commonsense action.

In this connection it should be noted that real private investigators never betray the confidence of a client or of the employer who entrusts them with legal and ethical responsibilities. The information obtained from a client is kept confidential. The relationship between investigators and clients, as Jay Armes puts it, "is completely inviolate, totally private."[10]

FOUR R's OF INVESTIGATION

There are four words of special significance to the private investigator that begin with the letter R: rapport, research, records, and reports.

Rapport

Rapport is harmony with humanity, accord with fellow human beings. It lies at the heart of all effective communication, making good interviews a reality and good interrogations a possibility. Rapport is the secret of dealing effectively with people. All private investigators need to develop rapport with every person from whom they wish to receive information. Rapport breaks down barriers and puts the other person at ease. It warms up the communication lines and unleashes a flood of information.

Research

Research includes any careful and close search of written records, public and private, that are pertinent to the investigation. Some investigations will call for much more critical and exhaustive research than others. They may involve research in the public or law libraries in the appropriate legal volumes, directories, or other sources. Investigations may require private investigators to secure information from such sources as government agency records, documents, data banks, trade journals, loose-leaf services, and the like, or any other record or publication that can provide valuable information.

The need for research varies according to the nature of the assignment. It obviously takes more research to delve fully into the background of an individual being considered for a post of high responsibility than it does merely to check on the vital statistics and identification of another person. Sometimes a few telephone calls to key contacts may be all that is required. At other times private investigators may need to do a great deal of footwork and "eye-searching" to come up with the needed information. Chapter 4 deals with common sources of private investigators' information.

Records

An investigator's notebook is his most important investigative tool. In it he carefully records all his investigative activities and findings. Most investigators carry loose-leaf notebooks so new pages can be added as needed to accommodate new information.

Accurate report writing is based on adequate and precise field notes, clearly and concisely written, covering the investigation in complete detail. Notes are the raw materials out of which investigative reports are made. They are also the basis for investigators' testimony in a court of law.

Field notes provide a record of private investigators' original sources of information. Notes represent original source material. All ace private investigators have developed the ability to take down information with reasonable speed while it is being disclosed, in handwriting or printing that is clear and legible.

The camera is also an important tool for recording information. It provides visual documentation of the scene, vehicle, damages, injuries, papers, persons, and other objects of evidence. Pictorially documented evidence often carries considerable weight because it can be used to identify, clarify, and illustrate. Since informative details should be carefully and correctly recorded as they are obtained or immediately on their discovery, some investigators find hand-held pocket recorders to be useful.

The private investigators' records from handwritten notes, sketches, photographs, slides, moving pictures, or diagrams are the best recall aids. Notebook records of all pertinent details are vital when writing reports, discussing details of the investigation and findings with a client or private investigation firm, and when testifying in court. Without accurate and complete records the private investigators are "sunk."

Reports

Report writing, like record taking, is a vital part of all investigations. Reports document uncovered facts. Actually, reports are the only tangible product private investigators have to sell. Of course, they sell their abilities and services, but investigative results are revealed in reports delivered to the client. Some are concerned with a single incident or statement. Others may contain a long series of facts, informative data, activities, and findings. All should be accurate and factual.

The only way the client, supervisor, or other person can really know the results of the investigation is by reading the private investigator's reports. Information can obviously be relayed verbally but the final detailed disclosure of investigative findings is written out. Reports disclose what the investigators did and what they learned from what they did; and what, if any, evidential information they were able to obtain. Many investigations require a preliminary report, followed by progressive ones periodically throughout the investigation, and ending with a final closing report.

Obviously, before private investigators can write satisfactory reports, they must conduct satisfactory investigations. But the best investigations in the world could be ruined by poor reports. The private investigators' effectiveness is judged by the kinds of reports they write. Therefore they should master the basic principles of writing factually and accurately, as top-quality investigations deserve top-quality reports.

Reports communicate and inform. They provide permanent records of investigative findings. They are read and reread, analyzed, and consulted. They document private investigators' findings and can be referred to whenever it is necessary to explain those findings. Reports help determine what additional investigation may be necessary to complete the case and provide a complete summary of facts on which necessary decisions can be made. When cases go to trial, private investigators' reports can be very beneficial to attorneys.

FOUR S's OF INVESTIGATION

The last four of our fifteen key words that preview private investigation career activities begin with the letter S: surveillance, search, strategy, and security.

Surveillance

Surveillance, in the words of Charles E. O'Hara, is the "covert observation of places, persons, and vehicles for the purpose of obtaining information concerning the identification or activities of subjects."[11] Surveillance involves direct observation of the subject or place by the investigator. It is usually a secret observation of which the subject is not aware.

Surveillance is the art of keeping a close watch on the movements and activities of a subject or on a specific place. Both moving surveillance—on foot, in a vehicle, or on public transportation—and fixed or stationary surveillance are frequently used private investigation techniques. An undercover operation is a form of inside surveillance. The investigative techniques of the various types of surveillance and undercover work will be discussed in a separate volume and will not be commented on here.

Search

In a broad sense, all investigation may be described as a search. Investigators are involved in many kinds of searches—searching for persons and objects whose existence is known, but whose whereabouts are not; through public or private records and documents; for clues, leads, intelligence information, facts, and evidence; for witnesses to an accident, crime, or other happening; for information an attorney can use in a specific case; and so on. The search is always for evidential information that will enable private investigators to arrive at the truth of the matter. Techniques of the search include inquiry, observation, inspection, research, examination, and critical scrutiny. It may involve surveillance, sub rosa photography, or undercover operations.

The word search has its specific applications to each case. Constitutional protection against unreasonable searches and seizures is provided to all citizens by the Fourth Amendment as follows:

> The right of the people to be secure in their persons, houses, papers, and personal effects against unreasonable searches and seizures shall not be violated, and no warrants shall issue but upon probable cause, supported by oath or affirmation, and particularly describing the place to be searched, and the persons or things to be seized.[12]

The United States Supreme Court has ruled that the due process clause of the Fourteenth Amendment requires that any evidence secured by a search and seizure that violates the Fourth Amendment is inadmissible in a state court, just as it is in federal courts.[13]

SEARCH WARRANTS. A search warrant is a written order issued in the name of the people of the state by a justice or magistrate, and signed by him. It directs the sheriff or peace officer to search the specified premises for personal property (for example, allegedly stolen property, unlawful goods, or other incriminating evidence) and bring the same, if found, before the magistrate.

The warrant involves both the search itself and the subjective reasons for requesting it.

The warrant may also include bringing the persons occupying the premises to answer before the court for any evidence found. State penal codes provide the guidelines for the use and control of the legal process of the search warrant. Implementation of the warrant is generally consummated by law-enforcement personnel.

[Search warrants are not issued without probable cause. The written affidavit, or oral statement under oath, of the person(s) seeking the warrants must become a part of the court's records pertaining to the warrant. Affidavits or statements under oath must justify issuance of the warrant. They should be carefully drafted to stipulate the exact grounds on which the search warrant is sought, providing the magistrate with the facts of the case, not investigators' conclusions.

For example, an affidavit may be based on investigators' observations. In that event, it would state what it is that the investigators (the affiants) observed respecting the conduct of the subject or the suspect, as the case may be, that would warrant the issuing of a search warrant. The affidavit should also state where the search is to be made—the subject's person, premises, or other site that is named as a potential hiding place for incriminating evidence.

Other grounds for issuing warrants include explicit information received from the personal knowledge of a confidential informant who has established a history of providing reliable information. The nature of the information in such instances is important because an affidavit must provide a truly sufficient basis on which the magistrate can determine adequate probable cause in order to make the evidence admissible in a court of law.

Warrants may be invalidated if the court considers they were issued without sufficient cause. Defense counsels, of course, invariably seek to suppress evidence seized under search warrants whenever they can possibly find any grounds for irregularities, abuses, or insufficient cause.

Private investigators should be aware of the law-enforcement procedures regarding search and seizure. These laws are designed to implement the search for and the seizure of evidences of criminal activity. Search and seizure are usually performed by police officers, and the Fourth Amendment governs their action in enforcing the laws of the state. Generally, private investigators have no lawful authority to make a search of private premises or personal property, although they may on occasion be constrained by circumstances to issue an affidavit requesting a search warrant if they are engaged in investigating criminal activities. While specific laws pertaining to law enforcement do not apply directly to them, private investigators should nonetheless protect themselves by not violating the legal principles of the rights of privacy and security.

PROBABLE CAUSE. Before a search warrant is issued, there must be reasonable grounds for believing the proposed search would disclose evidence of guilt. In a sense the affidavit is the heart of the search warrant, and the heart of the affidavit is the sufficient probable cause. To constitute probable cause, the facts must be such that one could reasonably conclude the high probability of specified items of evidence being found within the premises or on the person of the party to be searched. In a criminal investigation this involves a strong suspicion of the guilt of the suspect.

The magistrate is obligated to issue a search warrant when he is satisfied that sufficient reasonable and legitimate grounds exist for doing so. The process of issuing and implementing a search warrant involves:

1. The affidavit (the sworn statement in writing)
2. The magistrate's issuing of the search warrant
3. The law-enforcement officer's search according to stipulations of the warrant
4. Issuance of a receipt for any property or contraband seized during the search
5. Return of the seized property or contraband to the magistrate who issued the search warrant

Both the affidavit and the warrant must contain a precise description of the premises or person to be searched and of the property, thing(s), or contraband to be seized. Search and seizure is primarily a method employed in criminal investigation, and only certain categories of property can be seized, including: (1) stolen or embezzled property; (2) property or things (weapons, tools, etc.) used to commit a felony; (3) property intended to be used as a means to commit a felony; and (4) any property or things that have evidential value to show that (a) a crime has been committed, or (b) that a specific person has in fact committed a crime.

No search of any house is permitted without a search warrant, except one on a limited basis, made by an officer in connection with a lawful arrest. If, for example, a suspect is arrested at his home, the arresting officer without a search warrant may conduct a search deemed necessary to seize any weapons that might be used against him or used to effect the suspect's escape; or anything that might prevent the hiding or destruction of evidence. This search is limited to the person of the arrestee and the immediate surrounding area that would be considered to be within his reach or control.

SEARCHES WITHOUT A SEARCH WARRANT. The Fourth Amendment to the United States Constitution basically requires that a valid search can only be made with a search warrant issued on demonstration of probable cause. The few exceptions recognized by law are confined to (1) limited searches made incident to a lawful arrest; (2) searches made with a valid free and voluntary consent of one who has the authority to grant that consent; and (3) searches made in a legally recognized emergency situation.

A search and seizure made incident to a lawful arrest must be reasonable. That is, it must be reasonably related to the cause for the arrest, be reasonable in its scope, have a definite objective, and (usually) be made contemporaneously with the arrest. The search must also be made in a reasonable manner without any physical or psychological coercion. The pat-down frisk for weapons is a common procedure of search incidential to arrest.

Search and/or seizure with consent is based on valid voluntary consent by one who is authorized to give such consent by virtue of his authority within the premises to be searched. These cases are examined closely by the fact finders in a case. As a rule, anyone who is in possession and custody of the property in question would have the right to consent to a search. Such consent is a voluntary surrender of the rights of the Fourth Amendment. The investigator making the search must have reasonable grounds for believing that the one granting the consent has the authority to do so. The extent of the search must not exceed the authority granted.

Emergency searches or seizures are acceptable when justified by necessity. For example, if police officers in search of narcotics are suddenly confronted with the possible removal or destruction of the illegal drugs, they may exercise an emergency exception and seize the drugs. If they waited for a search warrant the evidence would be gone.

Searches of automobiles or other vehicles are often justified under exceptions to the Fourth Amendment. The vehicles have great mobility, and if they are not searched immediately incident to a lawful arrest, the evidence may be forever lost.

UNREASONABLE SEARCH AND SEIZURE. Unreasonable search and seizure refers to violation of individual rights by searches made without the authority of the law and beyond reason. This would include any searches of unreasonable nature, even those made under warrants issued without adequate reason. It would especially refer to searches of an oppressive nature that would invade the subject's right to privacy, or violate the personal liberties of the one against whose person or premises the search was unreasonably made. States have statutes against unreasonable search and seizure.

PRIVATE INVESTIGATION SEARCHES ARE MANY AND VARIED. As indicated in our introductory comments, the word search has a variety of applications for private investigators. The search of a scene of an accident, injury, or crime, for example, is thorough and systematic. It should be conducted with great care so as not to damage any evidence.

Such scenes often reveal a number of evidential details and materials, including minute transfer evidence (fibers, hairs, fragments of broken glass, paint chips, foreign items of one sort or another) or footprints, fingerprints, palmprints, tool marks, tire impressions, pieces of cloth, buttons, blood, and other body fluids. Victims, vehicles, and suspects are all searched for transfer evidence. (Guidelines for making such searches are discussed in another volume.)

Private investigators are often required to search public records. Vital statistics, license information, real estate ownership records, for example, are all matters of record. A title search is made to determine who owns a parcel of land. Searches are made to determine mortgages, liens, or other encumbrances. Investigations of this nature are frequently necessary in civil disputes involving properties.

The private investigation career is a repeated search for evidence in one way or another. Half the battle is knowing where to search, and the other half is knowing how to search for the needed evidence. All private investigators should have information contacts with local custodians of public records and with those who have access to records that are not usually available to the general public, but which can be made available for investigative purposes.

Strategy

Strategy is primarily a wartime term that has been adapted to a peacetime profession. Strategy has to do with the art of employing resources. In the military sense it involves the deployment of armed personnel and equipment. It also involves large-scale planning and directing of operations and making necessary adjustments to area, action, and alignments.

Similarly, private investigators through experience in the application of the principles of investigation, develop tactful strategy in the art of employing their talents and resources in dealing effectively with people and in tracking down evidence. They adjust their strategy to the area, action, and alignments related to personal interviews, interrogations, and other procedures such as sub rosa photography, surveillance, and undercover operations.

For private investigators, strategy is divested of all warlike intent except in such matters as the war against crime and other injustices. Thus they should never look on their sources of information as enemies to be outsmarted. Only in very difficult cases will they be confronted with the need to outwit interviewees. For the most part, sources of information are private investigators' most important professional friends, and they should be treated on friendly terms as far as circumstances permit. But strategy will be called for in solving difficult cases and in interrogating uncooperative subjects. Experienced investigators become versed in the art of the strategic application of the techniques of investigation.

Security

Private security and private investigation are totally different fields of professional service, even though they occasionally may overlap. Security personnel are either direct employees of in-house departments or they are persons whose services have been contracted for with rent-a-guard and rent-a-patrol or other such agencies.

Security guards and patrol services are also made available by firms that operate both security and investigation agencies under the same general management. This accounts for the frequent identification of security operations with private investigation.

As a general rule, private investigative firms that also offer security services employ and train separate personnel for these services. The same trainee does not normally function in either capacity, but works to become a private investigator, security guard, or some other security service agent.

Most investigations are after-the-fact probes into the cause and solutions of civil, criminal, personal, professional, or business problems. Security, on the other hand, is a matter of protection of properties of the private sector. It seeks to guard against the presence of unwanted problems and to protect against both criminal and accidental losses.

Physical security is designed to protect business firms, industrial plants, institutions, government facilities, and other entities from unauthorized access, theft, espionage, sabotage, and other forms of damage or destruction from natural or manmade causes under both normal and emergency operating conditions. Security guards provide appropriate services when accident, fire, explosions, criminal or civil threats, or other emergencies occur.

Physical security is concerned with the maintenance of a safe working environment for employees, and the protection of an institution's real property, equipment, facilities, products, materials, valuables, and records. It takes into consideration the type of facility involved, physical layout and construction, critical areas, and areas of vulnerability.

Theft, industrial espionage, and sabotage are three major security hazards. Internal pilferage is considered the primary cause of commercial and industrial losses. Sabotage includes any willful act resulting in damage to, or destruction of, property; disruption of normal operations of the firm; or injury to personnel. Espionage is the theft of company secrets through the operations of an unscrupulous competitor or foreign nation.

Losses of funds, products, equipment, tools, stock, materials, industrial secrets, classified information, new product blueprints, and other assets and documents annually take a tremendous toll from the resources of commerce and industry. The presence of security personnel and the installation and use of protective equipment systems can result in considerable savings to large industrial corporations and institutions that otherwise would be vulnerable to the thief, the invading saboteur, or espionage agent.

It would take a whole volume to deal adequately with the duties and services of security personnel and with the types of sophisticated security equipment and systems currently available. Since this book deals almost exclusively with the methodology of private investigation, space does not permit comprehensive coverage of the role of security personnel. Private investigators should, however, understand the basic principles of private security, as their advice may be solicited by individuals or business establishments in planning a security program.

SKILLS OF INVESTIGATION

The fifteen key words already discussed should help put the private investigation career in perspective, but we are not through with our consideration of terms. In a sense, private investigators wear a number of hats during their careers, depending on the scope and nature of the assignments. The following additional key words describe the skills and activities of a typical investigator.

- Actor — In undercover work the investigator must be able realistically to act the role of his assumed personality, living the life of the person he purports to be.
- Analyzer — The private investigator analyzes information obtained, evidence discovered, and all investigative findings to evaluate in detail their merit, relevance to issues at stake, and specific contribution to the investigation, pro or con.
- Communicator — A considerable portion of the investigator's career is spent in communicating with other people, especially to obtain and also to impart information. Interviews, interrogations, consultations, and written reports all require this ability.
- Controller — This term is used in an investigative sense rather than in its usual reference to a comptroller, or financial officer. The private investigator must maintain control in every interview and interrogation, directing, guiding, and regulating conversation to keep the subject on the track. Control is an important element in every other investigative procedure as well.
- Describer — The private investigator cultivates his powers of description so that he can describe persons, events, scenes, premises, vehicles, objects, documents, and so on in such a way as to produce with words a mental picture.
- Detective — To detect is to discover the acts or action, existence, presence, fact, or the nature or character of. It may be observation of someone in the performance of an illegal act, detection of a clue that eventually leads to solving a civil or criminal mystery, finding physical evidence at the scene of an injury or crime, or detection of the hiding place of stolen property or the key contact for illegal operations.

- Discerner—A discerner perceives and understands differences and distinctions. It is by discernment that the private investigator identifies relevant evidence through the ability to recognize the significance of a remark, clue, or other evidential inference that may not be apparent to the noninvestigative mind. He has the discerning power to distinguish between fact and fancy, relevant and irrelevant items of information and is able to select facts from a mass of narrative and opinion. Discernment concentrates on perceptive accuracy in detecting evidence that is not obvious.
- Examiner—A private investigator examines potential evidence when he subjects a matter to investigative inquiry by looking closely at evidential disclosures of a witness or other interviewee, or when he interrogates closely. He examines physical evidence when he inspects a document or piece of evidence, or scrutinizes an object in search of a possible latent fingerprint. It should be noted that it is the forensic scientist in the criminal lab who is considered to be the expert examiner of items of physical evidence, but prior to his receiving the object, document, liquid, or whatever for scientific testing, the private investigator has first examined it to determine its potential evidential value. Whenever he tests answers by additional questions or investigates by close scrutiny, the private investigator functions as an examiner.
- Explorer—To explore is to investigate an area to make a discovery. The private investigator explores to discover facts, seeking, going after, scrutinizing the territory of the investigation, tort, or crime to arrive at the truth. The private investigator is an explorer in the field of evidence.
- Filer—The private investigator is his own file clerk, unless his agency has an effective filing organization in which trained personnel handle some of the work for him. Even then he will have his own personal filing to do. Investigation files are vitally important for the organization and preservation of evidential information. The private investigator keeps all his notes, records, reports, sketches, diagrams, photographs, and any other documentary evidence on file.
- Finder—The investigator finds evidence by searching for it. By inquiry, observation, examination, and research he unearths evidential data and information. Sometimes with luck he actually stumbles on some valuable evidence, or he may accidentally locate the person who can disclose the fact he is seeking. Mostly he finds or discovers, by reasonable systematic application of the methodology of investigation to the needs of the case by going to look for it.
- Gatherer—The investigative process is one of gathering together information and items of evidence to fit together the pieces of a puzzle. The investigator also intuitively gathers by deducing from inference. He gathers together all information accumulated from inquiry, observa-

tion, records, and physical evidence to compile as complete a factual record as possible to achieve the investigative objective.

- Identifier — The private investigator will often be called on to identify or contribute to the identity of a person, object, photograph, document, or other item admitted into evidence. To identify is to attest to, or to prove to be the same as purported or asserted.

- Inspector — An inspector critically inquires, observes, and examines. The term officially is applied to a police officer who ranks below a superintendent or deputy superintendent, and who is put in charge of a number of precincts. The private investigator, however, is an inspector in the sense of the root meaning of the word in that he scrutinizes situations, scenes, objects, documents, and anything else that must be viewed closely and critically.

- Interrogator — An interrogator verbally examines another by asking questions. The private investigator interrogates reluctant witnesses and others who do not voluntarily disclose the information to which they are privy. Suspects are interrogated.

- Interviewer — Interviewing is a great part of the private investigator's life. His face-to-face meetings with those who have knowledge of relevant facts are the primary means of gathering information from people.

- Listener — A successful private investigator cultivates the art of perceptive listening to a high degree to enable him to crystalize details of information obtained from those he interviews or interrogates. He never monopolizes conversations, he stimulates them and listens carefully to what the subject says, giving attentive heed to all points of relative significance.

- Measurer — Any private investigator involved in examining the scene of an accident, crime, or injury becomes a measurer of distances, size, length, width, and relationships that are necessary to disclose on his sketch of the scene. This includes the positions of victims, tools, weapons, vehicles, other objects of evidence and items of significance to the issue. Measurements are taken, for example, to disclose the distances between items and key objects within the scene such as furniture or equipment, and between items of evidence and the boundaries of the scene such as the walls of an inside room and the perimeters of an outdoor area.

- Noter — The private investigator is constantly recording by hand the information he obtains and the evidence he discovers. His notes consist of names, addresses, telephone numbers, places, impressions, memoranda, comments, descriptions, statements, observations, references, and evidential findings. His notebook is the private investigator's most constant and important investigative companion.

- Observer — All great investigators are observant, always taking notice of what is taking place. Quick and careful observation is an imperative of effective investigation. A private investigator's powers of observation are essential to all methods of investigation and are key factors in the techniques of surveillance and undercover operations.

- Persuader — A persuader is one who influences or convinces another to adopt a certain belief or take a certain course of action. The investigator often must tactfully persuade a reluctant interviewee or interrogatee to cooperate. Obviously, some people are more persuadable than others. The measure of tactful urging required is determined by the type of subject and the seriousness and complexities of the investigative circumstances.
- Performer — Effective performance is the acid test of all professions. A true performer continues to the finish, completing the investigation and accomplishing its purpose by means of whatever techniques are necessary.
- Planner — The effective private investigator preplans his methods and procedures in advance of investigative action, specifically to meet the needs of the assignment. This includes interviews, interrogations, surveillance activities, and whatever strategies he will employ to attain his objectives. The planner is a preparer — he always makes ready beforehand.
- Photographer — The private investigator is not necessarily a professional photographer, but he is a practical one. The camera is a vital tool of investigation, documenting evidence in pictorial form. The private investigator should be able to photograph persons, scenes, and objects, and should know enough about photography to be able to make his photographs accurate representations of the subjects.
- Questioner — Questions are the principal tools of interviews and interrogations. With them the private investigator draws out evidential information, clarifies details, probes for facts, and controls and guides the interview. To question is to ask, inquire, interrogate. Interviews, interrogations, and inquiries require skill in the art of asking clear information-obtaining questions.
- Reasoner — Good reasoning is right thinking. Investigation calls for reasoning with people and about evidence. One needs to reason agreeably and logically in order to communicate intelligently and to talk persuasively. Reason is the power to comprehend, consider, explain, influence, infer, deduce, and lead a subject into cooperative willingness.
- Recorder — The private investigator is a private recorder rather than a public one. He commits to writing or hand-printing the record of all information obtained and evidence discovered, by making entries in his notebook. He also records with the camera and by means of

sketches of scenes and diagrams to clarify his findings. He sometimes records with tape recorders, with the permission of the recordee, to preserve the interview verbatim.

- Report writer — Every private investigator writes up reports of his investigation and its results. The result is an account of his investigative activities and relates, usually in chronological order, his findings, information obtained, evidence uncovered, photographs taken, sketches or diagrams made, documents examined or secured, physical evidence collected, and so on. The report repeats the evidential information the private investigator has been told, describes any evidence found, and summarizes the investigation to date.
- Searcher — The private investigator's career is a continual search for evidence and for persons and items of information that will establish the pro or con of the matter. This involves examining public records, probing personal information, and using any necessary search procedure. Sometimes the searcher is also a researcher in public or law libraries.
- Shadower — A shadower follows subjects closely and secretly to watch and observe their activities for investigative purposes. Shadowing (or tailing) is one form of moving surveillance, performed on foot or in an automobile or other vehicle.
- Sketcher — A private investigator draws a rough draft of the chief features of a scene, machine, object, or other subject of investigation. Initially, the sketch may be rapidly executed at the scene to give the general outline, pinpoint specific items of significance, and to record important positions and measurements. It becomes the preliminary draft that forms the basis for the more accurate scale drawing to follow.
- Surveillant — A surveillant is one who keeps another under observation. Surveillance includes shadowing or tailing people on foot, by automobile, vans, or other vehicles, and keeping watch on places from fixed observation posts.
- Strategist — A strategist is a person skilled in the art of employing resources to overcome obstacles and attain objectives. The private investigator is a peacetime strategist to the extent that he is able to make well-thought-out moves or adjustments to cope with difficult problems. In war, stratagems are often tricks, ruses, or deceptive procedures to deceive the enemy. With the private investigator, strategy is less a matter of intrigue and more a tactical maneuver or skillful adjustment in order to draw out needed information, or to make the right countermove.
- Undercover operative — A private investigator who goes undercover becomes a secret investigator. An undercover operative, for example, may appear to be a regular employee of an industrial plant while under

contract to probe internal theft. He may infiltrate a subversive group, criminal ring, or syndicate to get the inside information to incriminate offenders.

• Verifier—To verify is to confirm or substantiate. The private investigator checks or tests the accuracy or exactness of, or exposes the errors in, information received. The private investigator is a verifier of the facts.

• Witness—A witness attests to a fact or event pertaining to what he has seen or heard, or otherwise knows about the matter. Whenever a case the private investigator is investigating is submitted for litigation in the civil courts or for prosecution and defense in a criminal court, the private investigator is called as a witness to bear testimony relative to his investigations and findings.

Many years ago Roger Babson referred to these six I's that lead to success: industry, intelligence, integrity, initiative, intensity, and inspiration.[14] In the light of our brief review of key words, we can understand the importance of Babson's words to a successful private investigation career. It takes these inner resources to master the techniques of investigative methodology, and since investigation is more of an art than a science, it can be mastered only in the field of experience.

NOTES

1. *Training key no. 3.* (Washington, D.C.: Field service division of the international association of chiefs of police, 1965), 1.
2. Lotz, W. *A handbook for spies.* (New York: Harper & Row, 1980), 35, 36.
3. Nolan, F. *Jay J. Armes, investigator.* (New York: Macmillan Publishing Co., 1976), 52.
4. Hormachea, C. R. *Sourcebook in criminalistics.* (Reston, Va.: Reston Publishing Co., 1974), 19, 20.
5. Kenney, J. P., and More, H. W., Jr. *Principles of investigation.* (St. Paul: West Publishing Co., 1979), 128, 129.
6. Ransom, H. R. *The intelligence establishment.* (Cambridge: Harvard University Press, 1970), 3.
7. Ibid., 3.
8. Ibid., 7.
9. Dulles, A. *The craft of intelligence.* (Westport, Conn.: Greenwood Press, 1977), 157.
10. Nolan, F. *Jay J. Armes, investigator,* 28.

11. O'Hara, C. E. *Fundamentals of criminal investigation.* (Springfield, Ill.: Charles C Thomas Publisher, 1973), 188.

12. Grossman, J. B., and Wells, R. S. *Constitutional law and judicial policy making.* (New York: John Wiley & Sons, 1980), 1351.

13. Ibid., 770, 772, 775.

14. Cerney, J. V. *How to develop a million dollar personality.* (West Nyack, N.Y.: Parker Publishing Co., 1964), 85.

II. INFORMATION SOURCES

Chapter 4

Information, Please!

———————————————————

"Lack of confidence and lack of information sleep in the same bed, locked in the closest kind of embrace. . . . Confidence is the son of vision, and is sired by information."

—Cornelius Vanderbilt, Jr.[1]

"Information systems of every size, shape and form have sprouted and grown like weeds in recent years."

—Arthur R. Miller[2]

The body of investigation cannot exist without information. Private investigators cannot function without their network of sources and contacts who provide access to information. The essence of all professional investigation is the gathering of relevant, accurate, factual, evidential information.

Whatever the investigative assignment may be, sources of information always exist. Sometimes they are very limited, at other times they are abundant. Some sources are created by the situation under investigation. Others are a matter of public and private record. Most major investigations require consultation with both people and records.

Some record sources come to light only during an investigation. Others such as government agency and private industry records are there all the time. They are either public or are available to private investigators through access granted by key contacts who have the authority to extend that professional courtesy.

Contacts and records provide a very important network of information to which private investigators can turn for basic background data. Both the advice and information supplied by key contacts can prove invaluable many times over. This chapter and the next are primarily concerned with sources of recorded information. We also consider informants who supply private investigators with inside information. But first some basic observations.

COMMUNICATION OF KNOWLEDGE OR INTELLIGENCE

Information is best defined as knowledge or intelligence derived from reading, observing, or instruction. This definition implies three major sources of information for the investigator: (1) his own observations of people, of real physical evidence, and of related activities, situations, and circumstances; (2) reading of public records kept by governmental agencies, and private records and documents kept by commercial, institutional, and industrial enterprises, and by individuals; and (3) listening to and recording information communicated by other people who have observed, participated in, or been victimized by the occurrence under investigation. The investigator's career is largely one of obtaining, verifying, and communicating information.

POTENTIAL SOURCES OF INFORMATION

The primary sources of information are (1) people, (2) scenes of any investigated happening, (3) public and private records, (4) documents, and (5) the varied forms of physical evidence. A great variety of information sources fall under these general classifications.

Information may be spoken, written (typed or printed), or physical. It may be something known, something to be read or seen, or something of a material nature. Sensory information is perceived by the senses — sight, hearing, smell, taste, and touch. The senses are the source of information perceived by persons who are present at an occurrence, happening, meeting, event, or any accidental or planned confrontation of a business or social nature. It is the various sensory observations or perceptions that provide the information perceived by witnesses who see and hear what takes place in a given incident, or who are otherwise informed by their senses. Sensory information is compiled by the investigator from personal observations, surveillance, and undercover activities. Victims provide vital (and often emotionally distraught) sensory information. Sensory information perceived by other persons is relayed to private investigators verbally in interviews and interrogations, as testimonial information.

People who act as sources of information include many kinds of individuals: witnesses, participants, litigants, victims, suspects, and accomplices and their friends, relatives, and business associates. These plus the numerous seeing-eyes and hearing-ears on the street observe and provide information on the events that later become the subjects of investigation.

There are two other sources of people information created by private investigators' own network. They are the contacts who make valuable records accessible, and the informants who provide inside information.

Written information is found in records and documents of various kinds. It may be obtained from a custodian of government records, or from an employer's personnel files. It may be a letter, legal document, contract, bill of sale, deed, record of telephone toll calls, counterfeit money, fraudulently endorsed check, or any one of scores of other documents. Public records provide personal, descriptive, statistical, license, and background information on individuals. All readers are aware of such agencies as the Bureau of Vital Statistics and the Department of Motor Vehicles, whatever their name in a particular state. Births, marriages, citizenships, drivers' licenses, vehicle registrations, property holdings, voter registrations, immigration and naturalization, and passport information are among the available records that contain considerable information of value to an investigator.

Private records are made up of personal, institutional, and business information, and personal or private enterprise documents of one sort or another. Companies, institutions, and associations of all kinds operating within the private sector keep varied and extensive records, including employment records, financial records, telephone call records, and other personal and business information. In addition, information on credit rating, financial strength, and other areas of profitability and growth is available from data sources.

Public and law libraries provide many printed sources of information in directories, registers, indexes, loose-leaf services, compilations of legal information, annotated statutes, and sourcebooks of specific information, some of which are detailed in Chapter 6.

Physical evidence reveals itself in a great variety of objects, substances, prints, marks, and impressions, which will be considered in some detail in subsequent books. Real or physical evidence speaks for itself. It is found by searching the scene of the accident, injury, or crime. It is also obtained through follow-up authorized searches of persons and premises for incriminating evidence. It is found in the search for transfer evidence, which, for example, may have been exchanged between vehicles, between vehicles and persons, in hit and run accidents, or between the victim and the suspect in a crime of personal violence.

Each case provides its own sources of information, which may include any one or all of the primary sources—people, records, and physical evidence.

THE AGE OF DOCUMENTATION AND INFORMATION

The twentieth century may go down in history as man's greatest age of documentation and information—and who knows how much more compiling of data lies just ahead. The proliferation of data banks and ever more sophisticated computerized information systems are technological signs of our times. Governments, businesses, and institutions have all rapidly become information-oriented, and there is more information on record about everyone today than ever before in our history. In the words of Anthony V. Bouza: "It is an age when more aspects of life become officially documented. We are identified by digits, credentials, licenses, credit cards, medical bracelets, and historical records of our activities from birth to death."[3]

Instead of privacy, "deprivacy" appears to be the trend. Individuals in the land of the free, the citadel of personal and private rights, sense the inroads data mania has made and will doubtless continue to make on their lives.

Arthur R. Miller, in *The Assault on Privacy,* refers to "The creation of techniques for the direct observation of living persons and contemporary institutions," and the "increased information gathering" that has occurred both within the federal government and the private sector over the past several decades.[4]

The advent of the computer has greatly increased our data-processing capacity. Taxation and social welfare programs have multiplied the quantity of recorded information on individual citizens. Institutions and industry are relying more and more on the increased availability of information that computer technology places at their fingertips. Miller calls data mania a social virus. In his comment on the Task Force Report on Science and Technology, he notes the rapid growth of information systems in recent times:

> As if spread with a magic nutrient, information systems of every size, shape and form have sprouted and grown like weeds in recent years. As they do, their managers demand greater resources, more data on file subjects, and increased consolidation of separately maintained records.[5]

This trend toward the computerized compiling of multitudinous information elicited Miller's concerned comment: "We must begin to realize what it means to live in a society that treats information as an economically desirable commodity and a source of power."[6]

The modern explosion of sophisticated data gathering increases private investigators' potential sources of recorded information, and also their responsibility in the interests of freedom to treat information justly and confidentially. The delicate balance must be maintained between the individual's right to privacy and information justifiably available for investigative efficiency. The machines that record and retrieve information are neutral. It is the responsibility of those who gather and disseminate information to make a clear distinction between its use and misuse.

All this documentation makes it much easier to gather information on a subject under investigation. It is possible to compile quite a dossier on a subject, including among other things his birthdate, citizenship, marital status, educational attainments, employment history, driving record, social and political affiliations, military service, criminal record (if any), and his family history.

MEANS OF OBTAINING INFORMATION

The private investigators' problem is to obtain information as investigative needs require. Most relevant information is obtained from persons and records of one type or another. Persons have to be interviewed or interrogated to obtain the information they are privy to. Records must be available or be made accessible.

People Information

The private investigator obtains his people information from:

- observing people
- interviewing people
- interrogating people
- consulting people
- contacting people who can furnish information
- reading and hearing about people

All private investigators observe people under diverse circumstances and in sundry situations. They observe them while personally communicating with them, while conducting surveillance, and while functioning as undercover operatives. They watch while they shadow on foot, as they tail vehicles, or as they observe them from a fixed observation post. Observation information comes primarily from what private investigators see people do or hear them say.

Inquiry information is derived by private investigators primarily from interviewing and interrogating. They interview willing witnesses and interrogate unwilling witnesses and suspects. They listen to the disclosures, accusations, accounts, descriptions, and observations. When necessary, they interview social friends, relatives, and business associates of subjects, and interrogate suspects, their accomplices, accessories, and friends.

Private investigators consult with their clients, fellow investigators, police, and others who can provide valuable information or counsel. They contact custodians and other persons who have access to vital data that are part of official records. Private information sources are tapped through cooperative contacts. All persons having access to relevant data are key sources of information. Information is often picked up from the people on the street. Many details about prominent subjects may be obtained from reading about them in one of the various *Who's Who* books or directories of corporate officials found in the public libraries. The private investigators may hear about a subject on an evening newscast, or receive a helpful tip-off from an informant. The Texas private investigator, Gene Blackwell, notes how the professional private investigator deals with real people in the real world, and in the process of gathering information "talks, observes, tails, listens to, photographs, records and in a hundred other ways contacts people."[7]

Information is sometimes acquired slowly—a clue here and a lead there followed by seemingly interminable inquiries here, there, and everywhere until the truth is known. At other times a great deal of information comes from a single source. Often the information is put together little by little.

Paper Information

The private investigator obtains his paper information from:

- *public* records
- *private* records
- *evidential* documents
- *reference* sources

Capable private investigators are not only people-conscious, they are record-conscious and document-conscious. Many reference sources exist in public and law libraries to which private investigators can turn for information. Records are found in government agencies, in business corporations, in financial institutions, in personnel files, and numerous other places. The importance of documents and the role they play in investigation is stressed by James V. P. Conway:

> Evidential documents encompass all documents, writings, typewritings, printings, and marks intended to prove, or capable of proving, any principal or collateral fact of investigative or legal interest.[8]

Conway rightly contends that evidential documents are "competent witnesses"[9] and that they may justly "unmask the guilty" or "exonerate the falsely accused" as they "uphold the truth" of their contents.[10]

Access to Records

Access to records may be (1) by right of public record, (2) by permission of the custodian, or (3) by court order. Public and private sources of information are especially helpful in obtaining descriptive data and background information on persons under investigation.

Permission to read public records is available for the asking. The private investigators initially establish rapport with custodians of government agency records and continue to maintain professional affiliation with these contacts. These initial personal contacts are important.

Access to records that are not public is a matter of professional courtesy granted by the person in authority. It is the responsibility of private investigators to establish their own personal contact with the custodian or the official who has authority over such records. Whatever person gives permission for the release of information becomes the private investigator's contact for that private source.

Access by legal process is available when warranted, when governmental or private records are not public, or when they are not made available by an uncooperative person. The usual procedure is to obtain the data by means of a subpoena *duces tecum,* which is a court order requiring the custodian of record (or other person) to bring the needed material to the court. Bank records, for example, are usually subpoenaed in this manner. Telephone toll records and medical records generally require a court order, with the exception that the law in some jurisdictions makes medical records available to the police in stipulated cases such as child abuse, or in the event of gunshot wounds, stabbings, and the like.

Whenever there is any doubt with respect to the availability of a record, private investigators should contact the custodian or the security director of the company or agency and ascertain the conditions under which the material may be examined or the necessary data obtained. It may be possible to secure permission to check the record, or have the custodian do so in the investigator's presence. If not, private investigators should secure the name of the official to whom the subpoena should be addressed.

The question of accessibility therefore depends in the first place on whether the record is public or private, and in the second place, if it is private, whether or not the one in authority will extend professional courtesy and grant private investigators permission to examine it. It should be obvious that much depends on how private investigators comport themselves in the presence of the one from whom they seek the information.

In the event the case under investigation ends up in court, all records necessary to the outcome of a case can usually be made available by legal process. In such instances, this can be handled through the attorney representing the investigator's client.

NOTES

1. Prochnow H. V. *The public speaker's treasure chest.* (New York: Harper & Brothers, 1942), 336.

2. Miller, A. R. *The assault on privacy. Computers, data banks, and dossiers.* (Ann Arbor: University of Michigan Press, 1971), 22.

3. Bouza, A. V. *Police intelligence. The operations of an investigative unit.* (New York: AMS Press, 1976), 57.

4. Miller, A. R. *The assault on privacy,* 20, 21.

5. Ibid., 22.

6. Ibid., 23.

7. Blackwell, G. *The private investigator.* (Los Angeles: Security World Publishing Co., 1979), 226.

8. Conway, J. V. P. *Evidential documents.* (Springfield, Ill.: Charles C Thomas Publisher, 1959), 1.

9. Ibid., 1.

10. Ibid.

Chapter 5

People Sources of Information:
Contacts and Informants

"The name of the game is contacts — having someone you can call for advice, for
help, for suggestions, for information."

— Jay J. Armes[1]

"It is extremely advantageous for a private investigator to be personally known
to local sources of public information."

— Gene Blackwell[2]

This chapter deals with two important sources of information — contacts
who are the custodians of information, or who are themselves in a position
to provide information or counsel; and informants who relay information from
their inside sources, or from knowledge they have gleaned from their own contacts or associations with persons who would normally not be reached by
private investigators.

CONTACTS

All successful private investigators create their own channels to recorded
information sources. From the very start of an investigative career, private investigators learn where they can find specific types of information and set up
their personal network of these contacts. Whenever specific information is

needed from a record that they have not used before, a new contact is established to add to that network. Informed private investigators are fully aware
that they must personally cultivate key contacts and compile records sources
as rapidly and surely as possible. Throughout their career they will continue
to add new contacts and acquire new potential sources of information.

The network of contacts includes persons from various walks of life: government agencies, law enforcement, the legal profession, business and industry,
the financial world, the professional world. In particular it includes persons
who are custodians of records that usually are not available to the public. As
a rule, private investigators have access to such records only by permission of
those having authority over them or by court order. Professional private
investigators know where to go and who to see, or who to call on the telephone,
for relevant data. Think of the confidence this kind of knowledge — and such
a network of contacts — can give investigators. Key contacts are also great time
savers, as they enable private investigators to secure information quickly, and
often provide the kind of information to which private investigators would not
ordinarily have access.

Contacts in Government Agencies

The first time private investigators need information from the public
records of some government agency they will find this seven-step procedure
helpful. They should:

1. Courteously present themselves and their credentials and state the information they need
2. Learn the name and position of the person who provides the information
3. Obtain the specific information required
4. Inquire as to what other information is available from the same
   agency
5. Find out if the person who helps them or some other individual would
   be the one to telephone when they again need similar or related data
6. Meet and establish rapport with the key contact person as soon as
   possible
7. Thank the person who has served them for his or her time and effort

In addition, there are three important factors to keep in mind.

1. Investigators must sell themselves to their contacts as well as to their
   clients. In investigation, good business relationships are built on
   trustworthy operatives who have successfully presented their integrity

and business efficiency to clients and contacts. The more genuine the private investigators' personality, the easier this will be.

2. Immediately on leaving the information agency, private investigators should make a complete record of: the information received; the name of the contact person; all information available at this source; and the name, address, and telephone number of the contact.

    If the information is first recorded in the notebook, it should later be transferred to 3 x 5 cards for filing purposes. The reason for this is clarified in the forthcoming section. The information source records should be complete, and should include all pertinent data that will expedite gathering similar information from the same agency in the future.

3. Successful private investigators always show appreciation to individuals who help them. The private investigators should always leave a contact with a warm feeling of importance and of being appreciated for services rendered.

Contacts in Private Agencies and Businesses

The big difference between public and private sources of information is that private investigators cannot take for granted that private information will be forthcoming. Cooperative contacts are the conduits, channels, or pipelines to private information. The key to winning cooperation is for investigators to be completely professional and trustworthy. Obviously, the contact must believe that investigators are reliable before he will release the desired information. The surest way to fail is to try to manipulate contacts. It is folly to blunder or bully. Investigators should know how to establish and maintain sincere, friendly, and respectful relationships, being frank, open, and aboveboard with their contacts.

Private investigators should be aware that the private contact will generally need more background about them and their need for information than is usually necessary when obtaining public information. In other words, the contact with access to private information will need to be assured of investigators' right to the information, and that whatever he discloses will be used in a legal manner. This may entail more explanation and reasoning on the part of the private investigators. The who and the why of the information and the manner in which it will be used are important to private contact.

The Importance of Knowing People

Ace investigators know a great many people, and a great many people know them, as their circle of influence constantly widens. This process of widening influence grows over the years, but it is begun in the early stages of their career.

(An important word of advice to those just starting out in their investigating career is to get to know people, and get people to know you. Make as many friends as you can. Make a personal effort to make new friends. Try to include some people who are important in your community among your circle of friends. A word of caution, however: be sure that your own integrity of purpose, your respect for the concerns of others, and your investigative capabilities warrant their friendship and trust.)

Knowing people is a stepping stone to creating good contacts. Whoever private investigators contact on any case anywhere in the world—someone in law enforcement, an attorney, a custodian of vital records, an investigator, or a person in some other capacity who has been a liaison in the investigation—should be added to the network of potential contacts. The private investigators should, of course, also be willing to be contacts also, and reciprocate the favor.

Why People Are Willing to Be Contacts

It is a responsibility of custodians of public records to make information available on request according to regulations. Beyond that responsibility lies the deeper reasons for contact cooperation with trusted private investigators, especially by those who guard more highly confidential sources.

Among the reasons for contact cooperation are these given by Richard H. Akin:

1. They know the investigator and his work.
2. They like the investigator per se.
3. They know the investigative profession.
4. The investigator may be able to do something for them.[3]

Akin's list focuses on the contact's personal knowledge of investigators and their profession. When a contact likes private investigators and respects them and what they are doing, he will usually make the requested information available.

The Investigator-Contact Relationship

Mutual trust and respect should exist between contact and investigator in a relationship based on professional friendship and confidentiality. The private investigators' discretion, credibility, and integrity are the three essentials to this relationship. When private investigators receive confidential information from a contact, they respect that confidentiality and protect the person's identity to spare him any embarrassment. A confidential contact must never feel that investigators are taking unfair advantage of him and his willingness to cooperate. Professional private investigators know that every contact is very important and they treat each one accordingly.

When a lengthy research of records is required, private investigators should not expect the contact to do all the work. In such instances private investigators should go in person and do the research from the records the contact makes available. When a quick check is needed on readily accessible data, the telephone can be used.

The need for contacts in key places will become more apparent as the investigative career progresses. The private investigators who are specializing in certain areas of investigation will need contacts in related positions. All private investigators are well advised to develop a dependable contact inside a law-enforcement agency, especially those who become involved in criminal investigations. Law-enforcement agencies have prompt and legal access to identification records, arrest reports, accident reports, missing persons files, m.o. (modus operandi) files, and numerous other records and information. The spectrum of contacts will be directly related to the diversity and scope of any investigation.

The secret of an efficiently functioning information network lies in maintaining good rapport with contacts. When the relationship is strong enough, a considerable amount of nominal data over a period of time can be secured over the telephone. This saves time. When private investigators do have to go out to see contacts or research records, they can organize and preplan the route to reduce travel time and the need for backtracking.

The private investigators should only write for information when distance or regulations require a written application. If, for example, they need information from some distant federal agency source, it is advisable first to write for any forms that may be needed and directions as to the procedure to follow. If time is of the essence, they can telephone for the forms and get them in the mail as soon as possible.

Beginning private investigators should remember that all ace investigators create their own network of contacts. This is the secret of their ability to gather key data quickly and efficiently. Courteous, friendly, businesslike, and confidential dealings with contacts expedites the flow of information. Some investigators have been able to acquire a great deal of information over the telephone. On your contact card it is well to include the birthdays and anniversaries of your contacts so you can send them a card of remembrance and good wishes.

Another contrasting source of information for the private investigator is his informants. Informants are as practical in private investigation as they are in law enforcement, particularly in the investigation of fraud, scams, burglaries, embezzlement, and other crimes.

INFORMANTS

Criminal informants are sources of intelligence on criminal operations and activities. They provide inside or close contact information and are a frequent source of investigative leads.

The primary advantage to be gained from the use of informers is twofold: (1) informers can supply otherwise unavailable inside information, and (2) they function naturally in an environment where their undercover activity is not suspected or detected.

Persons who inform on criminals usually live on the fringe of the criminal world or in it. They may themselves be petty criminals or borderline offenders. They may be reformed criminals, parolees, or other illegal operators turned informant. Police recruit informants from criminal elements or from persons closely connected with criminals. Sometimes an anonymous informant turns out to be one criminal informing on another.

The basic premise for the use of informants is well stated by James Q. Wilson in his comments on FBI informants: "If information is to be obtained from criminal sources without arousing suspicion, the informant and not the agent will have to do it."[4] The only other way would be for the investigator to go undercover and seek to infiltrate the criminal community.

Noncriminal confidential informants may include persons who operate, or are employed by, establishments frequented by criminals, such as bartenders, hotel managers, waitresses, and other employees, or frequenters of criminal hangouts. A frightened ex-girlfriend or ex-wife may tip off private investigators or cooperate with the police in testifying against the criminal activities of the ex-boyfriend or ex-husband. Jealousy, revenge, and money are all motivating factors. Some inform to curry favor with the law, or to obtain lesser sentences for crimes they have committed.

The term informants is primarily used to designate those who periodically inform on criminal, illegal, or subversive activities. Ordinary citizens who may report something of an unusual nature are not generally classified as informants in the usual sense of the word. Confidential sources of information also involve people who work in legitimate professions, businesses, or occupations. These would include both contacts and occasional informers. An informant is one who has proved his ability to supply significant and trustworthy information.

Actual cases of the effective use of informants abound. Wilson tells how the FBI solved the 1972 robbery of New York City's Hotel Pierre through an informant's tip-off. The thieves had apparently stolen at least four million dollars worth of cash and jewels. The theft was "masterfully planned and executed," but the thieves made the mistake of taking the jewels to a fence who was actually a "high-level FBI informant."[5] The informant is thus the intelligence link to inside the criminal world.

Various types of leads may make the solution to a criminal case possible:

1. A victim may accurately identify a suspect.
2. A thief may try to sell his loot to a suspicious buyer.
3. A knowledgeable informant may inform on the suspect.
4. An effective investigation may uncover leads that ultimately identify the perpetrator.

According to Wilson, informants serve three functions. First, they provide leads with respect to a suspect's behavior, identity, or criminal intentions, or they may inform as to the location of loot. Second, they "deceive other criminals" by "introducing them to undercover agents" who pretend to be criminals, or by "stimulating" criminals to "commit a crime while being observed by agents." Wilson notes that such informants are sometimes called "participating informants." Their third function, Wilson says, is to testify in court as "informant defendants" against their "criminal accomplices."[6] Wilson is referring in particular to the use of informants by federal law-enforcement agencies.

In most cases informants are not called on to testify in court. The primary reason is that their identity usually must be kept secret to preserve their informant status. Also, most informants are not about to risk criminal retaliation by identifying themselves as witnesses in a court of law.

The Legality of Informants

All private investigators involved in criminal investigations and wishing to capitalize on the leads informants can provide should become familiar with the complex law that regulates the use of informants. There are fine weights in the balance between ensuring a fair trial to the accused and maintaining the effectiveness of criminal investigation.

The first legal principle is that the use of informants is constitutional and has been consistently supported by the Supreme Court. In *Hoffa* v. *United States,* the Court ruled that the Fourth Amendment does not protect "a wrongdoer's misplaced belief that a person to whom he voluntarily confides his wrongdoing will not reveal it."[7] The Court also upholds the right to protect the anonymity of informants.

In most cases, informers remain anonymous. As we have said, their identity is protected for two basic reasons: (1) to perpetuate their informant status and (2) to protect them from possible reprisals. Consequently, the defense does not have an absolute right to demand that the informant who provided the damaging testimony against his defendant appear in court to testify in person.

If, however, the informant's testimony is vital to the outcome of the case, he may either have to appear in court or the case itself will have to be dropped. If an informant does testify he must identify himself, and as a witness he is subject to cross-examination. Cases involving an important informant are usually dropped so as not to expose the individual and thus nullify his future value and possibly even jeopardize his life.

The FBI frequently guarantees informants anonymity, and as Wilson notes, even throws out good cases to protect these sources.[8] This is doubtless one reason for the FBI's highly successful use of informants and the cooperation it receives from them.

The effectiveness of law-enforcement agencies depends to some degree on the amount of inside information and leads they receive from their informant network. The same can be said of private investigators engaged in investigating various types of crimes. Informant information can prove very helpful in locating the whereabouts of suspects, in identifying the perpetrators of a crime, or in providing clues for the solution of an undetected or unsolved crime. Informants frequently provide the starting tip off for a criminal investigation.

Investigator-Informer Relationships

Criminal investigators need to develop special skill to use informants effectively and to maintain a rather tenuous relationship with them. The private investigators should always deal with informants strictly on a business level, not on a social one. Investigators must carefully avoid involvement that might in any way tend to make them accessories to criminal activity. Similarly, they should avoid tactics that might bring a possible charge of entrapment against them.

All private investigators should take every reasonable precaution to protect the identity of a confidential informant in order to maintain that person's value as a continued source of information. An informant's name is not usually listed in agency information files, but a code name or number is used as a confidential means of reference. The identity of the informant to whom the code refers is known only to the investigator and his supervisors. All contacts with the informant, whether by telephone or in person, should be covert — unobtrusive, private, and secret, and even these are held to a minimum. Each meeting is always at a different time and in a different place. For telephone contacts, informants should memorize an unlisted number. In addition, private investigators should not contact an informant in the criminal community in which they live. The informant will usually reach the investigators when he has inside information. Alert private investigators are aware that criminal elements and syndicates also have their own intelligence operations that include the detection, identification, and punishment of informers.

Informers' Motivations

The two primary motivations for criminal informants are leniency and money. A participant in a criminal or illegal act may turn informer to obtain leniency with respect to a lesser sentence for the charges brought against him. He may inform on his accomplices, or he may provide valuable information about others involved in serious crime. Wilson notes that narcotic agents tend to recruit their best informers from among the "twists" who, when faced with the threat of going to jail, become informants to "work off a beat."[9] In addition, they are usually paid a small amount of money.

Many informants sell their services for money. Although the threat of confinement may turn an arrestee into an informant, Wilson tells us that the FBI recruits "more informants with money than with leniency."[10] Because private investigators are not engaged in law enforcement, they are not in a position to offer leniency, and therefore informants usually sell their information to private investigators for a fee.

Parolees sometimes become informers to help support themselves until they can find legitimate employment and become reestabished in society, or until they tragically return to crime. Sometimes an informer may sell his information in the hopes of getting a friend or relative off the drug habit, especially if it helps to get revenge against the dealer.

Some additional reasons that informants may help law-enforcement investigators are to (1) gain favor with the law, (2) escape harassment, (3) obtain intercession, (4) eliminate a competitor, or (5) get personal revenge. They may help private investigators for money, jealousy, revenge, fear, competition, or personal reasons.

Informants may be classified according to motive.

1. Mercenaries inform for money or some other form of material gain.
2. Frightened people inform for their own protection and well-being. The source of their fear may be a criminal enemy, a rival, or an associate who has committed a criminal act.
3. Women usually inform because of jealousy, revenge, or a guilty conscience. A jealous girlfriend may inform on a boyfriend who has confided in her about his criminal activities or she may wish to ease her own conscience for associating with a criminal. An ex-wife may inform for revenge on the criminal activity of her ex-husband.
4. Rivals inform to eliminate competitors in order to profit further in their illegal activities.

The three types of informants referred to below are usually problems for the police rather than private investigators. Sometimes the motivations may be deceitful, as in the case of:

PROBLEM PEOPLE

1. Double-crossers actually seek to gain information rather than to provide genuine leads. They invent some informative excuse for contacting the police.
2. False informants make up information for the police in an attempt to appear to be on their side. They hope that as a result of their information they will not be suspected of any wrongdoing.
3. Self-benefiting informants give out underworld information to gain favor with the police. The information in such instances may be genuine.

There are two other types of informants who usually contact the police on their own volition. The first of these is the law-abiding person who operates a legitimate business. He does not want his business place to become a hangout for a criminal element or the underworld. He has observed a growing patronage of these people or overheard criminal negotiations transpiring within his premises. He may inform so that he can preserve a legitimate business atmosphere.

The other type is the anonymous informant who may live and work in or out of the underworld environment. He reveals his information either by anonymous telephone call or unsigned letter, usually to the police. Private investigators who have become prominent in criminal investigation might receive such a call or letter. Anonymous letters may be written by well-meaning citizens who do not wish their identity to be made known. Both the police and private investigators are aware that all anonymous calls or letters are not the work of "crackpots," but sometimes provide valuable leads.

Many law-abiding citizens are unfortunately reluctant to communicate information pertaining to criminal activity, either because they fear reprisals or simply do not wish to become involved. Such people who inform do so for different reasons, including (1) patriotism, (2) to aid the cause of justice, (3) to defend human rights, (4) to make their community a safer place, (5) to protect a loved one, (6) as an act of self-defense, or (7) as revenge for some criminal act against their family, a loved one, or their business.

Voluntary and Involuntary Informants

The role of informant may be voluntary or involuntary. A key objective of the voluntary informant is money. He may offer for a fee to supply information that can lead to the solution of an unsolved crime, or to the location of stolen loot or a wanted person. The risk usually determines the price of providing information.

An involuntary informant is frequently one who is reluctant to implicate himself because of his own participation in criminal activities or association with suspect(s). He may be a professional criminal who, because of his enmity against law enforcement and criminal investigation, is simply unwilling to assist the police, or even the private investigator. This type of person becomes an informer to obtain more favorable consideration if caught in a legal jam.

Informant Information Requires Corroboration

An informant is useful only when his information is reliable and his leads are valuable only when they have been verified. Therefore each bit of information he provides should be checked out as far as possible. In addition, informant information must be corroborated to become admissible evidence.

As an initial test of an informant's reliability, private investigators can ask him to get information they already know and have verified. If the informant fails to pass this test, the chances are he is not dependable.

Corroborative evidence usually must be obtained through further investigation to substantiate the informant's information. The informer may only provide a lead to be followed up by the investigator. An informer's statements ordinarily are not accepted as legally accurate or adequate, and without corroboration his testimony is likely to be thrown out of court in a trial proceedings. Corroborative evidence also solves the problems of validating disclosures and of maintaining the anonymity of the informant.

Informant information may be a starting point for an investigation or a helpful contribution to its successful solution. It frequently becomes a basis for further investigation. When the informant discloses names, addresses, and street numbers, it is usually quite easy for private investigators to check them out through their information network and personal verification. In criminal cases information must be verified cautiously, such as when tracking down a felon's hiding place or the storage place of accumulated loot.

Fair Dealings with Informants

A fundamental axiom of private investigation is "always be fair." This principle applies to all private investigators' dealings with all persons, including informants. Consideration and ethical procedures of decency always apply. The private investigators' professionalism may be put to the test in their arm's-length relationship with an informant who resides within the criminal environment or has direct contact with the underworld. Private investigators maintain secrecy and protect the informant's identity to lessen the danger of retaliation, unless a court order requires them to do otherwise. Professional private investigators respect an informant's point of view, never misrepresenting or misquoting him. They never make any promises they do not intend to keep or have no authority to implement.

The private investigator-informant relationship calls for considerable tact and patience. It is not advisable for private investigators to rush the informant, interrogate him, or take notes in his presence except for recording addresses, telephone numbers, or other precise data they would not be expected to remember. Confidential inside information is usually recorded afterward for the obvious reason that the informant is less apprehensive about communicating when his words are not being taken down before his eyes.

While private investigators can sympathize with the informant's problems, they should not become personally involved. They should show appreciation for worthwhile information, but not pay off the informant until his information pays off for the investigation. They should be scrupulously fair and exact in financial dealings, whenever possible getting a receipt from the informant for payments made or expenses reimbursed.

Experienced private investigators generally adhere to the following basic rules regarding their relationship with informants:

1. Keep all contacts secret and always protect their identity.
2. Deal with informants fairly, truthfully, and tactfully.
3. Avoid embarrassing, offending, or arguing with informants.
4. Do not pry into the informant's private life.
5. Always keep control of the relationship and any communication situation.
6. Verify all informant information as far as possible, or seek corroborative evidence.
7. Pay exactly and promptly, but only on the proved reliability of the information.

The legitimate law-abiding operator of a business, or citizen informing on criminal activities, should also be protected from criminal retaliation. Sometimes private investigators will need to help the citizen feel self-justified in his act of informing, building up his confidence that he is doing the right thing for the community and for himself. Just as with the informant who operates on the fringes of criminal life, private investigators always let a private informer know that they intend to keep his identity unknown.

Sources of Private Investigators' Informants

The extent of the criminal investigation activities largely determines where private investigators build their information network. Street operatives develop an informant network in places where people meet to talk and socialize, and where the criminal fringe elements may be found. They look for informers among people who are in a position to observe illegal activities or to overhear questionable and suspicious conversations.

Beyond the area of the criminal informant lies a wide world of potential informers who can play a helpful role in private investigators' detective activities. Investigations often do not involve criminal situations. Private investigators may be digging up evidence for any one of many types of civil investigations. In such instances private investigators expand their informer network beyond that of the criminal fringe or criminal participant. Informants of the wider scope can be found everywhere in high and low places, in schools, churches, department stores, financial institutions, and industrial complexes—in other words, in all walks of life.

Potential informers include all persons who are in a position to observe and have contact with the public. They often find themselves in a key spot at public happenings and can either inform or be witness to some aspect of the event. The following list is typical of the types of people who may be able to provide clues or inform:

- Airline clerks, hostesses
- Barbers
- Bartenders
- Bell hops
- Building managers
- Bus drivers
- Cab drivers (trip sheets)
- Camera girls
- Car hops (drive-ins, etc.)
- Custodians
- Dance hall operators
- Dentists
- Doormen
- Elevator operators
- Garagemen
- Gas station attendants
- Hairdressers
- Hat check girls
- Hostesses
- Hotel clerks
- Janitors
- Maids (bars, hotels, motels)
- Mailmen
- Neighborhood children
- News venders

- Night watchmen
- Operators of street businesses and entertainment houses
- Paper delivery boys
- Parking lot attendants
- Parolees and probationers
- Physicians
- Pool hall operators
- Public utility servicemen
- Railroad ticket agents, conductors
- Shoe shine operators
- Street venders (all-night stands)
- Switchboard operators
- Tradesmen (delivery services)
- Waitresses and waiters

Most private investigators employ both paid and unpaid informers. The paid informants are the regulars of the information network. The private investigators' $50 bill has the same appeal to the mercenary informant as the policeman's $50 bill. Investigators who are employed by a private agency will be expected to follow the firm's policies with respect to the use of informants and their payment. Payment is only made on the delivery of worthwhile information. The amount is generally based on consideration of the value of the information to private investigators and the risk taken by the informant.

When private investigators are working on a specific case they seek out voluntary unpaid informers on the street who, because of their proximity to an event or knowledge of the circumstances, can provide pertinent information. These sources can be very helpful, particularly in solving a troublesome case.

Knowledgeable private investigators are always aware that the "eyes" and "ears" along the street may have seen and heard a great deal that can be of value. These eyes and ears can be extensions of private investigators' own perceptive powers when they capitalize on the information they have to provide.

When undertaking an investigation of an accident, crime, or event in a given area, the private investigator concentrates on what the multiple eyes of the street may have seen in that area. He canvasses the street to determine who they saw, what they saw, when they saw, and how they saw. What did they see? When and where and how did they see it? Whom did they see doing what to whom? Whom did they see taking what from whom? The seeing eyes on the street belong to potential informers and to potential witnesses. The private investigator's problem is to find the eyes that saw and the ears that heard.

Consider the vast variety of the eyes of the street. There are the eyes of the street traffic and of sidewalk pedestrians; the eyes of businessmen located along the street and of their employees; the eyes of the customers in the stores, shops, bars, restaurants, show places, and elsewhere, and of operators and personnel of those establishments; the eyes of clerks, waitresses, doormen, venders, service, and delivery persons; and the eyes of residents of the street. Finally, there are the eyes of the street watchers; those persons who watch the street for hours at a time, some of them day after day and even a few at night.

Some of those eyes on the street are bound to be sharp eyes — eyes that quickly see and register what happens. Some eyes are in the right place at just the right time to get a good view. It is to these eyes on the street that private investigators turn to help them to piece together the picture of exactly what took place. From the mouths along the street private investigators learn what the eyes of the street have seen and what the ears of the street have heard.

NOTES

1. Nolan, F. *Jay J. Armes, investigator.* (New York: Macmillian Publishing Co., 1976), 57.

2. Blackwell, G. *The private investigator.* (Los Angeles: Security World Publishing Co., 1979), 155.

3. Akin, R. H. *The private investigator's basic manual.* (Springfield, Ill.: Charles C Thomas Publisher, 1976), 20.

4. Wilson, J. Q. *The investigators. Managing FBI and narcotics agents.* (New York: Basic Books, 1978), 68.

5. Ibid., 61.

6. Ibid., 62.

7. Ibid., 68.

8. Ibid.

9. Ibid.

10. Ibid.

Chapter 6

Paper Sources of Information: Records, Documents, and Publications

"Knowledge is of two kinds. We know a subject ourselves, or we know where we can find information upon it."

—Samuel Johnson[1]

"The investigator should make full use of *certified copies* of pertinent public records, such as court records and records of criminal convictions. . . . Copies of pertinent documents and private or business records should always be obtained as well as an affidavit from the custodian of the records . . . explaining what they are and attesting to their authenticity."

—Anthony M. Golec[2]

A considerable amount of evidential information is found in public and private records and documents and in various types of publications. We have considered the contacts and custodians who make these paper sources available to the investigator. We now look at the information these sources can provide and where it may be found.

Recorded sources of private investigators' information are found in local, state, and federal government agencies, and in records and documents kept within the world of finance, business, and industry. The private investigators' efficiency will be greatly enhanced if they know where to go for needed information.

GOVERNMENT SOURCES OF INFORMATION

Local, state, and federal government agencies maintain an incredible amount of recorded information. Some records are public, others are available under stipulated conditions and are made available when the objective of the investigation is in accord with these conditions. Still other records are privileged and generally unavailable. Confidential and top secret material is protected by law.

Of interest to the investigator is the fact that some government agencies are also investigative agencies in their own right. They employ their own operatives to help enforce the laws or regulations pertaining to their respective jurisdictions, or to investigate reported violations of such regulations. Their records include master lists and data compiled from their investigations.

Many important information-gathering government agencies are noninvestigative. They do, however, provide a broad spectrum of personal and property information useful to the investigator.

The location of specific government agencies is not uniform in all states. A similar bureau or department may have a somewhat different name and location depending on the jurisdiction. The fee for the search of certain records may also vary from state to state. Investigators must therefore develop their own record search, location, and contact activity. The following guidelines should prove helpful in determining where certain information may be found. When private investigators know what information they need and where it is likely to be recorded, the problem of locating it is greatly reduced.

When information of public record is to be submitted as evidence in a court of law, whenever possible private investigators should obtain certified copies of the data. In some jurisdictions, however, an order of the court is required to remove a transcript of a record of conveyance of real property, or even of any other record. In such instances the private investigators should gather all the information with the number and/or description of the document that will verify it. Then if a transcript of the document is needed in court, the court order will be issued. This matter can be handled through an attorney.

Public Records of State and Local Agencies

The principal available public records most frequently used by many private investigators are listed and commented on below.

DEPARTMENT OR BUREAU OF MOTOR VEHICLES. The words Motor Vehicle(s) usually appear somewhere in the title of this department, which may be known as the Department of Motor Vehicles (DMV), the Motor Vehicle Division, the Commissioner of Motor Vehicles, or some other name. A few states have different offices for drivers' licenses and auto registrations. To obtain driver or motor vehicle license or registration information, private investigators should contact the state's registration office by whatever name it is known, having all basic data at hand to expedite the process. Some jurisdictions follow the policy of informing the owner if information has been requested and by whom. In some states there are companies that will acquire that information in their own name, for a fee.

Driver and vehicle registration files provide information regarding operators' licenses, certificates of title, motor or serial numbers, license plates, and data on vehicle ownership. Data include description, key vital statistics, and residence addresses of applicants for an operator's license. Information may also be available on driver limitations, license revocations for accidents resulting in fatalities, or for driving while intoxicated and other moving violations.

BUREAU OF VITAL STATISTICS. The Bureau of Vital Statistics (sometimes called the Marriage License Bureau) records births, marriages, and deaths. It is frequently referred to as the city clerk's office. The city clerk usually maintains commercial license information as well. When private investigators go to this bureau in search of statistical data about anyone, they should have as much specific information as possible. This is a basic axiom when seeking information from recorded data. The sooner the person or persons are identified, the quicker the information can be obtained. One must always have some information to get more information.

For marriage records private investigators usually contact the State Division, Office, or Bureau of Vital Statistics, or Bureau of Records and Statistics. In a few states they may need to contact the Clerk of the Court, the County Clerk, or County Recorder where the marriage license was issued. The private investigators should have the full name of both the bride and the groom, as well as the data and place of the marriage ceremony. Marriage records are a good source of information on both the bride and groom, such as names and addresses, occupations, dates and places of birth, and prior marital status.

When investigators know the date and place of the marriage they can often find additional information in a local newspaper. Newspaper reports of weddings usually list the names of close friends and relatives and important people who attended, as well as the new residence of the couple. In the case of a church wedding, the name of the clergyman who officiated will be listed in the newspaper as well as in the church records, along with the names of the witnesses.

The Related-Information Principle. Whenever private investigators secure information from a given source, they should not fail to check out any additional related data that source may also provide. Statistical sources are a good example of this related-information principle of investigation.

Birth records are often very helpful to investigators. It is very rare that a missing or wanted person or a subject under investigation for either civil or criminal matters will go so far in his cover-up attempts as to seek to change his birth date. Birth records are an item of identification that verify the date and place of a person's birth. As such, they also have tracing value. In addition, birth records may provide such identification data as:

1. Name of the attending physician
2. Background information on subject and family
3. Mother's mailing address at the time of the subject's birth
4. Place of birth (if it was a hospital birth, the hospital records may provide additional leads)
5. Father's name, age, birthplace, and occupation

Related information also has identification value. It may be sufficient to start a background inquiry. Many public information agencies are sources of both specific and related information.

When investigating a wrongful or suspicious death, private investigators should check the death certificate for investigative leads. They frequently include the father's name and the mother's maiden name (data needed to establish descent and rights of inheritance). The certificate indicates the deceased's Social Security number. The name and address of the funeral director, and of the person who provided the information, and the location of the cemetary are usually noted. Both the funeral director and the cemetary records may provide additional information.

MUNICIPAL, COUNTY, STATE, AND FEDERAL COURTS.   Courthouse records cover civil, criminal, juvenile, equity, and probate proceedings. They disclose the disposition of civil and criminal actions. They also record divorces, citizenships granted, and legal changes of names.

For divorce records private investigators will usually contact the clerk of the court (superior, county, or district) in the county where the divorce was granted. In a few states they will contact the Bureau of Vital Statistics. The private investigators should be aware that the more details they can furnish regarding the person(s) under investigation, the easier it will be for the custodian of the records to locate the information. This is especially true if private investigators have to write for the information from a more distant court. When requesting a copy of a divorce record the following should, as far as possible, be supplied:

1. Full names of the former husband and wife
2. Former addresses

3. Present addresses of both parties (if known)
4. Date and place of the divorce
5. Type of divorce decree granted (if known)
6. Either ages at the time of divorce or the dates and places of birth of both parties

Court records of divorce proceedings may contain information of medical importance or allegations regarding character or behavior. Interviews may be advisable with the attorneys for both parties, and with the ex-spouse and witnesses.

Space does not permit classification of courts that function within the American system of jurisprudence. The private investigators will be aware that the civil courts have been established for the adjudication of controversies between plaintiffs and defendants, or the enforcement of private rights and redress for private wrongs. Criminal courts are charged with the administration of the criminal laws and the punishment of public offenses against the peoples of the state.

Between them they keep records of all civil and criminal proceedings, as well as personal and business adjudications of various kinds, including those pertaining to the laws of bankruptcy, probate, deeds of trust, personal injuries, sales contracts, and so on.

Courts have degrees of judicial powers and jurisdictions indicated by their names: municipal, circuit, appellate, and supreme courts of the state, as well as the federal district courts, courts of appeal, and the U.S. Supreme Court. Probably the best place for private investigators to begin is the county courthouse, where they will often find most of the business and personal information of a judicial nature.

COUNTY FARM BUREAU (STATE AGRICULTURE DEPARTMENT). Atlases and plat books are periodically published by most counties. They show the boundaries of townships within the county and identify the owners of all land within the county. Sometimes owners are identified both on individual township maps and in an alphabetical index.

Plat books and atlases are of specific value in identifying the owners of rural property and in locating rural addresses. They also reveal ownership, acreage, and location of farms. County agents can provide maps and corresponding information. Some departments also keep data on air activities of Flying Farmers and other pilots employed or hired by them.

COUNTY ASSESSOR AND RECORDER'S OFFICE. The name of the recorder's office varies in different states. This office maintains data on property ownership, both personal and real property, and property assessments for taxation purposes. The precise legal description and location of property can be found in these records. The recorder's office also maintains records of real estate deeds, mortgages, and related documents.

BOARD OF ELECTIONS. The election board maintains a list of all registered voters in the county. Precinct books can determine how long a person has resided in any area. These background data are also helpful in cases involving citizenship issues. The board provides names and addresses, length of residence, and former residence.

LICENSING AUTHORITIES (MUNICIPAL, COUNTY, AND STATE). All licensing authorities maintain records and information regarding applicants and types of licenses granted. These agencies are important when it is necessary to check on whether an individual under investigation is legally operating a professional service or business that requires a license. Both commercial and professional licenses are involved. Some licenses require that the licensee meet prescribed standards. Agencies usually have on record a considerable amount of related information.

BOARD OF EDUCATION. Board of Education records include administrative action information affecting employee and/or student personnel, identification of administrative personnel, school attendance records, student participation in athletic activities, and so on. Similar information is available from the deans of admissions of colleges and universities.

A Subject's Educational Background. Educational records available from institutions attended by the subject are always helpful in investigating scholastic attainments and educational qualifications. These sources include high school, college, university, and alumni records. They often disclose ancillary information on a subject's personality, scholastic aptitude, and campus activities.

Alumni records are a source of information on what a subject has done since graduation in his or her chosen trade or profession. Often they indicate the present business, professional, or employee status of the subject, and in many cases list an up-to-date address. Fraternity and sorority records may reveal the subject's personality influence and ability to work with others.

By consulting with a subject's former (or present) teachers, educational guidance counselors, principals, professors, or even college presidents, private investigators may be able to glean information relative to the subject's character, dependability, and integrity, as well as his educational record.

Locating Subjects with School-Age Children. The school system is helpful when private investigators wish to locate a subject who has children of school age. If the subject has moved, private investigators can consult the old school the children attended. Copies of school records will doubtless be forwarded to the new school as a matter of record. By locating the school where the children are now in attendance, private investigators have a direct lead to locating the subject.

City and county boards of education maintain complete files on their school systems employees, both professional and nonprofessional. These records can be helpful in locating and identifying teacher personnel within the county or city. Educational records include those of school boards or local departments of education, of educational institutions attended by the subject or the subject's children. Locating the educational institutions a subject has attended is usually not too difficult, since many employment records require that the applicant identify schools attended all the way from high school through university.

STATE VOCATIONAL REHABILITATION AGENCIES. Rehabilitation agencies include state boards of vocational education. These agencies maintain considerable background medical information, including diagnosis and treatment of those who benefit from their services. They are also a source of information on state job training endeavors. Public welfare agencies maintain similar information.

PUBLIC LIBRARIES. The main public libraries in cities across the continent are veritable reservoirs of reference information. Directories, registers, loose-leaf services, encyclopedias, trade journals, and standard reference guides provide private investigators with volumes of commercial and industrial information, as well as data on prominent people in finance, education, science, and industry, to name a few professions. The names of some key directories and reference works that appear later in this chapter will give the reader an inkling of the mass of information on record in public libraries.

All libraries have card index files where investigators can check the location of any book by book title or by author. By checking the files they can determine what may be available on a particular topic. Whenever private investigators are not sure where to look for information, they can go to the information or service desk and ask the desk clerk where to find the specific information they need.

Maps, atlases, catalogues, geographies, and travel guides can prove helpful in national and international investigations. Investigators will find that many libraries contain volumes dealing with forensic science, criminal justice, and related topics, along with case history accounts of investigator-detectives solving their difficult cases. Libraries found on the campuses of universities and in a number of professional associations and government agencies are also sources of valuable books and documents.

LAW LIBRARIES.   Law libraries abound in information on legal, judicial, and statute matters. They contain annotated volumes on the civil and criminal codes of the states, journals of the state senate and assembly, up-to-date indexes of federal regulations codes, and county and municipal codes. While most of the information is more applicable to the work of attorneys and jurists, these libraries contain much of benefit to private investigators, especially legal investigators.

The law library is the obvious place to go for information on the many codes that regulate our society. It contains volumes on many classifications of law such as commercial, constitutional, corporation, labor, public, public land and mining, consumer protection, real estate, premises liability, military, torts, and all the civil and criminal laws of the state. The law library has information on civil procedure in civil courts, and criminal defense procedures in criminal courts.

Private investigators can find helpful information on specific cases all the way from bankruptcy to worker's compensation. There is a great deal of legal information applicable to investigative procedure in personal injury and product liability cases. There are volumes on all kinds of legal matters, court procedures, legal definitions of words and phrases, and legal forms used in proceedings and transactions.

Reference information is available on negligence, trespass, fair trading, contracts, trusts, patents, trademarks, copyrights, libel, slander, the rights of privacy, usury, equity, property rights, and the laws of evidence. Add to this the law reports, law reviews, and volumes on the statutes of other states and other countries, and private investigators have available a great mass of legal information that can be helpful in certain types of investigations. In numerous tort situations, knowledge of the legal principles and procedures involved helps to complete a successful investigation.

MAYORS' OFFICES.   In many of the larger cities, well-staffed mayors' offices provide information and assistance relative to city ordinances, departments, committees, inspectors, public works, property data, policies, and procedures. Lists of city government personnel are usually available, indicating heads of departments.

Government Investigative Agencies

Government investigative agencies that conduct their own investigations within the scope of their respective jurisdictions have compiled a tremendous amount of information in their records.

ATTORNEY GENERAL.   State attorneys and county or district attorneys investigate state and county law violations. Information includes names of persons who have been prosecuted and those who have been considered for prosecution. When relevant to a criminal investigation, this information can prove valuable to the investigator.

COUNTY SHERIFF. County sheriffs and county police departments investigate violations of county and state codes, both motor vehicle and criminal. They maintain arrest records.

MUNICIPAL POLICE DEPARTMENT. The police department is the law-enforcement agency that deals with violations of local municipal and state codes, motor vehicle code, and criminal code. It handles complaints filed with the department through its precincts.

Local police files and arrest records contain a great deal of information that is generally not available to private investigators in most jurisdictions, at least not without an understanding contact and a legitimate cause. An exception is likely to be made when private investigators have been employed by the victim to investigate criminal acts, in which case pertinent information may be made available. When a criminal case that is dormant in police files comes under private investigation, the information is usually more readily obtained. Whenever private investigators are working on an active case they will need to coordinate their investigative activities with those of the police.

Professional private investigators who do criminal investigations have been able to establish good working rapport with the police, particularly when their investigation complements police efforts. If the case is not considered to warrant considerable police attention, the investigation, if any, may be left to private investigators; or if the law-enforcement personnel are too undermanned to cope with investigative demands, a qualified private investigator known to be both capable and dependable may be called in on an investigation.

Law-enforcement records are maintained on local, state, and federal levels. Police departments and sheriffs' offices keep some records on offenders they arrest and investigate. Local records usually include identification records (photos, fingerprints, descriptive data); records on known offenders (check passers, confidence men, sex offenders, and narcotics dealers); descriptions of lost and stolen articles; files on duplicate pawnshop tickets; and files on accident reports, missing persons, gun permits, field interrogation cards, and modus operandi. Arrest reports contain descriptive data on arrested persons, and crime reports designate crimes reported to the police. Access to these non-public records is a matter of professional courtesy in cases of cooperative investigation, or of confidential contact.

STATE POLICE AND THE HIGHWAY PATROL. State police and Highway Patrol personnel deal with motor and criminal code violations that come under the jurisdiction of the state. In addition to the material compiled on these violations, including fingerprint data and descriptive information on statewide offenders, the state law-enforcement system generally maintains probation and patrol records, statewide firearms registration, license records, and prison records.

COUNTY CORONER. This office conducts autopsy hearings and postmortem examinations in fatal accidents, homicides, and suicides to determine the cause and responsibility of death, and the nature and extent of any injuries or disease suffered by the deceased.

STATE MOTOR VEHICLE DRIVERS' LICENSE BUREAU. The title of this office varies among the states. It is responsible for investigating driver violations, and keeps records of such cases, with related vital statistics and relevant information.

MUNICIPAL FIRE MARSHAL. The fire marshal's records apropos of investigative needs concern arson investigations and repetitious fire losses, with the names of known arsonists and pyromaniacs (firebugs).

HEALTH OFFICER (DEPARTMENT OF LICENSES). This department maintains a list of medical certificates of employees who perform personal services for the public (waiters, food dispensers, cooks, barbers, etc.) as a means of protecting public health. The department also provides information on sources of contagious diseases.

STATE BOARD OF HEALTH. This is a potential source of information in medical malpractice cases. This board maintains disciplinary records and complaint records relative to persons associated with the healing arts.

STATE PAROLE AND PROBATION BOARD. This office keeps background information on persons prior to their being sentenced, and complete records on probation and parole actions.

STATE AND COUNTY FISH, GAME, AND FIRE WARDENS. These are the wardens who act to preserve natural resources and wildlife. They maintain records on violations of laws and regulations pertaining to their respective jurisdictions.

OTHER STATE AGENCIES. Each state has its own offices of the government departments to which private investigators can apply to determine information relative to the matters under investigation. These agencies include departments of consumer affairs; health, housing, and community development; and industrial relations, to name a few. To investigate matters that involve government agency records, private investigators can simply check the telephone directory for a local office and make contact to determine what may be available.

UNIQUE LOCAL RECORDS.   In addition to the information systems that are common to all cities, counties, and states, there may be records that are unique for a specific city or county. For example, the records of the county clerk in Reno, Nevada, contain data on every divorce granted there. Local records pertain to matters that are germane to their own areas. Unusual local records may be native to the area in which the private investigator lives and works.

Federal Government Agencies

Most federal government agencies maintain centralized records. The authority for the release of information remains at the seat-of-government level. Investigators should try to keep abreast of local, state, or federal legislation that affects the disclosure of any level of government records information.

Some of the records kept by the agencies listed below are confidential and secret. Others may be made available on a need-to-know or professional courtesy basis. Some agencies provide investigative career opportunities.

CENTRAL INTELLIGENCE AGENCY (CIA).   The investigative division of the CIA serves a number of important functions. It investigates those who are considered for potential employment by the federal government. It maintains a master index of all persons so investigated, and of all U.S. citizens who are employed in foreign countries. The CIA is an important agency of the Executive Office of the President. It is responsible for foreign intelligence, and for protecting America's secret intelligence information sources.

DEPARTMENT OF STATE.   Two divisions of the Department of State maintain significant master lists. The Investigations Division of the Office of Security has a current index of all persons it has investigated for fraud or for passport and visa purposes. The Passport Office of the Bureau of Security and Consular Affairs maintains a master list of passport applicants. A significant amount of personal data is included in passport application files, including proof of birth and U.S. citizenship.

DEPARTMENT OF THE TREASURY.   Master indexes are maintained by three of the investigative and enforcement agencies of this department:

1.   The Bureau of Customs keeps current a master index of names of persons engaged in import and export activities, both legal and illegal.

A name search of the master index will disclose which district office
has the enforcement records pertaining to a specified subject.

2. The intelligence division of the Internal Revenue Service (IRS)
    maintains a master name index from law enforcement actions it has
    taken to collect federal income and excise taxes. Investigators seeking
    information from this list should provide the Social Security number
    of the subject and of the subject's spouse, as well as the name, to
    facilitate the search. Investigators must first obtain the written
    authorization of the taxpayer before the IRS will provide certified
    copies of the income tax returns filed by the taxpayer.

    The Alcohol Tax Unit of the Bureau of Internal Revenue main-
    tains records of the violations of laws relating to the manufacture,
    storage, and sale of alcoholic beverages. The Bureau also enforces
    the National Firearms Act.

3. The United States Secret Service, another division of the Treasury
    Department, maintains a master index of its law-enforcement actions
    involving violators, or alleged violators, of laws relating to (1) coins
    and currency (counterfeiting) and (2) obligations and securities of the
    United States and foreign governments.

    The Secret Service also operates a Protective Intelligence
    Division that contains a master list of persons who have written
    threatening letters to the President of the United States or other high
    government officials. This list includes any known individual who is
    deemed to be a potential threat to the safety of the President. District
    offices of the Secret Service record names of persons in the above
    categories who reside within the geographical areas over which their
    field offices have jurisdiction.

DEPARTMENT OF JUSTICE. Two separate branches of the Department
of Justice maintain valuable data for certain types of investigations. The first
is the Federal Bureau of Investigation (FBI). Its Records Branch maintains a
master index of all persons investigated by the FBI under any of its
responsibilities for (1) internal security, (2) law enforcement, or (3) tort claims.

The Identification Division of the FBI serves as a national clearing house
for criminal identification records. Data include master indexes of persons
arrested and of those wanted and sought for criminal violations. This is the
division that operates the FBI's famous fingerprint classification system, which
includes fingerprint cards of (1) persons arrested for violations of law and (2)
those processed for government employment or military service.

The second important branch of the Department of Justice, as far as
private investigators are concerned, is the Immigration and Naturalization
Service (INS), which maintains all immigrant and alien records. Both its

Inspection Service and its Border Patrol provide significant data relating to aliens and to citizenship applications.

The master index maintained by the Inspection Service in Washington, D.C., includes names of all aliens lawfully residing in the United States as well as of all applicants for citizenship. The names of naturalized citizens are also included in the master list. The index card on each person discloses the location, by regional or district office, of the naturalization investigation records, as well as the federal court that conferred citizenship. This agency also maintains the passenger and crew lists of all ships using U.S. port facilities.

The Border Patrol maintains its master index of names of all persons investigated (or under investigation) for illegal entry or illegal border crossing, and any possible illegal operations across international boundaries of the United States. Such investigations include surveillance of pilots and aircraft involved, or suspected of being involved, in clandestine Mexican border crossings. The INS registers and fingerprints all known aliens. Its alien registration files contain valuable background data.

POST OFFICE DEPARTMENT. The department's Bureau of Chief Postal Inspection maintains its master index of names of all persons it has investigated for mail fraud and violations of the U.S. Postal Laws and Regulations. Geographical indexes are kept by the Postal Inspector-in-Charge at regional headquarters, and by the Resident Postal Inspector at large post offices.

The Postmaster or Superintendent of Mails at the local post office is the one to contact for forwarding addresses or change-of-address information. Investigators must present proper official credentials and be prepared to pay the required fee for such information.

DEPARTMENT OF LABOR. The Department of Labor Bureau of Employees' Compensation maintains a master index of claimants for worker's compensation benefits under the Federal Employees Compensation Act (FECA). The benefits are provided for civil employees and officers of the United States who are injured in the performance of their duty. The Employees' Compensation Appeals Board maintains its list of claims that have been appealed from the final decision of the director of the Bureau.

DEPARTMENT OF HEALTH AND HUMAN SERVICES. The information records of three separate entities of this department (formerly the Department of Health, Education, and Welfare) are worthy of note. The Bureau of Drug Abuse Control of the Food and Drug Administration maintains a master list of addicts (persons addicted to the use of habit-forming drugs) and of the violators of narcotics laws and regulations. The Public Health Service has a Bureau of Medical Service that operates facilities for the treatment and possible cure of narcotic addicts, including hospitals for drug rehabilitation and outpatient clinics. This Bureau keeps the medical records of patients or inmates.

The Social Security Administration issues Social Security account numbers on request. These numbers are valuable items of information. There are nine digits in the Social Security number, divided into three groups separated by hyphens, with three digits in the first group, two in the second, and four in the third, for example, 000-00-0000.

The first three digits identify the area from which the number was issued (with the exception of the 700 series). The next two digits indicate the group number (Social Security numbers within areas are broken down into groups). The last four digits simply comprise the numerical series within each group from 0001 through 9999. The areas of issuance as designated by the first three digits of the number are as follows:

Initial numbers	State of issuance
001-003	New Hampshire
004-007	Maine
008-009	Vermont
010-034	Massachusetts
035-039	Rhode Island
040-049	Connecticut
050-134	New York
135-158	New Jersey
159-211	Pennsylvania
212-220	Maryland
221-222	Delaware
223-231	Virginia
232-236	West Virginia
237-246	North Carolina
247-251	South Carolina
252-260	Georgia
261-267	Florida
268-302	Ohio
303-317	Indiana
318-361	Illinois
362-386	Michigan
387-399	Wisconsin
400-407	Kentucky
408-415	Tennessee
416-424	Alabama
425-428	Mississippi (also 587)
429-432	Arkansas
433-439	Louisiana

Initial numbers	State of issuance
440-448	Oklahoma
449-467	Texas
468-477	Minnesota
478-485	Iowa
486-500	Missouri
501-502	North Dakota
503-504	South Dakota
505-508	Nebraska
509-515	Kansas
516-517	Montana
518-519	Idaho
520	Wyoming
521-524	Colorado
525	New Mexico (also 585)
526-527	Arizona
528-529	Utah
530	Nevada
531-539	Washington
540-544	Oregon
545-573	California
574	Alaska
575-576	Hawaii
577-579	District of Columbia
580	Virgin Islands
581-584	Puerto Rico
700	Railroad employees with special retirement act

The Social Security card is not actually an identification card, even though there is a growing tendency to use it as such. It is not considered a reliable source of identification, however, because of the ease with which it may be obtained. Military ID numbers are the exception when they are the same number as the individual's Social Security number.

The amount of individual Social Security benefits and the account records of those covered by Social Security insurance are privileged by law and not generally available to investigators. The Social Security Administration will provide a photocopy of an original application for a Social Security number and any changes of information subsequently made in that application, provided such a request is accompanied by written authorization of the person whose original application is desired.

DEPARTMENT OF TRANSPORTATION. The National Driver Register Service of the Bureau of Public Roads maintains a central index of those whose driving privileges have been withdrawn for (1) driving under the influence of intoxicating liquor or (2) conviction of a driving offense that resulted in a fatality.

The U.S. Coast Guard – Intelligence Service maintains a master index of (1) persons associated with the maritime industry and (2) those investigated in connection with (a) its licensing activity or (b) its law enforcement activity.

FEDERAL RECORDS CENTER. St. Louis, Missouri, is where the Federal Records Center is located. It is operated by the General Services Administration, which administers the National Archives and Record Service. The Federal Records Center maintains a national locator file of all current federal civilian employees, including the inactive personnel files of former employees. Any request for location of the current duty station of a federal civilian employee should be accompanied by Social Security number, full name, and date and place of birth.

SELECTIVE SERVICE SYSTEM. The state director of the Selective Service System (SSS), with headquarters located at the state capital, maintains a master list of all Selective Service registrants who were residents of the state at the time of registration. The state director will furnish the identity and location of the local Selective Service Board that has the registrant's category classification and jurisdiction over the registrant.

CIVIL SERVICE COMMISSION. The Commission's Bureau of Personnel Investigations keeps a master index of (1) persons investigated for federal employment and (2) certain contractors working on federal projects who require security clearances.

The Commission's Bureau of Retirement and Insurance – Medical Division maintains a master list of applicants (1) for civil service employment and (2) for disability retirement resulting from physical or mental disabilities.

FEDERAL LAW-ENFORCEMENT RECORDS. Federal law-enforcement records are maintained by specific agencies for their own use and to aid local police. They include:

1. National Crime Information Center (NCIC) — This center operates a computerized system of nationwide information covering:

    • Stolen and suspect vehicles
    • Stolen license plates
    • Stolen articles
    • Missing firearms
    • Stolen securities

- Stolen boats
- Wanted persons
- Missing persons

The center also operates Computerized Criminal History (CCH) files.

2. Identification Division of the FBI — The FBI's Fingerprint and Criminal Identification File is a national clearing house with over 200 million fingerprint cards on file, including those of serious offenders.
3. Drug Enforcement Administration (DEA) — This administration provides automated intelligence records on known and suspected drug dealers and their aircraft.
4. El Paso Intelligence Center (EPIC) — This center functions as the intelligence compilation service of the Immigration and Naturalization Service (INS).
5. Bureau of Alcohol, Tobacco and Firearms (ATF) — The firearms division maintains records of firearms dealers and manufacturers. Its registry includes persons who lawfully possess heavy weapons, including machine guns.
6. Bureau of Prisons maintains background records on former and current federal prisoners.

There are numerous criminal justice intelligence systems of both natural and state dimensions. The NCIC referred to above provides quick computer access to national listings of stolen autos, stolen property, and wanted persons. Illustrations of state systems include the Police Information System (PINS) of California, which deals primarily in wanted persons and wanted vehicles; and the New York State Intelligence and Identification System (NYSIIS). The NYSIIS and California State Intelligence Systems are geared to provide state-wide information relative to criminal histories, modus operandi, sex and narcotics offenses, gun registration, and fingerprint and name identification files. All of these systems have been established as an aid to law enforcement and are not generally available to private investigators except through law-enforcement and legal channels on a need-to-know or professional courtesy basis.

OTHER RECORDS. The United States Coast Guard maintains a listing of all persons serving aboard U.S. merchant ships. The Bureau of Narcotics keeps records of all licensed handlers of narcotics, such as physicians and druggists.

The Attorney General of the United States has compiled a list of subversive organizations that are suspected of planning to overthrow the government of the country. Attempts are often made by subversives to infiltrate other legitimate and nonsubversive organizations and transform them into "fronts" for their activities.

Criminal Justice Records

Before moving to the private sector sources of information, a word regarding criminal justice records is appropriate, particularly to private investigators involved in criminal investigations. Criminal justice records are valuable sources of information on criminal histories, prior crimes, and accurate descriptions of repeat felons.

Any fugitive from justice, or wanted person with a prior criminal record, will have on file rather comprehensive records of his history to date. Data include a complete and accurate physical description, the modus operandi of any previous crimes, along with the fugitive's fingerprints and photographs at the time of his last arrest. All relevant facts uncovered in any past investigations will be recorded, with information pertaining to previous accomplices in criminal ventures and close relatives, including known ex-wives or ex-girlfriends.

The department of corrections will have further information if the offender has previously spent time in prison. In addition to the prison's personal information on the subject, data include the names of friends, cellmates, and visitors, and the subject's institutional history.

The parole board will have information if the subject has been paroled or if he has been placed on probation. In addition to the basic criminal justice and prison records, the parole authority will have information regarding the subject's current residential address and employment during the period of parole. It will also have a record of references issued on behalf of the former felon.

Criminal justice records are found within the various law-enforcement agencies and the criminal courts. Private firms compile their own records pertaining to criminals and criminal activities they have investigated. The largest compilation of these files within the world of private investigation is credited as belonging to the Pinkerton Agency, which is said to have 1.5 million files on known criminals. The credit for this system goes back to Allan Pinkerton's day when he began his files long before the age of modern information gathering.

Government Personnel Lists

Government agencies maintain their own official personnel and security files and provide lists of employed personnel in their departments. The information is available for city, county, state, and federal agencies, and is invaluable in locating individuals in government service.

FEDERAL GOVERNMENT. Four publications of the federal government provide government personnel data: (1) *United States Government Organization*

Manual, (2) *Federal Register,* (3) *Book of the States,* and (4) *Congressional Directory.* The last is published semiannually, and contains detailed biographical data on federal government personnel. It gives the names of committee members and of top-ranking personnel of executive departments.

Departments and agencies of the federal government also maintain their own agency civilian personnel records and employee dossiers. The scope and volume of the records vary with agency requirements and any need for security clearance. Some department records are more detailed than others in describing the functions of their personnel.

STATE AND CITY GOVERNMENTS. State *Blue Books* and directories provide similar information on state officials. *Civil Lists* give the names of all personnel on the city payroll. Names are usually listed according to department affiliation. Some civil lists are sources of considerable municipal employee information. They include the name and address of each person employed, his or her job or position title, salary, previous positions held, date entered city service, and dates of any promotions. In cities that do not publish such a list, the information can usually be obtained from the payroll department or from the civil service municipal employee card files.

This completes our resumé of some of the principal government information records. Some of these records are public. Some are privileged and not available as a rule. Others are obtainable through private investigators' contacts. A few are top secret and restricted.

PRIVATE SECTOR SOURCES OF INFORMATION

A great many sources of information may be found in the private sector. All private businesses and commercial and industrial firms keep records, as do private organizations, associations, institutions, and agencies. Business and financial publications compile significant information. Files, records, documents, contracts, transfers, bills, titles, deeds, financial statements, and data services record key information on almost every significant transaction of the private world of free enterprise. Add to this the numerous periodicals and publications that carry information of one kind or another and the result is a formidable array of potential sources investigators can probe as needs require.

PRIVATE INDUSTRY EMPLOYERS. All corporations, organizations, institutions, associations, and companies that employ management, departmental, clerical, and labor personnel have on file applications for employment and personnel records. These contain a significant amount of personal data including related educational and employment history. If the employer is a defense contractor, these files include security clearance for employees.

From the records contained in the personnel files of former employees, private investigators can extract valuable information regarding a subject's former employment and employers, the nature of his work, former addresses, references, and other pertinent data. Past history information often provides leads to present activities. Investigators who probe this type of information will sometimes encounter former supervisors or co-workers who know where the subject is living or working currently.

Sometimes a private investigator has to talk with a manager about one of his current or former workers or with a president of a firm regarding one of his managers, or they may need to discuss some investigative matter involving the firm itself. It may be an interview about problems with industrial espionage, the cooperation of management in a security survey, or a lawsuit.

When a private investigator wants information from a business firm, it is usually best for him to contact top men, the president or chief executive officer, the executive vice president in charge of operations, or the general manager. The private investigator will generally receive a more friendly reception and secure greater cooperation from executive personnel than from middle or lower management levels.

When a private investigator contacts a middle management person on an important matter, he will be dealing with someone who probably does not have the authority to act on behalf of the company. His responsibility will be limited to the area of his operations and the workers who are under his jurisdiction. If he has to relay a message or request to higher officials, it may be far less effective than it would have been had private investigators gone directly to those officials in the first place. The private investigator always seeks to deal with people who have the authority to act, and not with those who have to secure permission from their superiors.

If a private investigator is referred to a lower management level by a top executive he will then have the request of the superior office on his side, which will make the interview more effective. Even if, because of the circumstances of the investigation, the private investigator does not anticipate real cooperation from a company executive, it is still advisable to go to the top; the private investigator may be surprised at the information he is able to obtain. Sometimes minor information can be obtained from lesser officials, but for all major investigative needs it pays to go to the top.

TELEPHONE COMPANY RECORDS.   Telephone directories are effective references for locations, both local directories and those of any other city involved in the investigation. They are invaluable in skip tracing and locating missing persons. Telephone information services are helpful when a subject's name is not yet listed in a directory. People who are presumed to be lost have frequently been found listed in a telephone directory in some other county or city, near or far away.

Local directories of past years provide information relative to the time a subject resided locally, principally, the address for which the telephone service was provided. This information can provide a starting point for address tracing. A check can determine if the local telephone company keeps a library of old directories; these are usually made available to authorized investigators.

In addition to the regular alphabetical names directory, telephone companies frequently publish reverse directories that list subscribers according to street addresses. Such a directory is very helpful when private investigators want to identify the subscriber at a specific address or make a background or neighborhood check.

Toll tickets used for billing long-distance calls can be obtained by filing a court order; this is not difficult for the investigator to secure. This procedure establishes the authenticity of toll tickets as evidence. Such tickets provide dated records on the subject's long-distance calls and the telephone numbers called. Telephone credit card calls also provide excellent tracing records. Both the number of the telephone from which the call was made and the number called (and possibly even the name of the person called) will be listed. Telephone credit card information includes calls made from public telephones.

Local telephone company offices may for a fee scan their files for past addresses and telephone numbers of a specified person.

COMPUTERIZED CREDIT BUREAUS. Computer technology plays an ever increasing role in the gathering and dispensing of information. Data bank firms treat information as a commodity to be marketed to companies and organizations that are members of or subscribers to their systems.

A division of TRW, Inc., TRW Credit Data, is one of the leading examples of computerized retail credit bureaus. It responds to telephone inquiries from subscribers, which are primarily firms or institutions that extend credit to their customers, clients, patients, and others. A computer printout of the borrower's credit record and any significant data pertaining thereto is promptly received by the subscriber. Reportedly, the average response time is two minutes. The TRW Credit Data is a computer-based credit reporting agency with millions of records and thousands of subscribers. Its profits are realized from the sale of information from its computerized files. Both operators and subscribers must identify themselves to the computer by number.

The Retail Credit Company of Atlanta, Georgia, is said to be the largest of its kind in terms of files and information services. Other firms specializing in preemployment records include Hooper-Homes, Dun and Bradstreet, and Fidelifacts. It is claimed that Equifax, Inc. (formerly Retail Credit) maintains files on nearly 50 million Americans, which probably rates it near the top as a consumer investigation service.

CREDIT AGENCY RECORDS. Private investigators frequently need to conduct preemployment, credit, and background investigations. The Fair Credit Reporting Act regulates the conditions under which information is released from credit agencies in an effort to maintain fairness and impartiality and respect for the consumer's rights to privacy.

Section 604 of the Act sets forth the permissible purposes for which consumer reports may be released. A consumer-reporting agency may furnish a report under any of the following three circumstances: (1) in response to a court order, (2) in accordance with the written instructions of the consumer, and (3) to a person the reporting agency believes will use the information disclosed for legitimate purposes in connection with:

1. A credit transaction involving the consumer, an extension of credit, review of credit, or collection of an account
2. Employment consideration
3. Underwriting insurance involving the consumer
4. A consumer's eligibility for a license granted by a government agency, when it is required by law to consider the applicant's financial responsibility
5. A legitimate business need for the information in a business transaction involving the consumer

All applicants for credit and consumer information must identify themselves and certify the purpose for which the information is sought. They must also certify that the information will be used for no other purpose. There are several other stipulations of the Act with which investigators should familiarize themselves before seeking such information.

RETAIL CREDIT BUREAUS AS SOURCES OF NEW LOCATION INFOR-MATION. When a person moves to a new area and seeks credit there, his request is cleared with the local credit bureau. When they find no credit transactions in the new area of residence, the local bureau contacts the credit bureau of the city or county in which that person previously lived.

Operatives involved in missing-persons or skip-tracing investigations can possibly trace the relocated person through credit bureau requests. If the private investigator knows from which city a bureau requested credit information, he knows where the person moved. If the individual has left town without meeting his financial obligations, a creditor may be able to help obtain information regarding the transfer of credit data.

FINANCIAL INSTITUTIONS. Investigations may require information from banks, savings and loan companies, finance companies, or other financial institutions. Generally, these companies are reluctant to release information relative to customer accounts. To do so could lead to lawsuits. They will, of course, cooperate when presented with an authorization signed by the customer for the release of the data. Financial company officials usually want to be assured that the information will not be used in any legal proceedings unless it is first subpoenaed. The subpoena relieves the institution of voluntary responsibility in the matter. Banks can release records to a law-enforcement agency or an investigator looking into the illegal use of bank drafts or other financial instruments.

Contacts in banks and financial institutions must be treated with discretion. When investigating fraudulent financial activities, private investigators should carefully consider the most prudent manner in which the institution(s) involved can cooperate. Good investigators are likely to obtain cooperation within legal limits when they show concern for the best interests of both the institution and the client.

INSURANCE COMPANIES. Insurance companies warrant special reference. Although they have their own claims investigators, they frequently hire private investigators in cases of suspected insurance fraud or false disability claims. In such instances the company provides the investigators with the necessary information on a confidential basis to enable them to pursue their investigations intelligently.

Insurance fraud involves both the policy holder's fraudulent acts and claims against the insurer and white-collar fraud within the industry itself. Phony accidents, false injury claims, arson, the burning of property for financial gain, automobile theft, and other crimes against insured property and insurance carriers anually take a heavy toll. Whenever private investigators are called in to investigate such activities they will have the full cooperation of the insurance company in providing any evidence of fraud or other related information.

When investigators seek medical information from life insurance files, they usually need authorization for the release of such information signed by the policy holder.

CHAMBERS OF COMMERCE. Chambers of Commerce often have voluminous information on commercial and industrial establishments located within their areas, as well as considerable related information on trade and industry as it affects their communities. Many of them publish valuable lists and guides. Some of these are so extensive as to list all the business firms within the area, with the names of presidents and other key officers, their addresses, and telephone numbers. A manual of that type can be of considerable help to investigators.

A Chamber of Commerce may also have lists of manufacturers and international traders operating within its localities, and references pertaining to specific businesses. It will often have trade journals covering industries important to its region.

BETTER BUSINESS BUREAUS. The information available at Better
Business Bureaus is limited. Its data are developed because of any one or more
of three different situations: (1) the bureau has received a prior request for
such information; (2) a business or industry has volunteered the information;
or (3) the bureau has had a complaint lodged against the business. Private
investigators can always check to determine what information may be available.

INSTITUTIONAL, ASSOCIATION, AND SOCIETY RECORDS. All institutions, organizations, associations, and societies keep records. Some of these
are confidential and others are neither confidential nor public, but may be made
available on a need-to-know or professional courtesy basis. Such records may
be of real value in cases involving members, patients, or personnel of these
organizations. This category would include professional, business, and membership societies of one sort or another, ranging all the way from the American
Medical Association and the American Dental Association to local chapters
of Alcoholics Anonymous. The multiplicity of these societies increases the
potential sources of information.

Multiplicity of Data Banks in a Free Society

Many persons have become deeply concerned with the vast amount of
data being compiled on individual citizens in our free society. To what extent
is the rapidly growing computerized data industry invading one's rights to
privacy? This question emphasizes a critical problem confronting our freedom.
Any serious misuse of this enormous amount of data could trigger a national
crisis. The federal government's computer inventory is staggering, and the
growth of computerized information retrieval systems within private industry
has been phenomenal in recent decades, adding to the deepening concern.

On the other hand, electronic analysis and retrieval of criminal histories
can prove a real boon to the cause of justice. Moreover, the records of state
government agencies such as those of the motor vehicle department and bureau
of vital statistics are essential to the knowledgeable functioning of modern
society.

Weekly, monthly, and annually, multiplied millions of decisions are made
about individuals by business enterprises of one sort or another, employing
key personnel, granting retail credit, or dealing with persons in business
transactions that call for the evaluation of credit, employment, and other
capabilities, based on available accurate and complete information. Business
firms are continually drawing information from commercial reporting and
retrieval services operating within the private sector, in addition to their own
compilation of data. Banks, retail merchants, lending institutions, employers,
insurance companies, and those conducting preemployment, preinsurance, and

premerger investigations all seek information from private firms who commercialize it.

Credit bureau information is compiled from numerous sources, including banks, landlords, employers, property records, court records, credit references, and any trade publications listing the subject's name, position, and related data. All these are potential information sources for investigators as well.

After compiling information from the above, and from the usual government agency and private sector sources, credit bureaus can provide a considerable amount of data pertaining to the individual's history and credit record, including occupational and residential history, number of dependents, financial status, bank references, loans and credit extended, litigations (if any), and the manner in which the subject pays his accounts.

PUBLISHED SOURCES OF INFORMATION

Public and law libraries stock many useful published works, some of which may prove very helpful in specific types of investigations. Publications include directories, registers, indexes, continually up-dated loose-leaf information services, and numerous volumes dealing with specialty subjects. The sources referred to in this section represent only a fraction of the information research potential provided by these libraries.

Financial and Business Publications

Financial, business, industrial, and professional publications abound with a wide range of information. For private investigators involved in related investigations, there are numerous comprehensive sources dealing with corporations, industrial products, securities, commodities, banks, and other financial and business data.

City libraries have many of the standard financial and business references, some of which are listed below. Space does not permit detailed description of their contents. A few basic works are described to a limited degree, others are listed under suitable headings. Often the name of the publication itself will be clear indication of the field it covers.

Standard and Poor's and Moody are two big names in published loose-leaf services on financial data. Any private investigators involved in financial investigations needing information on corporations and their security issues can find a mine of information in the many volumes published by these two information services.

CORPORATIONS. Standard and Poor's *Corporation Records* includes both a daily news compilation of corporate data and an analysis of each corporation called corporation descriptions. These descriptions include: (1) capitalization, (2) corporate background, (3) bond subscriptions, (4) stock data, (5) earnings and finances, and (6) consolidated balance sheet data.

CORPORATE PERSONNEL. Standard and Poor's *Register of Corporations, Directors, and Executives* and Dun and Bradstreet's *Reference Book of Corporate Managements,* including directors and officers, are both valuable reference works for identification and capsule resumés of key corporate personnel.

CORPORATE STOCKS. Both Moody and Standard and Poor's provide ample data on corporate equity (stocks) and debt (bonds).

Standard and Poor's *Stock Reports* is an analysis and ranking of common stocks of the various corporations. This includes a significant amount of easily referenced data, including important corporate developments and business and financial information.

MILLION-DOLLAR FIRMS. Dun's Marketing Services, a division of Dun and Bradstreet, publishes the *Million Dollar Directory* in three separate volumes. These directories provide information on U.S. businesses with a net worth in excess of $500,000. Volume 1 covers 45,000 of the top companies ranked according to their net worth. Businesses are listed in three separate categories: (1) alphabetically, (2) geographically, and (3) by product classification. Volumes 2 and 3 list approximately 37,000 additional firms.

MANUFACTURERS. The *Thomas Register of American Manufacturers* is a sixteen-volume set of data on the nation's manufacturers. This is an excellent reference in product liability cases. In Volumes 1 through 8 the products and services of these companies are listed alphabetically. Volumes 9 and 10 provide company names, addresses, ZIP codes, and telephone numbers. Volumes 11 through 16 include catalogues of the firms, bound alphabetically, many of which illustrate key products.

RETAIL STORES. Fairchild's Financial Manual of Retail Stores is published by the book division of Fairchild's Publications, New York. This volume highlights primary data on the great retail chains and stores, including officers, directors, business activities, transfer agents, stock exchange on which their stock is listed and ticker symbol, the number of stores in the chain, revenues, common stockholder's equity, income account, assets, liabilities, and statistical summary. The *Thomas Grocery Register* is a three-volume set on supermarket chains and wholesalers. Volume 3 lists 60,000 companies alphabetically.

BANK DIRECTORIES. The *Rand McNally International Banker's Directory,* published in Chicago, contains an excellent description of the Federal Reserve System with its member banks and branches, together with color maps showing the boundaries of the Federal Reserve districts and district banks. It lists the key banking authorities in America, including the Board of Governors of the Federal Reserve. The *Directory* includes check routing numbers by city and area, automated bank clearing houses of the nation, names of bank holding companies, and data on all the banks and branches operating in America, including their financial statements.

Polk's World Bank Directory, North American edition, lists directory data on banks in the United States, Canada, Mexico, the Caribbean area, and Central America. The international edition is published annually at midyear. The publisher is R.L. Polk and Co., Nashville, Tennessee.

BUSINESS CREDIT RATINGS. The *Reference Book* of Dun and Bradstreet lists the names, financial data, and credit ratings of manufacturers, wholesalers, and retailers in the United States. Lists are arranged by states, cities, and towns, including references to the type of business and the year it was founded. Subscribers to the service can secure detailed credit reports on specific firms. Dun and Bradstreet publish a number of directories comprising their Business Reference Library.

Multiple Sources of Financial and Business Information

Public libraries abound with sources of business information of which the following is but a sample.

FEDERAL RESERVE BULLETIN. This is the best single source of banking and monetary statistics and policies.

WHO OWNS WHOM. Published by the Directories Division of Dun and Bradstreet, it lists the subsidiaries and associate companies of parent companies. Anyone investigating the link between a parent company and its subsidiaries will find this volume helpful.

BUSINESS PERIODICALS INDEX. It is published by H. W. Wilson Co., New York City.

NATIONAL FACULTY DIRECTORY. Gale Research publishes this in two volumes that contain an alphabetical list with addresses of approximately 524,000 members of the teaching faculties of junior colleges, colleges, and universities in the United States. This source is a helpful reference for locating faculty members of national educational institutions above the high school level.

DOING BUSINESS IN THE UNITED STATES. A multivolume looseleaf service edited by J. J. Spires contains practical guidelines relative to business operations and regulations. It includes the general business law and the Uniform Commercial Code. Volume 6 contains a glossary of business terms.

UNIWORLD. Uniworld Business Publications, Inc., publishes this directory of American firms operating in foreign countries. Dun and Bradstreet International of London and New York publishes a directory of Europe's 5,000 largest companies.

WORLD GUIDE TO TRADE ASSOCIATIONS. A list of more than 46,000 trade associations in all parts of the world. The *Guide* is published by K.G. Saur of München, Germany, and New York City.

Space precludes our listing other types of reference works. The above is sufficient to illustrate the broad spectrum of published information available.

City Sources

Many cities no longer publish encyclopedic directories because of their high cost. Los Angeles, for example, has not had such a directory for many years. Where they are published, they are a valuable investigative tool.

Most of the large directories over the years have been published by the City Directory Division of R.L. Polk and Co. They provide reference to residents, businesses, and other city organizations. It is estimated that over 70 million persons are listed in these volumes, representing residents in covered cities and communities who are over eighteen years of age. Personal data include name, address, marital status, occupation, place of employment, and telephone number. Directory information normally covers three areas: (1) alphabetical directory, (2) street directory, and (3) type of business.

Comprehensive city directories are an excellent intelligence tool, as they reveal updated information on a subject at the time each new directory is compiled. By using both current and previous directories, private investigators can run a check on a subject's personal history. The comparison of data will thus disclose job or position changes, address changes, and significant movements within the city.

In some directories widows are so identified, along with the name of their deceased husband. All directories usually include the wife's name when listing the name of a married male. In the street directory streets are listed numerically (or alphabetically as necessary), including the number of each building and names of the occupants. City directories provide a quick reference for locating persons, business firms, institutions, and professional establishments.

Many large cities publish their own directories of all the departments of the city government, with the names of officials and bureau heads, and the location of police precincts, schools, license bureaus, courts, jails, and so on. These may be published in lieu of the larger city directories, or in some cases in addition to them.

NEWSPAPER MORGUES. Copies of old newspapers are often valuable in investigating cases that were given newspaper publicity. They may contain clues or leads private investigators can follow up, and may in fact name persons who could be contacted as potential witnesses. They may also provide helpful address information and even some descriptive details. Most papers maintain so-called morgue copies for at least one year or more. Also private investigators may be fortunate to have in their area one of those rare daily papers that provides an indexed catalogue of information found in past issues.

Safety Information Sources

Safety organizations and publications provide a considerable amount of information on safety standards and accident and fire protection. Sources include the National Safety Council of Chicago, which publishes the *Accident Prevention Manual* and the monthly *Safety Newsletter;* the National Fire Protection Association of Boston, publisher of the *Fire Protection Handbook;* the American National Standards Institute of New York City, issuer of the *ANSI Reporter;* the American Society of Safety Engineers, Park Ridge, Illinois, publishers of the monthly *ASSE Journal.*

Other publications include *Dangerous Properties of Industrial Materials,* by Van Nostrand Rheinhold, New York City; the *Machine and Tool Blue Book,* by Hitchcock Publishing Co., Wheaton, Illinois; the *Safety and Accident Prevention in Chemical Operations and Manufacturing Processes,* by John Wiley and Sons, New York; and *Best's Safety Directory,* by A.M. Best, Oldwick, New Jersey.

In industrial accidents, information and sometimes helpful assistance can be provided by the unions and labor organizations involved. Traffic safety information can be had from the National Highway Traffic Safety Administration of the Department of Transportation located in Washington, D.C., or from New York's Society of Automotive Engineers, Inc.

Professional and Business Associations

The Gale Research Co., Detroit, Michigan, publishes an *Encyclopedia of Associations,* which lists national organizations of the United States under seventeen different categories, with a composite alphabetical index. Gale also publishes the *Encyclopedia of Business Information Sources,* which lists organizations providing sourcebooks, periodicals, and handbooks dealing with various kinds of business information.

Section 1 of Gale's *Encyclopedia of Associations* lists national trade, business, and commercial organizations; section 3 legal, government, public administration, and military organizations; and section 4, scientific, engineering, and technical organizations. These three sections illustrate the *Encyclopedia*'s national coverage of associations in many different fields. It also contains data on Chambers of Commerce, labor unions, and educational and religious organizations.

Some associations of interest to private investigators that are described in the *Encyclopedia of Associations* include the following:

INTERNATIONAL ASSOCIATION OF ARSON INVESTIGATORS (MARLBOROUGH, MASSACHUSETTS). This association publishes the quarterly *Fire and Arson Investigator.*

AMERICAN SOCIETY OF QUESTIONED DOCUMENTS (HOUSTON, TEXAS). This is a membership society for professional document examiners in private practices and public service.

INDEPENDENT ASSOCIATION OF QUESTIONED DOCUMENT EXAMINERS (CEDAR RAPIDS, IOWA). The association provides qualified examiners to assist justice in the examination of documents.

FEDERAL INFORMATION CENTER PROGRAM (FIC). Part of the General Service Administration of Washington, D.C., this is a directive information center. It directs those lost in the maze of the federal bureaucracy to the right office for the service or information they are seeking. The FIC operates centers in forty-one cities. An additional forty-three cities have toll-free tie-lines connecting to the nearest FIC office. It also publishes information on federal information centers.

SOCIETY OF PROFESSIONAL INVESTIGATORS (ELMHURST, NEW YORK). It is a membership society for investigators with at least five years of experience for an official federal, state, or local government agency, or quasi-official agency.

CITIZENS' LEGAL PROTECTIVE LEAGUE (CLPL) (ST. LOUIS). The League provides basic training in court procedures for Americans who wish to represent themselves in court without hiring lawyers.

RETORT, INC. (PRODUCT LIABILITY) (CAMBRIDGE, MASSACHU-SETTS). Among other services, it conducts research in the liability of industry for injury and damages resulting from product use. It publishes a bimonthly newsletter. RETORT is an acronym for reason and equity in tort.

NATIONAL ASSOCIATION OF LEGAL INVESTIGATORS (NALI) (EAST ALTON, ILLINOIS). This association issues an investigative handbook and specializes in the investigation of personal injury cases.

NATIONAL ASSOCIATION OF FIRE INVESTIGATORS (CHICAGO). This is a membership organization with emphasis on improving the skills of persons engaged in the investigation of fires.

INTERNATIONAL ASSOCIATION OF CREDIT CARD INVESTIGATORS (NOVATO, CALIFORNIA). The association specializes in the investigation of criminal violations of credit card laws.

Two other associations should be mentioned: the American Federation of Investigators (AFI) and the American Society for Industrial Security (ASIS).

This list is not exhaustive. Some associations limit their membership to those who have investigated for agencies of the federal government or to former intelligence officers. Such societies can help private investigators establish contacts with reliable persons who are in a position to provide counsel, assistance, or information. New associations are being added from time to time. Alert private investigators are aware of any such developments taking place within their areas.

All professional associations and organizations keep their own membership records and related data. Directories of the American Medical Association (AMA), the American Dental Association, and religious and denominational directories and yearbooks are illustrative of types of professional records. The *American Medical Directory* published by the AMA provides a reference list of all physicians. Hospitals' and doctors' records are usually privileged and are available only on a demonstrated need to know basis or by court order.

All business associations keep records pertaining to their line of business. The records of automobile associations are typical. National automobile associations include the American Association of Motor Vehicle Administrators (AAMVA), which maintains up to date information on out-of-state violations of motor vehicle codes; and the National Driver Registration Service (NDRS), which lists the names of drivers whose licenses are under suspension or revocation. The National Automobile Theft Bureau (NATB), headquartered in Palos Hills, Illinois, may prove helpful in the identification and recovery of stolen automobiles.

Telex Communications

Jaeger and Waldermann publish an *International Telex Directory* listing the international call numbers for worldwide communications through ITT. The Telex-Verlag, Jaeger and Waldman firm, located in Damstadt, Germany, publishes an English edition that should be available in city libraries.

Who's Who Publications

The leading publisher in the *Who's Who* categories is the Marquis Who's Who, Inc. of Chicago. They publish such works as *Who's Who in America, Who's Who in the West, Who's Who in Finance and Industry,* and so on.

These books provide capsule biographies of prominent persons within the categories covered by the specific volumes. There are references to achievements, education, marital status, and current addresses. Some *Who's Who* sources may give addresses and telephone numbers not listed in telephone books. One will often find information in these brief summaries helpful in investigating any person listed in a *Who's Who* volume, and in providing good starting points for investigations in "cold clue" situations. *Who Knows What* lists specialists in almost every field by specialty and by name.

Directories of Private Investigators

The *Regency International Directory* is a worldwide directory of enquiry agents, investigators, private detectives, security services, and similar agencies. It is published by Regency Directories International Publications Limited, Newtone House, 127 Sandgate Road, Folkestone, Kent, England. The *Regency International Directory* is really a compilation of more than a score of separate directories that include the names and addresses of operatives in nearly fifty countries of the world. Some listings also include telephone numbers.

The *Directory* is an excellent source of information for those seeking investigative-detective personnel or agencies in other parts of the world and is a handy manual for private investigators involved in international investigations. A recent copy contained the following compilations:

1. A general directory of all seven of the professional services covered listed by countries and cities of the world. The seven categories of services identified by code letters after the person's or agency's name are as follows:
   DC — debt-collecting agencies
   EG — enquiry agents

IN — investigators
PD — private detectives
SS — security services
SE — status enquiries
TP — trade protection societies or services

2. The geographical directory is followed by several other volumes including the rosters of state, national, and international associations of private investigators and private detectives. This compilation covers most of the countries of Europe, South Africa, and the associations of six American states and of Quebec, Canada, plus rosters of the World Association of Detectives and the Council of International Investigators. The twenty-first volume is a worldwide alphabetical listing of enquiry agents, investigators, and private detectives. The number of compiled directories may vary somewhat from edition to edition.

Rosters of U.S. Attorneys

The *Martindale-Hubbell Law Directory* is an eight-volume reference source containing geographical rosters of members of the bar and attorney firms for the fifty United States. It is published by Martindale-Hubbell, Inc., Summit, New Jersey. Volume 8 contains law digests of various states and countries; the Model Business Corporation Act, the Uniform Commercial Code, and several other Acts. The *Directory* is very helpful when there is need to locate attorneys for legal services in other cities and states.

Finding Source Materials for Specific Investigations

City law libraries can be very helpful to investigators seeking research material on certain types of cases. Take for example these four: accident, contract, personal injury, and product liability cases. Private investigators will find multivolume information sources on these and other types of cases in a good law library, as well as legal source material on most types of civil investigations, criminal prosecution, and defense. Here are four compilations that deal specifically with the four categories:

1. Accident cases — The Lawyers Co-Operative Publishing Company, Rochester, N.Y., publishes a multivolume set, *Handling Accident Cases,* by Albert Auerbach. Volume 3 deals with products liability, and Volume 4 with automobile accidents.

2. Contracts — *The Law of Contracts* is a treatise on contract regulations by Samuel Williston. The third edition is by Walter H.E. Jaeger. The publisher is Baker, Voorhis & Co. Inc., Mount Kisco, New York.
3. Personal injury — Matthew Bender of New York and San Francisco publishes several volumes on *Personal Injury — Actions, Defenses, Damages.* This comprehensive source of information is helpful in coping with the increasing number of personal injury cases filed each year.
4. Products liability — Matthew Bender also publishes several volumes on *Products Liability* by Louis R. Frumer and Melvin I. Friedman. Individual states may have a publication dealing with product liability laws, such as the *California Products Liability Actions,* which contains helpful investigative guidelines. While all four sources are legal works, their complete indexes give private investigators access to the specific information they are looking for.

Public and law libraries provide so many information sources that private investigators usually can find valuable guidelines on almost any matter that becomes a subject of investigation.

THE "HOW" OF INFORMATION

Since investigators are only as good as their information, it is most important that they become thoroughly familiar with the practical "how to" aspects of the process of gathering information. They should know:

1. How to activate sources of information
2. How to obtain information
   - from people,
   - from records and documents, and
   - from scenes and physical evidence
3. How to record information
4. How to analyze information
5. How to verify information
6. How to report information
7. How to preserve information

Information gathering is the key to investigative success. It includes searching records; making inquiries; interviewing and interrogating persons; examining scenes, documents, and objects; and making observations of persons and places by shadowing, tailing, photographing, and observation-post surveillance activities, and by undercover operations.

The Importance of Recorded Information

The main thrust of this chapter is the importance of recorded information to the investigative process. Access to a tremendous amount of public information provided by various government agencies is comparatively easy once investigators have established contacts with key people. The same is true with respect to establishing contact in private industry with those who are custodians of potentially valuable information.

SOURCES-OF-INFORMATION FILE

All successful private investigators maintain an up-to-date filing system as an aid to placing key sources and contacts at their fingertips. The system recommended here is patterned after the card directory files of public libraries. The following basic suggestions should prove helpful in setting up referenced source files.

1. Use a separate file card for each specific information source. Only then can it be readily located. To list different types of information on the same card, even if they are in alphabetical order, can add to the confusion. In addition, some items can potentially be listed under several letters of the alphabet. For source file purposes 3 X 5 cards are recommended.

2. Three separate filing classifications on each information source will expedite locating key information. The three-card cross-referenced system requires separate files as follows: *available information, source location,* and *contact name.* Consider the advantages of the three-card, three-file system. It enables one to check files for any of the three classifications. If you remember the name of the agency or firm but not the telephone number or address, check under Source Location. To determine if you have a file card on the specific type of information you need, check under Available Information. To find the telephone number or accuracy of a contact's name, check the Contact's Name file. These illustrations show the adaptability of the three-file system to investigators' information, and how it expedites speedy information checks.

3. Cross-reference each card to the other two cards pertaining to the same source of information. The Available Information card should contain cross-references to the Source Location and Contact's Name cards, and so on. The usual procedure is for each card to contain basic data on all three areas. All three cards could contain essentially the same information with one basic difference—the caption would be headlined for each of the three files.

4. Caption each card according to the file in which it belongs. Use capital letters or underline the titles. Each card in the Available Information file is headed with an item of information such as *Births* or *Deeds,* for example. Begin the heading for each card in the upper left-hand area of the card. The top of each card in the Location file gives the name and address of the government or private source, with its ZIP code and telephone number(s). At the top of the cards in the Contact's Name file appears the name of the person to see, telephone, or write, as the case may be, with the telephone number and extension or department designation that helps to reach him directly.

    In other words, titles on Available Information cards are all specific types of information. In the Location File the titles are all names of agencies, departments, or firms where the information is found, and their precise locations. In the Contact's Name file the titles are all names of persons to contact for precise information.

5. Arrange all file cards alphabetically in each of the three files. This can be done with a separate set of alphabet divider cards for each file.

6. Each item of information, each agency or firm name, and each contact should have a separate card. By adhering to separate cards throughout the three-file system, it becomes a simple matter to keep them alphabetically in their respective files. Some information agencies will be able to supply more than one type of information. Even if you should list all available data from a multi-information source on a card with cross-references, it is important to make out a separate card for each type of available information. By so doing, that information record will be readily available. Each information card will include data on where and from whom information is available, plus a cross-reference to the other two cards.

7. Each file card should highlight the data that pertains to its title. The Source Location files, for example, highlight the name, address, ZIP code, and telephone number of the agency, organization, company, or service from which the information is obtainable. When the same agency provides more than one type of information, these can be cross-referenced to other files. Cards in the Contact's Name file highlight the name of the person to be contacted, telephone or extension number if all calls come through a general switchboard, and other helpful guidelines, with cross-references to the information that contact can provide.

The advantage of the three-heading, three-file system is its quick reference to any of the three basic facts one should know about information sources: type of information, location of the information-providing agency, and the person to contact. Cross-referencing cards duplicates some information, and making out three cards takes a bit more time, but the system pays valuable dividends when it is in operation. It puts contact, location, and information specifics at your fingertips without having to remember which cards contain the items you want.

Some private investigators prefer to provide identical cards for all three files, changing only the headings to designate the file to which a card belongs. They may underline items pertaining to information, location, or contact. Others prefer to have each card contain only the basic data for that file, plus the important cross-reference to other cards. Two things are important: the heading on the card should identify the file to which it belongs, and the data on the card should be accurate.

The simplest procedure to use in implementing a filing system is for private investigators to take three file cards whenever they record any specific information source. On the top of one card they should headline the type of information, at the top of another card the location of the information source, and at the top of the third card the name of the party to contact. Include on each card sufficient information to tie together all three cards pertaining to that source, either by stipulation or reference, or both. File each card in its respective source file.

Additional Mobile File Cards

Some private investigators set up an additional set of mobile cards, to be carried with them during investigations, listing their most frequently used sources. Pertinent data are all included on the same card—information source, location, and contact. This does not replace, but is in addition to, the three-card file. Mobile files are not part of the three-card system, which should not be mutilated by removing cards. Data from the basic, permanent file should be transferred to the mobile cards, and should be restricted to pertinent, on-the-job information. A source file is a reference source. Its cards are on file for reference purposes only and should never be taken away. Information from them can be transferred, when necessary, to private investigators' notebooks or to "mobile" source cards.

Checking Information Source Files

When a private investigator is given an investigative assignment, he analyzes the issues involved and the types of information that will be needed to complete the assignment. What information will be obtained from interviewing other people? What information is already a matter of public agency or private sector records? Where must he go to get that information? Who can he telephone? Who can he see? How many answers can he find in his information files?

The private investigator turns to his information files and finds that one item on the list of information he needs is available from a contact. He checks his Contact file, gets the phone number, calls him, and soon has what he needs. He is not certain as to the availability of another item of information. He checks his Information Available file to see if he has anything listed in that category. If not, he will have to go in search of it.

There is another record the private investigator should check at a specific agency, but he wishes to confirm the address before he leaves. He does this by going directly to the Location File. He may also need to check the Contact File. He is soon on his way, knowing where to go and who to see to get the information he needs.

The private investigators success depends to a considerable degree upon the quality of his information. His two general sources are public and private. Contacts are the channels of private information. It is the private investigators' responsibility to determine the location of public sources of information.

In the words of Fuqua and Wilson, "Developing contacts is a lengthy process, but knowing where to find public information is only a matter of careful preliminary research. The well-prepared investigator knows where information in general is kept, and what kinds of information are kept where. If he knows this, he will have a head start on finding something particular. If he does not, he will be like a man looking for a needle and not even knowing which haystack to search."[3]

NOTES

1. Johnson, S. From James Boswell's *Life of Johnson. The Oxford dictionary of quotations.* 2nd ed. (London: Oxford University Press, 1964), 272.

2. Golec, A.M. *Techniques of legal investigation.* (Springfield, Ill.: Charles C Thomas, Publisher, 1976), 38.

3. Fuqua, P. and Wilson, J.V. *Security investigator's handbook.* (Houston: Gulf Publishing Co., 1979), 17.

III. OBSERVATION, DESCRIPTION, AND IDENTIFICATION

Chapter 7

What Do You See When You Look?

"While . . . recognition of persons can be achieved by remembering such things as voice, gait, clothing and mannerisms, by far the most powerful means of recognition is by perceiving, storing and retrieving aspects of facial configuration."
— Brian Clifford and Ray Bull[1]

"Observation is more than seeing; it is knowing what you see and comprehending its significance."
— Charles Gow[2]

In his book, *Allan Pinkerton, America's First Private Eye,* Sigmund A. Lavine records Pinkerton's description of a stranger who became the subject of his first investigative assignment. The significant fact about Pinkerton's observations, which he so clearly recalled, is that they were mentally recorded during just one brief, unobserved, apparently careless glance at the stranger. It is impressive to note the number of physical identification factors the investigator observed in that one glance[3]:

1. Nearly six feet tall
2. Weighing "fully two hundred pounds"
3. At least sixty-five years of age
4. Standing "very erect"
5. "Commanding" appearance
6. Dark hair "sightly tinged with gray"
7. "Very prominent" features
8. A "very large" nose

9.   An "unusually" large mouth
10. "A pair of the keenest, coldest small gray eyes I have ever seen"
11. Wearing a "large, plain gold ring" on one finger of his left hand

Eleven items of identification observed and described from one look at the subject — a remarkable score from one who had no previous training in developing the capability of perceptive observation.

Not many persons have the natural ability to observe keenly and adequately, and to describe clearly and accurately an individual they have seen or an event they have witnessed. Most people have failed to cultivate and develop their powers of observation, description, and identification. In no profession are these powers more vital than in the career of investigation. They are also criteria for evaluating the reliability and credibility of the testimony of eyewitnesses. Just how accurate and adequate was their perception? How complete and accurate is their recall? Estimates of witness reliability differ considerably, largely as a result of the varying ability of individuals to perceive, recall, and describe what they observed.

SENSORY POWERS OF OBSERVATION

To observe is to take specific notice of. Investigative observation may be defined as vigilant, perceptive sight. To be vigilant is to be alert and watchful, and cognizant of what one sees. The process of perceiving is the consciousness of persons, objects, events, and scenes. Perceptions come through the senses, principally, the eyes and ears.

The vigilant observer sees what the heedless onlooker misses. Seeing and awareness of seeing combine as a source of knowledge and information that results from being alert, awake, alive to evidential facts. True observation, then, is mentally recognized and recorded seeing. It embraces awareness of perceptions registered by the five senses: sight, hearing, smell, taste, and touch. Sense perception conveys information to our minds. Resulting impressions and discernments have a sensory basis on which mental judgments are made or intelligent conclusions are reached.

Sight

The human eye is a most fruitful source of personally obtained information. Investigators' eyes must be trained for adequate and accurate observation. In evaluating their powers of observation, private investigators should ask themselves: Is my visual observation accurate? Is it adequate? Do I see sufficiently, clearly, and correctly? Correct visual observation identifies. It also enables the mind to record mental pictures for later identification. The visual recording of evidence is an important basis for description.

Observation is also the faculty of taking specific notice of the physical characteristics of persons, of the multiple facets of events, of the physical evidence at accident, injury, and crime scenes, and of whatever relevant data and evidential information apply to any assignment or case. Private investigators seek to develop that capability of keen and comprehensive observation that is cognizant of both the total picture and the significant details.

Hearing

Hearing is the second most important human faculty for investigation. The ear records normal, unusual, and significant sounds. When trained it can also help to estimate distance by sound. Through the ears one can make note of conversations, remarks, exclamations, promises, agreements, and contracts. It is also possible to identify sound effects of gunshots, explosives, crashes, brawls, and the like. Ear-witness testimony may prove to be of great value, especially in cases where there are no eyewitnesses.

Touch, taste, and smell usually play a lesser role in detection, but they have their evidential uses. Examples include the smell or taste of narcotics; or the touch of some physical evidence that registers the impact of its significance, such as an explosive device, weapon, or tool used to burglarize a business office.

PSYCHOLOGICAL ASPECTS OF OBSERVATION

The following psychological factors have a direct bearing on the ability to observe clearly, accurately, and adequately:

- Attention
- Awareness
- Emotional reactions
- Shock, stress, and surprise
- Perception capacity
- Selectivity of perceptions
- Mental recording and storage
- Understanding

Attention

Attention implies focusing the mind on what is seen. A mind out of focus can never accurately record evidence. Attention gives special consideration to what actually occurs. That consideration is the measure of the attention factor. Professional private investigators sense the value of close and continuous attention as a means of acquiring knowledge of any given situation.

Attention normally precedes perception. We cannot discern what we do not heed. When attention and perception do not come naturally, because they have largely been left unused, they must be activated and developed by sheer will power and by intelligent practice. It may be necessary at first deliberately to focus attention until it becomes habitual.

Awareness

Awareness is the conscious recognition of what is transpiring. Without awareness we bypass evidence, totally unaware of its existence. We remain ignorant of information of which we should become knowledgeable, and thus we fail to become conscious of the presence of clues that might help us solve cases. Only when we are aware of a fact and perceive its significance are we in a position to understand its meaning and import.

Emotional Reactions

Emotional reactions can greatly reduce perception capability. In their book *The Psychology of Person Identification,* Clifford and Bull note, "Emotion has a disorganizing effect on both perception and memory." They also note Berrien's contention that "Excitement blurs accuracy."[4] Observational ability and accuracy are negatively affected by emotional excitement or disturbance.

SHOCK, STRESS, AND SURPRISE. The shock referred to here is that sudden agitation of emotional or mental sensibilities. A jolt to the sensibilities can adversely affect the rational powers of observation, at least temporarily, leading one to overlook at least some of the details of reality.

Stress can be created by accidental, injurious, dangerous, or criminal circumstances, with a resulting divergence of perception away from actuality. Strain and pressure then tend to cloud the details of the stressful event.

Attention is diverted or reduced by anxiety reactions created by threatening situations. Psychological stress can adversely affect sensory input. Stress factors should be carefully weighed in evaluating the testimony of a witness, particularly with respect to serious criminal offenses.

Any event that places a witness under stress, shocks his senses, or produces some strong emotional reaction creates a psychological barrier that could considerably impair the accuracy and clarity of both sensory input and later memory of the event. Reaction affects perception, conception, and memory. Stress and shock should especially be considered in dealing with witnesses to crimes or other upsetting events.

It is also true that when one is caught by surprise, the very unexpectedness causes some part of what is happening to escape notice. The surprise element may temporarily immobilize perception, and it may be a few moments before a witness recognizes what is actually taking place. When that awareness dawns, part of the event has already passed.

Perception Capacity

The capacity to perceive varies a great deal with different persons. Some are keenly perceptive; others are more oblivious to what goes on about them, and a few can take in a large number of significant details regarding any person or event. Many others are only aware of the scary, the dramatic, or the unusual that may penetrate their inattention. Private investigators should constantly develop the accuracy of their sensory input.

To be an effective witness it is important really to see and mentally record what actually transpires, or to hear correctly and remember what is heard. Any impairment of sight or hearing (poor sight and defective hearing) results in less awareness, reduced perception, and incomplete information—or worse, inaccurate information. "People differ in perceptual capacity due to sensory deficits."[5]

The ability to perceive, however, involves more than the possession of good sensory faculties. Perception records a mental photograph of at least a portion of what occurred, or of who did what to whom. A perceived act must be stored in memory to enable one to witness to the fact of that act. Thus perception is both the process of obtaining knowledge through the senses and apprehension of that knowledge by the mind. The senses should alert the mind to focus attention on and mentally record what takes place in an observed event.

SELECTIVITY OF PERCEPTIONS. The fallibility of perceptions is increased by their selectivity. All that is seen is neither fully perceived nor mentally recorded. The human mind consciously or unconsciously selects that which it deems worthy of recording. Generally, whatever makes the greatest impact or impression on the consciousness is mentally recorded and later most readily recalled. Clifford and Bull note that recent research supports the belief that people "select what they will pay attention to and remember."[6]

Therefore private investigators should recognize the fallibility and limitations of human perception. Some people have considerable trouble in giving perceptive attention to what is happening around them. Nearly all persons are perceptively selective and much may escape their attention. They only register a fraction of the total sensory input; and their minds record only a fraction of what is registered. The result is an incomplete picture of what happened, and at best a partial identification of the person(s) involved. If private investigators seek to have the witness fill in the gap, the tendency too often is to invent the fill-in. When private investigators are fortunate enough to have a number of witnesses, they can compare their narration of events and answers to key questions to draw out the common elements of their testimony.

People sometimes tend not to see and hear actions and words that are clearly presented to their senses. They may even tend to see and hear what did not actually occur or what was not said. As a result, they may not even remember things that did happen, but may substitute in their place things they imagine to have occurred. In such instances both senses and memory data are obviously fallible.

Mental Recording and Storage

Even a witness with keen sensory input may still fail to record mentally much of what was seen. The recording and storage functions may be distracted by such things as interference, obstruction of view, emotional shock, excitement, fear, or other forms of mental distress that can screen out considerable information. How capable were the witness's recording and storage functions? Did he record with reasonable accuracy a visual image of what and who he saw? The better these functions, the better the chances of good recall.

The strength of the initial mental impact of the recording will affect the length of time that memory storage and recall remain reasonably operative. Factors that have an effect on the initial storage will have a delayed effect on recall, in that they limit the amount of information that is recorded. The mind is not a camera, or even a photocopier. Only a comparatively few people have what is sometimes called a photographic memory.

Understanding

Understanding is also a critical element of perception. Was the witness mystified as to what was actually taking place or did he clearly understand the events? The better the situation is understood, the more accurately it is recorded. The mental capacity clearly to comprehend what is transpiring is a definite factor in perception and memory. Private investigators have an advantage over most witnesses in that understanding grows through experience and familiarity with similar situations.

Problems of witnessing may be those of inattention, partial or complete obstruction of view, mental or emotional distress adversely affecting reception of sensory input, lack of perceptive capacity, meager selectivity of perceptions, failure to record mentally and store for future recall, or lack of understanding as to what actually happened. Investigators who understand the psychological problems of achieving perceptive observations are better able to cope with the shortcomings of witness testimony, and are more likely to overcome these psychological handicaps when developing their own powers of observation.

Recall

The accuracy of sensory input and the ability of the witness mentally to store visual images are vital elements affecting the accuracy of testimony. Reliability and accuracy depend on the ability of the witness to perceive, record, remember, and recall.

The authors of *The Psychology of Person Identification* define recall as "a measure of retention in which no external help is given to the recaller in his attempt to retell what he saw or heard."[7] Obviously, recall is more difficult than mere recognition. To recognize a face one has seen before is usually not too difficult. To recall the separate features of that face from one's impressions without seeing it again or without a photograph is decidedly more difficult.

When a witness is asked to describe the person he saw at the scene of the event, and that person is neither in a police lineup nor represented by a photo, the witness must depend solely on his memory's recall ability. Whether or not he can do so will depend on to what extent he can recall the initial visual impressions the subject made on his memory.

In private-investigator/witness interviews, recall is usually aided by cues. After the witness has reported whatever impressions he can remember, private investigators jog or cue his memory by asking questions relative to potential identification factors of facial features—eyes, mouth, nose, forehead, and other factors such as the shape of the subject's head, or his gait. For example, the question, "Can you describe the shape of the subject's head?" is a memory jog or cue that may help the witness recall something he had not thought of in his general description by causing him to retrieve a visual impression that was temporarily lost. The questions, however, must not be leading questions, that is, they should never influence the reply of the witness, whether it be the description of a person, event, vehicle, scene, or object.

There are degrees of ability to recall. The extent of recall is a matter of how long and how accurately the memory can retain the original sensory input. It is also a matter of how accurately that input was mentally recorded. Thanks to practice and experience as observers, private investigators have an advantage in their recall efforts that most witnesses do not.

Since private investigators always have their notebooks handy and invariably record their observations and details of sensory input, they do have external help to fall back on to refresh their minds and stimulate recall. A simple notation may, in fact, cause a rather comprehensive flashback. Without such written support, and possibly without the recognition of the importance of what was seen, the eyewitness would naturally find it more difficult fully to recall the initial input.

FACTORS AFFECTING PERCEPTION, MEMORY, AND RECALL

Both the internal reactions of the witness and "the external social situation can markedly alter the accuracy of recall for a seen person or event"[8] in terms of initial perceptions; recording, retention, and recall; and description and potential identification of what and who was seen. There are ten key factors that affect the completeness and accuracy of the testimony of a witness.

Key Factors

1. The nature of the occurrence.] Different kinds of happenings — accident, fraud, injury, tort, crime, or whatever — may affect observers differently. The impact of the occurrence may be maximal or minimal: it may call forth considerable attention or little attention, it may produce a strong observer reaction or a weak one. The external nature of the event can create reactions in the witness that affect both his perception and memory. It may determine, at least to some extent, how indelibly or how vaguely the facts of the event were registered in his mind.

2. The unexpectedness of the event.] Was the witness caught by surprise? Had some of the action already transpired before the witness was aware of what was happening? To what extent did the surprise factor throw the perceptive abilities of the witness off guard and render them temporarily inoperative?

3. The length of visual exposure to the action.] How long did the witness observe what was taking place? The length of exposure to the action has a direct bearing on sensory input. Brevity reduces the number of details observed. For example, when a face appears out of the blue and disappears with equal suddenness, a witness has to be on the alert for that face to be etched on his memory. As a general rule, the longer a witness observes an event, the more likely it is that greater numbers of details will be recorded and possibly remembered, and recalled with correspondingly greater accuracy.

4. The viewing situation.] Was the witness a bystander, near to or distant from the event, a victim, passer-by, or investigator? Viewing situations vary greatly. Was the observer a pedestrian, or was he riding by in an automobile? Was he standing waiting for a bus, or for a stoplight to flash green? Was he at the immediate scene or some distance away?

Different viewing situations can create a variety of emotional or objective reactions, depending on the measure of concern and the nearness to or involvement in the action. It is not difficult to sense the different reactions of an eyewitness, a victim, an accomplice, and an investigator, all of whom may by chance be observing the same happening. If the key witness is also the victim, his emotional trauma is considerably greater than if he had merely been a bystander.

5. The psychological impact of the occurrence on the observer.]Real life situations are often emotionally charged, especially those that are contrary to the norm. Emotions sometimes supersede objectivity and color the impressions of the witness. Stress, tension, fear, outrage, anger, and shock all have a powerful reactive influence on the human mind and its objectivity. As already noted, anxiety reactions invariably tend to diffuse both perception and memory. The total emotional atmosphere of any event or situation must be taken into account in evaluating witness testimony.

6. The rapidity of the action.]How quickly was the act consummated? The more rapidly events occur, the less detail is mentally recorded. Too much escapes observation because of speed, even for trained observers, because rapidity of action challenges sensory input. A face in motion does not permit the same detailed study as a static face of a photograph. The ability to perceive and record motion is affected by the speed of the motion.

7. The perceptive attention capability of the observer.]Accurate perception requires concentrated attention. Any measure of inattention leads to impaired perception and results in one seeing without really observing. Perception involves focused, concentrated attention to and awareness of what is happening. The extent of attention or inattention directly affects the amount and accuracy of the details mentally recorded. If the witness directly focuses his mind on what is occurring, his eyes faithfully record that occurrence; otherwise much of his sensory input is lost to memory.

8. The objectivity of the observer's perceptions.]What percent of what the witness saw was objective reality, and what percent was subjective reaction? One must be objective to focus attention on external facts rather than on subjective reactions, feelings, prejudices, or judgments. Subjective criteria can so easily falsely color interpretation.

9. The complexity or simplicity of the occurrence.]The more complex, intricate, and detailed the occurrence, the less complete is the scope of observation. Observers only mentally register a portion of what transpires in any complex situation. The more people involved in

the action, the more difficult it is to remember facial features or other identifying characteristics, and to keep from confusing the different persons. The multiplicity of details increases the numbers that pass unnoticed, or that fail to become a part of recollection of the event. Any intricacy or mystery pertaining to the happening complicates the observer's understanding and objective perception. The more simple and less complicated the occurrence, the more likely its most obvious facts will be remembered.

10. The visibility factors affecting the observations. Good or poor visibility obviously contributes to good or poor observations. Poor visibility may be due to weather conditions or to physical obstructions of the observer's view. Have surrounding trees or heavy foliage hidden part of the action? Has a construction project or a commercial sign obstructed part of the view? Was the witness in a good position with a clear view of the scene? Did he have unobstructed visibility? From his position could he be expected to observe clearly what happened? Is it reasonable to assume that from his viewing position he could actually see what he claims to have seen?

These ten basic factors clearly indicate how external happenings and the internal ability of the witness visually and mentally to encompass them affect the clarity, accuracy, and completeness of observations and their later recall.

The Role of Observation in Person Identification

Efficient private investigators develop a person-identification orientation in observations of other people. They take specific note of precise identifying features. This ability is essential, for example, in surveillance activities to ensure that the private investigators will not suddenly find themselves tailing the wrong person.

In interviewing witnesses or clients, private investigators often seek descriptions. In skip tracing and the search for missing persons, private investigators obviously need the best possible description if they are to locate the right individual.

The correct identity of a suspect is vitally important in criminal investigations, as mistaken identity could result in wrongful conviction. Innocent people have gone to prison because they have incorrectly been identified as culprits. In felonious cases great care should be taken not to depend on inadequate identification.

If private investigators have no personal acquaintance with a subject and there are no photographs to study, they depend on verbal descriptions by those who know the subject or have seen and observed him. Often the matter of identification is based on the testimony of witnesses, even though the credibility of even an eyewitness is not a foregone matter of fact.

Since verbal descriptions largely depend on visual observations, one must be concerned with aspects or features of personal appearance that provide identification. The description of unique personal characteristics is the usual means by which persons are identified when neither their presence nor their photograph is available. Identifying characteristics include:

1. Facial features and characteristics
2. Shape and size of head; amount, description, and color of hair
3. Build, posture, body shape
4. Characteristic physical movement
   a. Gait — manner of walking, running, or foot movements
   b. Gesture — motion of the limbs or body used for expression
   c. Unusual moving habits: nervous twitches, limps, short steps, extremely long stride, etc.
5. Abnormal appearances
   a. Scars, tattoos, birthmarks, etc.
   b. Handicaps, disfigurements
   c. Extremely sickly, bent over, out of shape, abnormal size
6. Voice — distinctiveness of human voice
7. Identifying mannerisms

Identifying marks and scars and facial features are generally considered to be among the most important identification factors. A person's voice is also significantly helpful in some instances, but it can be altered somewhat in an attempt to hide identification, as is frequently the case in telephone ransom demands made by kidnappers. Abnormal appearances are effective identification characteristics, but with the exception of scars, tattoos, and other marks, they are comparatively rare. When private investigators are shadowing a subject, how that subject appears from the rear is a primary matter of continued identification; gait then becomes a key identification factor.

Detailed Descriptions for Person Identification

Minimum descriptions are of very little value. General classifications of a subject by sex, race, height, weight, and approximate age are not specific enough to identify one person among others who may equally fit the general description.

One needs to obtain as much detailed descriptive information as possible to be able to recognize a missing or wanted person or a suspect. The more specific the items of description are, provided they are reasonably accurate, the better. The problem is that it is often very difficult to get precise descriptions from witnesses or others who have only seen the subject for a brief period. It is even a problem for some people to describe a person they know quite well.

No single description from any one witness will ever include all of the potential identification clues listed in the next chapter. Investigators should be aware of potential facial clues. The recall description and subsequent recognition may be primarily a matter of the characteristics of one or two prominent features, or a combination of facial features that gives a unique appearance to the face. Person identification is greatly aided when there are some outstanding characteristics of face or form that set the subject apart as different from other persons. Often there are no such prominent identification features. In such cases more detailed information may be needed.

Anything unusual that a witness may recall may be an important identification factor. It may have to do with the subject's characteristic movements or posture, facial features, or physical structure. It could be his speech or peculiar manner of speaking. The more prominent or unusual characteristics may be, the more readily recognizable they will be, and the more effective they will be in terms of identification.

NOTES

1. Clifford, B. R., and Bull, R. *The psychology of person identification.* (Boston: Routledge & Kegan Paul, 1978), 71.
2. Montapert, A. A. *Distilled wisdom.* (Englewood Cliffs, N.J.: Prentice-Hall, 1964), 264.
3. Lavine, S. A. *Allan Pinkerton, America's first private eye.* (New York: Dodd, Mead & Co., 1963), 12.
4. Clifford, B. R., and Bull, R. *The psychology of person identification,* 18.
5. Ibid.
6. Ibid., 186.
7. Ibid., 19.
8. Ibid., xii.

Chapter 8

The *Portrait Parle*

"... faces are but a gallery of pictures. . ."

—Francis Bacon[1]

"It is the common wonder of all men, how among so many millions of faces, there should be none alike."

—Sir Thomas Browne[2]

Portrait parle is a French term meaning word picture of a person. The term literally means "spoken picture." It is applied to verbal descriptions only, primarily those of facial features. Alphonse Bertillion, the developer of the Bureau of Criminal Identification at the Paris Prefecture, and once called France's greatest detective and "father of scientific detection," is said to have originated the term.

Portrait parle is sometimes loosely used in reference to the total physical appearance of a subject; primarily, however, it embraces precise recognized and recalled facial characteristics.

"The face of man," according to Schopenhauer, "gives us fuller and more interesting information than his tongue."[3] Not only does the face reveal character, attitudes, and the life history of a person up to the time of observation, it has its own identifying physical characteristics, with which we are now concerned. Any extreme feature has recognition and identification value. The more medium, neutral, or normal the appearance, the less memorable are the features.

Portrait parle descriptions generally start at the top of the head and work downward over the face. There are times, however, when a striking stand-out feature may first catch the eye, and thereafter become the essential item of description. These are frequently described first before proceeding with the overall portrait parle.

HEAD CHARACTERISTICS

While the human face is generally considered to be the most recognizable and descriptively identifiable part of the verbal picture, the head itself may have identification characteristics of its own. There are at least seven potential identification factors that relate to the head, the forehead, and the hair — or lack of it.

1. Shape. The six basic classifications of head shapes — flat back, bulging back, round, pointed, egg-shaped, and flat top — are illustrated in Figure 8-1. A peculiar head shape may be an identifiable and describable departure from these shown here. Does the head, for example, have an unusually high crown?

Figure 8-1.   The six distinctly different head shapes illustrate how the shape of a subject's head can contribute to identification.

HEAD SHAPES:

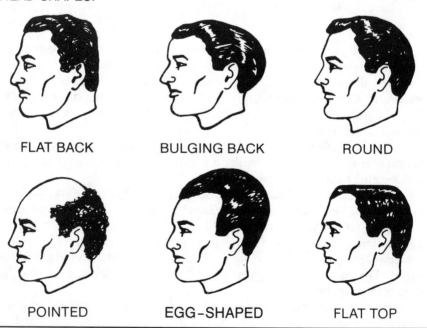

FLAT BACK   BULGING BACK   ROUND

POINTED   EGG-SHAPED   FLAT TOP

2. Size. Head sizes are broadly classified as large, medium, or small. A remarkably big head or an unusually small head are strong identification factors. Both the length and width of the head could be of significance, for example, long and narrow or short and wide.

   How the subject carries or holds his head may be an identification clue, such as some peculiar manner or significant angle. There may be a significant or characteristic tilt forward, backward, or to either side.

3. Width and height of the forehead. A glance at section A of Figure 8-2 will help visualize the three basic classifications of forehead widths: wide, medium, and narrow.

   Some foreheads are quite noticeable because they are unusually wide or very narrow. This identifying factor is also related to the shape of the face, which is considered later.

   Forehead height is another feature that contributes to identification. Again this is particularly true when the forehead is very high or unusually low.

4. Slope of the forehead. Forehead slopes are illustrated in section B of Figure 8-2. A forehead may recede to the hairline, it may have a vertical appearance from the nose to the top of the head, or it may have a prominent bulge. Receding or bulging foreheads are the most readily noticeable because they again represent more extreme characteristics.

5. Forehead scars or marks. Some persons are quite easily identifiable by unusual scars, slashes, or marks on the forehead. This is one of the key places to look for identifying scars or marks, as it is an area frequently injured in childhood falls. In addition, natural marks have identification value, especially when they are quite prominent. Is the forehead heavily wrinkled? Do the wrinkles run horizontally across the forehead, or vertically up and down?

6. Hairline. Both total baldness and the extent and location of partial baldness have identification value (Figure 8-3). It should be remembered that wigs can cover up characteristic hairline features should the subject attempt to disguise himself. Was the subject bald or partially bald? Where—front, back, top? Was the hairline receding? To what extent?

7. Hair color and style. The color of the hair should be noted even though a wanted person, for example, could easily dye his hair and temporarily change its color. Similarly, a woman can drastically change her hair style. There are, however, basic aspects of the hair to make note of. Is the hair long or short? How long, how short, shoulder length, crew cut, etc. Is it straight, curly, wavy, kinky, or shaggy? Is it parted? Where is the part? Is it combed straight back? Is it neatly combed, disheveled, or unkempt? How long are the sideburns?

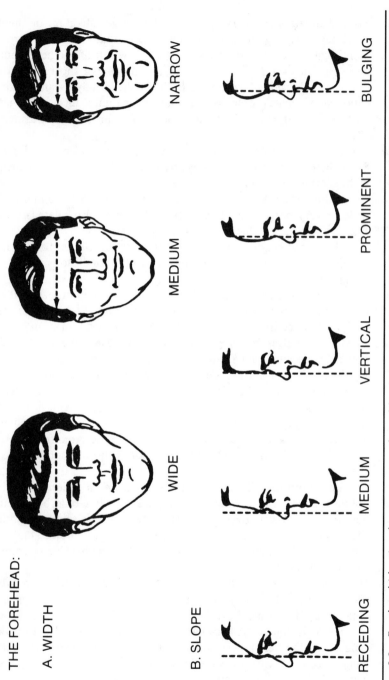

Figure 8-2. Forehead identity clues are primarily width, slope, and height. The three forehead widths (top row A) emphasize the identification value of a very wide or a very narrow forehead. Row B sketches five types of shapes with terms used to describe the slope or contour line.

DEGREE OF BALDNESS:

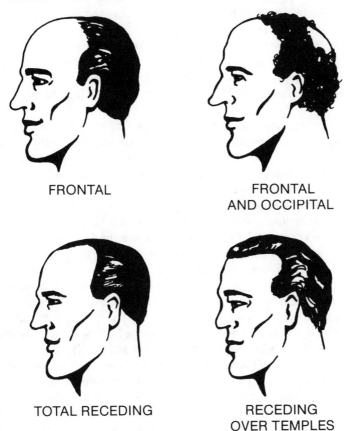

| FRONTAL | FRONTAL AND OCCIPITAL |

| TOTAL RECEDING | RECEDING OVER TEMPLES |

Figure 8-3.   Partial baldness is more frequently encountered than total baldness. The figure illustrates some of the most common forms of the varying degrees of baldness and receding hairlines.

What is the contour of the hairline along the top of the forehead or above the eyes? Is it fairly straight across or does it form an irregular outline? Does it overhang the forehead or come to a peak part way down? Does it peak in the center, or over the left or right eye? Some hairlines have a fairly round appearance. Others have irregular curvatures. Another factor is the amount of hair at the hairline edge. Is it thin or heavy? Any unusual outline or appearance created by the hairline can be an identification factor.

THE FACE

Persons are primarily recognized by their facial features. Every face is unique, displaying its features both individually and in combination and interrelationship with all the others.

In *The Psychology of Person Identification,* Clifford and Bull analyze the findings of tests made by a number of different specialists over recent years to determine the primary aids to identification. They state that the face is the "basic means of recognition"[4] and "the most salient feature of a person's being."[5]

Identification may result from (1) the total impact of the face, (2) isolated and unique facial features, or (3) the combination and interrelationship of the facial features. Sometimes we perceive faces in their totality. Sometimes we perceive features that stand out sufficiently to provide a strong identification factor, such as piercing or very attractive eyes, a prominent nose, or protruding forehead. At times we may see a whole face before we begin to note individual features. At other times, when certain features are more impressive or more prominent, we take note of them before we see the face as a whole. Initial attention often focuses on the eyes and the mouth. These and the nose frequently have specific identification value.

The probability is that faces are remembered by the basic structure together with salient features that stand out. Good or evil faces also have identification impact. Researchers have found that the most attractive faces have the highest recognition value as well as the highest recall potential. The least attractive faces were next in recognition and recall value, and the in-between neutral faces that were neither attractive nor repelling had the poorest recognition impact, and therefore the poorest recall potential.

Police often have victims or eyewitnesses try to identify a suspect in a police lineup of potential suspects or by looking at the police album of photographs (so-called mug shots). When recall is fuzzy or the initial perception poor, people will as often as not pick the wrong person or be unable to identify anyone.

Sometimes on the basis of the verbal descriptions given by a victim or eyewitness a police artist can create a striking facial similarity. In private investigation the emphasis is on being able to recall, rather than on recognizing a person in a lineup or police album. Sometimes, however, private investigators are aided by photographs as well as verbal descriptions. For example, a client might provide a comparatively recent photograph of the person he wants the private investigator to find.

Mistaken identity has sometimes resulted in a miscarriage of justice. If it leads to a wrong conviction in a criminal case, it creates a dual tragedy: an innocent person is unjustly found guilty, and the guilty culprit still remains at large.

Facial Characteristics for Identification

Differences in facial appearances involve both total views and specific characteristics. Facial characteristics to be considered in identification include:

1. Shape
2. Size
3. Mobility
4. Prominence of certain features
5. Shape or appearance of specific features
6. Markings, scars, moles, birthmarks, etc.
7. Complexion and skin texture
8. Attractiveness or unattractiveness
9. Arrangement and interrelationship of facial features
10. Expression—pleasant, unpleasant, kindly, cold, etc.
11. Character—good, evil, honest, sly, etc.

Obviously, a fleeting view does not allow time for an analysis of all of these characteristics. Any and all of them, however, are potential identification clues.

SHAPE. The general shape of the face may be round, square, oval, rectangular, or triangular. It may be broad, long, or full (Figure 8-4). The more extreme shapes are the most readily recognized because they represent a greater departure from the usual, for example, the triangular face with the narrower apex at the top of the head and the wider lower jaw. Its identification value, with the interrelationship of the features arranged within this shape, is quite evident. The shape of the face is a general identification factor, as well as a positive aid in an artist's sketch. Within this general outline, individual features can be indicated.

SIZE. The size of the face is not usually as important an identification factor as its shape, unless it is unusually large or abnormally small. There are certain types of faces, however, in which size in combination with shape provides positive identification value. The four primary size categories are very large, small, unusually long, and very short.

MOBILITY. With over one hundred muscles, the face can have remarkable mobility. Mobility is characterized by ease of movement. Mobile features readily express changes in feelings. The more mobile the face, the more versatile and changeable it is and the more quickly it responds to stimuli. This is easily observed in face-to-face communication such as interviews and interrogations or when a victim is personally confronted by the culprit. A face

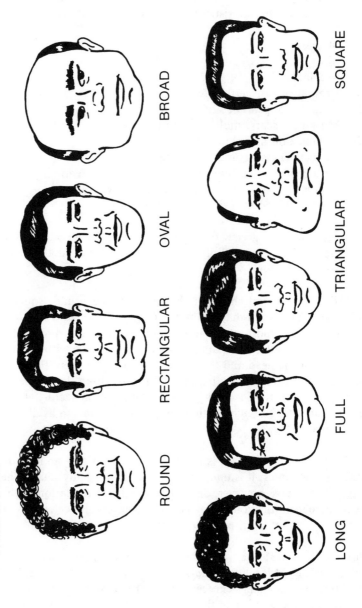

FACE SHAPE:

ROUND   RECTANGULAR   OVAL   BROAD

LONG   FULL   TRIANGULAR   SQUARE

Figure 8-4. The shape of the human face and its characteristic features are the primary means of identification. These nine readily identifiable, distinct shapes provide a starting basis for the description of facial features.

is sometimes subject to involuntary movement such as twitching or a spasmodic contraction of the muscles. Twitching is observable in the quick jerk or sudden, short, and quick motions. Any unusual mobility characteristic of the face can be an identification clue.

PROMINENCE OF SPECIFIC FEATURES. The most notable aspect of some faces is the prominence of one feature; occasionally, several features may stand out. Those features could be very large eyes or a long, prominent nose.

The identification value of specific features may mean that they are prominent, conspicuous, or noticeable, attractive or unattractive, or that they have some other unique appearance. The word salient is used to describe outstanding features in relation to the whole face.

SHAPE OR APPEARANCE OF SPECIFIC FEATURES. All facial features have their own identifying characteristics. At times these are very noticeable, at times they so blend in with the other features that they largely escape detection. Prominent features as described above are unique primarily with respect to size in relation to other facial features. Any way in which a feature appears different or strange because of shape, size, appearance, or placement makes it stand out from the other features and is a factor in identification. Sometimes comparatively normal variations in shape or appearance may also have identification value because of their effect on the face, and the fact that they are significant enough to be detected by an observer.

FACIAL MARKINGS. Facial markings and scars of one kind or another have high identification value, especially when they are prominent. Markings include scars, slash marks, scabs, moles, skin cancers, birthmarks, tattoos, freckles, fresh or healed wound marks, and any other forms of blots or injuries. Facial deformities such as marred or missing features have strong identification value, as do an excessive number of age lines.

COMPLEXION AND SKIN TEXTURE. The appearance of the facial skin is a factor to consider. What is the skin hue, tone, and color? Is the skin fair, very fair, dark, or very dark? Is it soft, delicate, smooth, rough, leathery, dry, moist, oily, or sunburned? Is it white and pale, or red and inflamed? Is it an olive color or a greenish yellow hue? Many terms can describe the condition of the complexion and texture of the face. A face may be dusky, ashen, pallid, wan. It may be tanned, freckled, or pockmarked. The presence of acne, pimples, or inflamation of the skin should be noted. Skin identification factors are observable in close-up situations such as in the case of a victim who is for some minutes face to face with an attacker, or in the case of an informant or other person identifying someone personally known to him.

ATTRACTIVENESS OR UNATTRACTIVENESS. The more pleasant and attractive a face appears, the more easily it is remembered. Pleasantness and attractiveness have drawing power and tend to register themselves on the memory. A very unpleasant or unattractive face also has an impact on the memory.

Facial beauty is a strong recognition and recall factor. It is natural that people more easily remember the faces of beautiful women and handsome men. They also tend to remember, but sometimes in a distorted way, frightening faces. A face that strikes fear into one's heart tends to etch itself on the memory. The emotional stress of the confrontation, however, may affect the later recall, resulting in a description more fearsome than the face really is.

Actually, faces with outstanding singular features are comparatively few. Most faces must be recognized or recalled for other reasons. A face that has no outstanding features, which seems to melt away into a sea of neutral or ordinary faces, presents the major recall problem. In such instances the recall is more general, for example, impressions of shape and overall appearance, with less emphasis on individual features. In such cases, in fact, shape and size of the face may be the best remembered identification clues.

ARRANGEMENT AND INTERRELATIONSHIP OF FEATURES. This identification factor considers the complete face. It specifically makes note of any unusual relationship among the features. Is there abnormal distance between the eyes? Is there a strange proportion in relationship of the nose to the mouth? Unusual interrelationships usually are detected between the eyes, nose, and mouth.

EXPRESSION. Facial expression sometimes aids recognition and recall. The problem with this identification factor is that expressions of emotions can be altered at will to a greater or lesser degree. Consequently, the identifying potential of an emotionally engendered expression may be only temporary, created by the events of the occasion.

The value of expression as an identification factor therefore depends upon its constancy. Expression of an inherent nature may have sufficient permanence to provide identification value. For example, does the face radiate personality and warmth, or is it cold and unexpressive? Is it happy or sad? Facial expressions, of course, can often reveal inner feelings, and may indicate attitudes and motivations that are significantly related to issues of the case.

CHARACTER. A face is more than structure, shape, and size, and unique appearance of eyes, nose and mouth. It tends to reveal inner character of the person who is living behind it. Facial character or attributes may have recognition value, for example, most people remember good or evil impressions.

A listing of the following opposites is sufficient to illustrate personality impressions made by human faces:

- Intelligent — stupid
- Mature — immature
- Warm — cold
- Honest — dishonest
- Frank — sly
- Naive — sophisticated
- Kind — cruel
- Good — evil

IDENTIFICATION VALUE OF SPECIFIC FEATURES

Psychological tests have been given by authorities in an effort to determine the principal identifying factors of the human face. Tests of recognition are, of course, much simpler than tests of recall. In one such test subjects reported that the eyes, nose, mouth, lips, chin, hair, and ears, in that order, best aided recognition. In another, the subjects selected the nose, eyes, forehead, and mouth as the primary recall aids.[6]

Investigators, however, are not operating in a controlled situation. They are dealing with real life situations and people. Here, the eyes, nose, and mouth frequently play the most important role in recall. Eye identification includes brows and lashes. Mouth identification includes the lips and teeth. The nose, ears, cheekbones, and chin also have potential for identification.

Eyes

The eyes are given a high rating in person identification, probably because they are primary instruments of expression, and because they are often the first facial feature noticed, particularly in close contact, where their shape, size, color, and expression are easily noted. According to Clifford and Bull, the 1975 Fisher and Cox findings indicated that "the upper features of human faces" contribute "more information for recognition than lower features." Their experiments indicated the "eyes contributed most to identification," which led to their conclusion that the "eyes are the most important facial features for recognition."[7] Smith and Nielson suggest that people look at each other with "a top to bottom" scanning of the face, while Munn says they focus on "the eyes and mouth."[8] In real life situations, witnesses apparently tend first to look at the eyes and mouth of a subject or at any unusually prominent feature, particularly in the upper portion of the face.

EYE PLACEMENT:

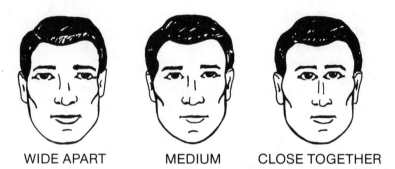

WIDE APART   MEDIUM   CLOSE TOGETHER

Figure 8-5. These faces show three distinctly different eye placements with varying distances between the eyes. The wide-set position of the eyes (left) and the close-
set eyes (right) diverge from the normal and are potential identification clues.

The positioning of the eyes is one identification clue. They may be closely
set or widely separated (Figure 8-5).

COLOR. The primary eye colors are blue, gray, brown, hazel, green,
and black. These colors may be more or less prominent or clear. Sometimes
they stand out with brilliant quality, sometimes they appear dull and lackluster.
Occasionally, the colors may be more unusual, such as pink and reddish yellow.
On rare occasions the same person's eyes may be of different colors, either
distinctly different or only moderately so. Different color eyes are a definite
identification clue.

Investigators should be aware that sometimes witnesses mistake colors
because of color association beliefs. They tend to associate blue eyes with blond
hair and brown eyes with dark hair, when in fact a blond person, for example,
may have green eyes, and a dark-haired person may have gray eyes. A witness
needs to take specific note of the color of the subject's eyes to be able to report
accurately, otherwise the tendency is merely to try to fit the color of the eyes
with the color of the hair.

SHAPE AND SIZE. The recognition of eye shapes can contribute to
identification. There are four basic shapes: round or oval, or slanted down or
up (Figure 8-6). When eyes slant down they go toward the nose. When they
slant up, they slant toward the temples.

The size of the eyes provides a distinct identification clue. All of us have
seen persons with very large eyes and some with very small eyes, and in each
instance the impact of this feature becomes a memory factor. Wide open eyes
tend to appear larger than those that peer out from behind partially closed lids.

THE EYES:

EYE SHAPES:

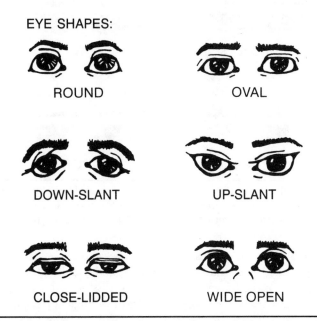

ROUND   OVAL

DOWN-SLANT   UP-SLANT

CLOSE-LIDDED   WIDE OPEN

Figure 8-6. Eye shape is usually either round or oval. The oval eye is somewhat egg-shaped. Eye positions may be level or the eyes may slant up or down. Close-lidded eyes and wide open eyes are identity clues. They are also physical aspects of the eyes' expression.

PUPIL SIZE AND PLACEMENT. The size and placement of the pupils may also be an identification factor in close-up situations. Pupils may be large or small. They may be placed high or low within the eye, or be reasonably centered (Figure 8-7). These are usually lesser identification cues not generally noticed unless either is extreme. Occasionally, something about the pupils, or a pupil, may call attention to itself. The moment any feature stands out, it becomes an identification clue.

EXPRESSION. The normal expression of the eyes in certain persons may have helpful identification value. As with facial expressions, momentary flashes of anger, resentment, or other emotions cannot be depended on as identification cues because of their transitory nature. Fairly constant expressions can be very revealing, however.

Are the eyes wide open or partially closed? Is the subject squint-eyed or cross-eyed? Are they serious, mysterious, frank, or apparently sincere? Or are they shifty, evasive, cold, or sneaky? Are they relaxed or penetrating? Any

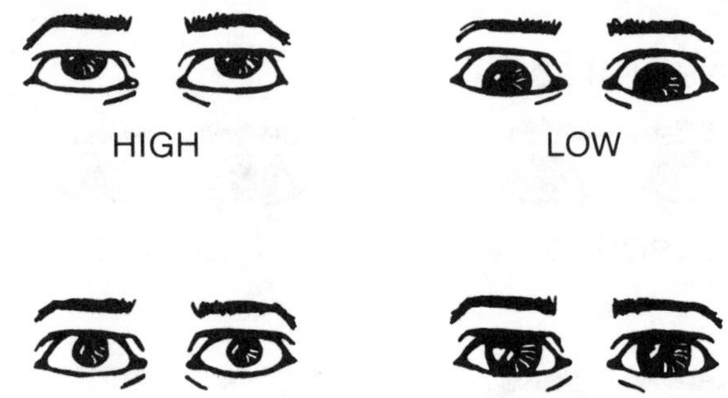

PUPIL SIZE AND PLACEMENT:

HIGH   LOW

SMALL   LARGE

Figure 8-7. Very small and very large pupils are noticeable in close-up confrontations. Pupils that are not centered in the eye tend to move higher or lower. Any extreme or divergent placement of the pupils can become an identity clue.

outstanding quality in the expression of the eyes should be noted. The eyes have long been called the windows of the soul, and usually they are the most expressive element of the human face. Their expressions are understood in all languages as is so readily seen when they flash in anger or speak in love.

Another factor to consider is the depth of the eyes in their sockets. Is this position normal, deep-set or sunken, or possibly bulging or somewhat protruding? The length and thickness of the eyelashes, and the condition of the eyelids may also provide clues if they in any way attract attention to themselves.

GENERAL CONDITION OF THE EYES. Do the eyes appear healthy and the eyesight good? Does the subject wear thick-lens glasses or highly magnified ones? Is there any other evidence of sight impairment? Are there any apparent eye malfunctions? Are the eyes clear, bright, and alive, or are they dull and unexpressive? Are they watery, puffed up, swollen, or bloodshot? Are they squinting, blinking, or twitching?

On rare occasions one may be confronted by a subject with a missing eye or a glass eye. Frequently the subject may be bleary-eyed, glassy-eyed, or dopey-eyed due to the consumption of alcohol or narcotics.

EYEGLASSES. Eyeglasses obviously are not a part of the natural features of the face. They can be important, however, when it is necessary for the subject to wear glasses at all times. Glasses are also changeable. A subject may have several pairs, including sunglasses for outdoors and driving a motor vehicle on sunny days, and more highly magnified glasses for reading or close work. While wearing glasses or not may be a quick way for a subject to change his appearance, he may find it more difficult to do so if he is in constant need of glasses. The subject would then have to have several styles to alter his appearance successfully, which would not likely be the case. Although glasses are not a permanent feature of the human face, their presence should not be ignored.

When the subject wears glasses, private investigators should note the type, color, shape, and style of the frames as well as the tint of the glass or plastic lenses. Are the glasses bifocals? Are the rims plastic or metal? Are the lenses of oversize dimensions? How thick are the lenses? Does the subject wear full-view glasses or only a halfmoon type? Does the subject wear contact lenses? Women may wear glasses with jewels, or their imitations, worked into the frames. The type and color of the real or synthetic jewelry should be noted.

COLOR AND SHAPE OF EYEBROWS. Eyebrows have identification value especially when they are unusually heavy, bushy, thick, or thin. Their shape can also be significant if they are very irregular, arched, or extremely straight. Some eyebrows slant down, some slant up (Figure 8-8).

Figure 8-8. Eyebrows that are very prominent, peculiarly shaped, or almost nil readily attract attention in face-to-face contacts. These seven types of eyebrows have potential identity recall significance.

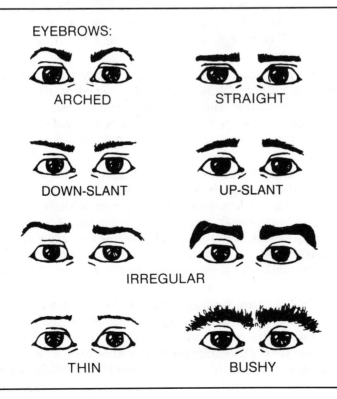

EYEBROWS:

ARCHED   STRAIGHT

DOWN-SLANT   UP-SLANT

IRREGULAR

THIN   BUSHY

They can be bushy or thin. Some are almost absent and are penciled in. Some have been plucked. There is also the matter of their length and width. Are they long, short, narrow, or wide? Is their color the same as the hair? Frequently a person's eyebrows will naturally be a different color or shade than his or her hair. When private investigators make description inquiries they should always determine, if possible, whether the color of the eyebrows is the same as or different than hair color.

Nose

The nose is often a salient feature. Anything unusual about its size, shape, outward projection, or appearance of its base could become an identification factor.

SIZE. Both the size and shape of the larger, more noticeable noses provide strong identification clues. Small noses, when they appear to be out of proportion with other facial features, are also quickly identifiable. Again, the medium-sized nose has little identification value unless it is completely out of proportion with other features, or some peculiarity of shape or projection makes it sufficiently unique to attract attention. A study of the nose illustrations of Figures 8-9 and 8-10 will highlight its most important identification features.

Noses may be short, medium, or long, wide or narrow, thick or thin. They may have small or flaring nostrils. An injured nose usually provides recognizable identification. Has it been flattened, twisted, or pushed out of shape? Any mark or observable injury should be included in the description of the nose. A crooked nose is also an identification clue.

WIDTH. One of the most noticeable features of the nose is its width. This is akin to size, because the wider the nose the larger the area of the face it covers. Narrow and wide noses are obviously more noticeable. Medium-width noses are considered normal. Narrow noses are usually moderately long but even when they are not, they appear to be because they allow more space for the cheeks. Wide noses, on the other hand, can spread across a sizable portion of the face just above the upper lip, as a glance at Figure 8-9 will show.

PROJECTION. How far does the nose project outward from the subject's face? Projection is an identifying factor, especially in the case of a long, protruding nose that thrusts or projects itself out from the levels of the eyes and upper lip. It is also significant for identification when the nose lies unusually close to the face, and fails to project itself a regular distance from

THE NOSE:

WIDTH

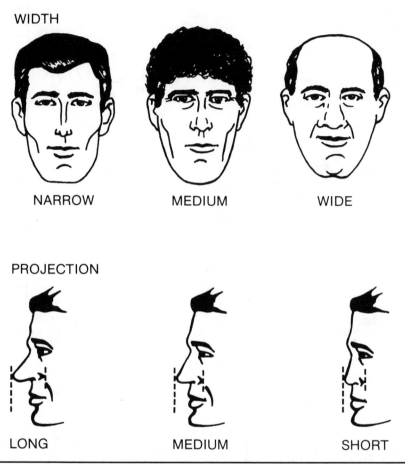

| NARROW | MEDIUM | WIDE |

PROJECTION

| LONG | MEDIUM | SHORT |

Figure 8-9. Width and projection are the two principal identity clues of the nose. Very wide and very narrow noses are readily detectable. Both the flat nose, which lies close to the face, and the nose that projects far outward from the face are identification clues. Prominent outward projection of the nose is especially noticeable.

the eyes and upper lip levels. Such a nose, if it also has a tendency to be broad, may be described as a flat nose lying close to the cheek level (see Figure 8-9).

The nose with medium projection tends to have a more symmetrical relationship with the eyes and mouth. In considering the length of the nose there are two factors to note: its facial length and the distance of its projection from the face.

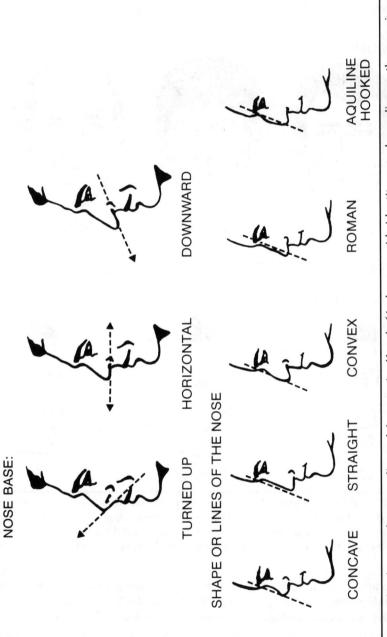

Figure 8-10. The shape and contour lines of the nose itself and of its base provide identity cues depending on the prominence or uniqueness of these lines. Illustrations of the three most common directions of the nose base line and of the five principal types of noses and their descriptive terms portray the usual identity clues.

BASE OF THE NOSE. If the base of the nose is turned up or down, as illustrated in Figure 8-10, the angle of departure is another identification clue. The tip of the nose, or its nostril base, has a direct bearing on its shape. Some noses come to a rather sharp point, others are rounded or even broad.

The shape of the base or tip of the nose affects the appearance of the nostrils, largely determining how much the nostrils show or to what extent they are hidden. Are the nostrils small or flared? Do they appear fully exposed to normal view? Is there any distortion in shape, or anything unusual about them?

SHAPE OF THE NOSE. The five most common nose shapes are illustrated in Figure 8-10. Descriptions help to provide a mental picture of the nose and related facial area. For example: the subject had a large hooked nose that dominated his face and almost completely hid its nostrils; or, the suspect had a very straight nose, perpendicular to the forehead line, and symmetrical in size, shape, and position with the other features. With many faces the line or shape of the nose is quite a prominent feature. Unusual shapes combined with unusual sizes, or pronounced shapes and prominent sizes, increase identification value.

The Mouth

The eyes and the mouth are probably the two most looked at facial features, as they are the principal media of expression and communication.

Since these two features greatly aid recognition, it may be reasonably assumed that they also may have a higher recall potential. On the other hand, attention directed to the mouth and eyes is primarily for the purposes of communicating and understanding expression, emotional reaction, and attitude, and not necessarily for encoding their physical characteristics within the memory.

CURVATURE AND SIZE. The curvature of the mouth, that is, its shape and contour, is an important factor of its appearance. Curvature, however, is variable because it is employed in the functions of speech and emotion. The configuration that persists as a permanent feature of the mouth may provide a cue for identification. Are the lines fairly straight, or bowed? Do they turn up or turn down at the corners? A very large or very small mouth is a significant identification factor. As in all facial features, any extreme in size or shape is readily identifiable because of its prominence (Figure 8-11).

THE LIPS. Descriptions of both upper and lower lips are included in descriptions of the mouth. One of the most frequently noted points of identification is the thickness or thinness of the lips.

Big lips tend to be full and thick. The upper and lower lips may vary

THE MOUTH:

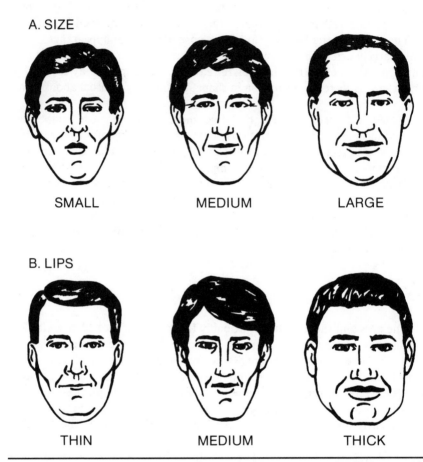

A. SIZE

SMALL   MEDIUM   LARGE

B. LIPS

THIN   MEDIUM   THICK

Figure 8-11.   Large and small mouths are identity clues, as indicated in row A. Their departure from the normal and their effect on the total view of the face create their identification values. Thin lips and thick lips (row B) have identity value for the same reasons.

considerably in size and fullness. Either lip may protrude beyond the other. Comparisons between the upper and lower lips of different subjects may invove a number of variations:

1.   Top lip medium; bottom lip full
2.   Both lips large, but bottom lip bigger
3.   Fat, chubby lower lip; top lip thinner
4.   Both lips thin, but lower lip a trifle wider

5. Bottom lip very wide compared with top lip
6. Top lip protruding; lower lip recessed backwards
7. Lower lip protruding; upper lip appears sunk backward between protruding lower lip and nose
8. Both lips well proportioned, but bottom lip slightly protrudes, and appears slightly fuller than top lip

Lips may also be well proportioned and evenly matched. Their shape may be comparatively straight, bowed, or somewhat irregular. Figure 8-11 contrasts thin, medium, and thick lips.

The expression of the lips should also be noted: a smile, a sneer, a pout. Do the lips droop? Are they tightly compressed? Are they relaxed, loose, and almost open? Are they fully open? Are the corners straight or do they turn up or turn down?

There are many characteristic terminologies used to classify types of lips, particularly those of a female: cupid, pouty, droopy, bloated, sexy, sticky, fat, cherub, and hot lips. But such cliches in themselves are not adequate descriptions, and one using them must precisely identify what is meant by the phrase by stipulating the characteristics that led to the use of the term.

The color of the lips can be significant. Are they full color, bloodless, purple, or anemic? With respect to women, the color of the lipstick can, of course, be altered. The extent of the coloring should be noted. Is it light or heavy, subdued or extreme?

As with other facial features, private investigators look for anything unusual, including such things as irregular lip structures, a cleft lip, scars, sores, or cancer. Symmetrical lips have no extreme characteristics, but their very symmetry or beauty in some instances may be an identifying factor.

MUSTACHES AND UPPER LIPS. The interrelationship of facial features should not be overlooked as possible identification factors. Whatever departs from reasonable symmetry or is out of proportion is usually noticeable. Any abnormally wide or narrow space between the nose and the mouth covered by the upper lip can be a peculiar identifying characteristic.

Both the width of the upper lip and its positioning relative to the lower lip may have identification significance (Figure 8-12). Sometimes the upper lip will protrude beyond the lower lip if the subject has buck teeth. On some faces the lower lip protrudes or extends further out than the upper lip. Extreme protrusion of either lip would be an identification factor. In this section we are primarily concerned with wide upper lips that show considerable space between the nose and the mouth.

Sometimes a wide space between the crest of the upper lip and the nose is made less apparent by the presence of a mustache. A mustache, of course, can easily be shaved off to alter the subject's appearance, although he may be

UPPER LIP:

LENGTH

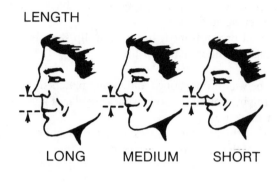

LONG   MEDIUM   SHORT

POSITION

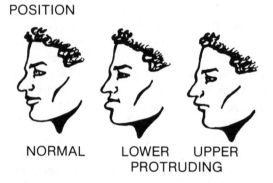

NORMAL   LOWER   UPPER
                      PROTRUDING

Figure 8-12. Lip identity cues include the space between the upper lip and the nose, the position of the lips in relation to each other, and their effect on the appearance of the lower portion of the face. The top group depicts variations in the length or width of the upper lip. The bottom group indicates the effect of lip protrusion on the appearance of the face. When either lip protrudes beyond the other it makes the face more readily identifiable.

reluctant to do so. In describing the human face one is well advised to concentrate mainly on the natural permanent features rather than on any addition that can be altered or removed; however, the mustache should not be ignored, as it could have a high identification value if it is of unusual style, shape, or size.

The principal styles of mustaches are illustrated in Figure 8-13. They include the special styles known as the handlebar, mandarin, and Kaiser. The ends of the handlebar mustache turn up like the handlebars of the bicycle, whereas in the mandarin mustache, the ends turn down, often to considerable

MUSTACHES:

SHORT-HAIRED

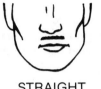 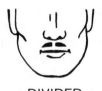

STRAIGHT CURVED DIVIDED

STUBBY

SQUARE ENDS POINTED ENDS ROUNDED ENDS

LONG-HAIRED

TURNED DOWN TURNED UP BUSHY

SPECIAL STYLES

HANDLEBAR MANDARIN KAISER

Figure 8-13. Mustaches come in many shapes, sizes, and styles. The twelve styles depicted cover most common types. The mustache is a removeable feature, but as long as it remains it can be one more identification clue.

length. The mandarin is frequently worn in combination with a tiny goatee just below the center crest of the lower lip. Many waxed mustaches have their ends twisted so that they extend almost straight out at both ends, sometimes nearly across the face. Even when the upper lip is largely covered, its width is indicated by the width of the mustache.

Each mustache style has its own features. Short-haired mustaches may be straight, curved, or divided in the center. Stubby mustaches may have square, pointed, or rounded ends. Long-haired mustaches may turn down or up, or present a bushy appearance. Any unique or extreme style of mustache is an identification clue, provided the subject does not shave it off or in some way drastically alter its appearance. If he is a wanted man, the mustache is likely to disappear. If he is not aware he is being investigated it will likely remain. The fact that a subject wears a mustache should always be noted, and the mustache described. Its description should include style, shape, length and color, and any other descriptive feature.

APPEARANCE AND CONDITION OF THE TEETH. The condition, coloration, and general appearance of the teeth can be important identification factors when they appear unusually good, abnormally bad, or in any way malformed. Missing, broken, and very discolored or irregular teeth are usually noticed. When the upper teeth jut out they are very noticeable.

Are the teeth irregular or symmetrical? Are they large, small, or medium-sized? Are the teeth out of proportion—a few large ones and a number of smaller ones? What is their general condition? Are they good teeth, or badly decayed? Are any broken or missing? Are there visible gold or gold-capped teeth? Does the subject wear braces to correct defects? What about the color? Are they white, yellow-stained, or dark brown? The color, shape, and size are all important. Are the teeth natural or false? Is the subject toothless, or nearly so? Do the teeth tend to fill the open mouth, or does a large portion of the upper or lower gum and root area show? Are the teeth badly worn, or do they appear in good condition? Are they readily seen or partially hidden?

Teeth may be described as long, broad, narrow, short, crowded, or with gaps between. Crooked and broken teeth are usually noticeable when they are in the front of the mouth. When there is nothing singular about the teeth, their color, size, and condition could best be described as normal.

Bone Structure of the Cheeks

Some people have prominent high cheekbones. Others are small-boned. When the cheekbones stand out enough to be noticed, this is clearly an identifying factor. The general appearance of the cheeks can be described as ruddy, full, sunken, thin, or fleshy. Cheek colors vary along with the general color of the face. They may be reddish, sallow, sickly yellowish, or artificially colored. The primary identifying factor is that of the prominent high cheekbones when they exist.

Ears and Earlobes

The usual ear shapes encountered are triangular, round, or rectangular (Figure 8-14). Ears are classified as large, medium, or small. Unusually large ears are readily noticeable. Extremely small ears may not be so obvious but may be sufficiently peculiar to attract attention. Irregularly shaped ears may attract attention.

Figure 8-14. These seven sketches outline the most common shapes of ears and earlobes. When the ears are clearly visible, their shape can become a contributing identity clue. Awareness of ear and lobe shapes is focused on extreme largeness or smallness.

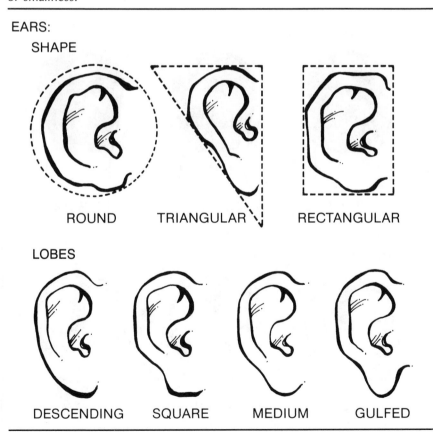

EARS:

SHAPE

ROUND   TRIANGULAR   RECTANGULAR

LOBES

DESCENDING   SQUARE   MEDIUM   GULFED

EARLOBES. The earlobes—the soft portion at the base of the ear—have their own identifying characteristics. They may be described as descending, square, rounded, or pointed, with a decided drop from the general ear-line. This condition is sometimes described as "gulfed" (Figure 8-14).

The lobes may be small, normal, or large. When earrings are worn, they should be briefly described even though they are a changeable item. Are the earrings small or large? Are they close to the ear or dangling? Have the ears been pierced? Briefly note the color, description, and apparent quality of the earrings.

Figure 8-15. Protruding ears generally provide the most obvious identity clue of this facial feature. Ears that project out and are largely separated from the head are noticeable and thereby become an identification factor. Ears that lie very close to the head also can become an identity clue. The positioning or setting of the ears on the head is a less noticeable clue, as illustrated in the bottom three sketches, which show ear location in relation to the eyes.

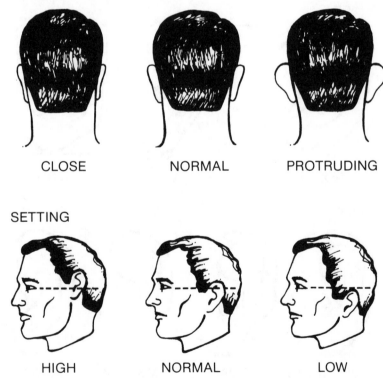

SEPARATION FROM HEAD:

CLOSE   NORMAL   PROTRUDING

SETTING

HIGH   NORMAL   LOW

PROTRUDING EARS. The closeness of the ears to the head or their separation outward from the head can be of significance, especially in the case of protruding ears. The further the ears stick out, the more obvious they become. They may be set almost against the head, be in a normal position neither close nor protruding, or they may protrude at various angles (Figure 8-15). The more outstanding the protrusion, the more significant from an identification viewpoint. Abnormally large and protruding ears have the highest identification value. Odd-shaped ears also attract attention and tend to be remembered.

SETTING OR POSITION OF EARS. The location or setting of the ears on the head, if in the normal position, will be directly to the rear of the eyes, with the eye level line running through the middle or slightly above the middle of the ears. Ears in a high position on the head will be just above the eye level line, or the imaginary line will pass through the ears approximately between them and the lobes. The position of ears set low on the head is located just below the eye level line (see Figure 8-15).

Chin and Jaw Characteristics

The size, shape, and appearance of the chin may have potential identification and recall value. Receding or jutting, protruding jaws are very noticeable and easily remembered. So are small pointed chins or large square-jawed chins.

A chin may be small and short, long and pointed, dimpled or cleft. The subject may have a double chin, or even what appears to be a triple one, as the flesh below the jaw multiplies itself. The hanging part of the double chin is also called the jowl, a term that is sometimes applied to the underjaw itself (Figure 8-16).

The jawline in some people is quite pronounced, clearly indicating the shape and structure of the jaw. There are actually two jaws or bony structures bordering the mouth: the relatively fixed upper jaw (the maxilla) and the hinged, moveable lower jaw (the mandible). The term jaw also includes the bones, muscles, and nerves surrounding the mouth that serve to open and close it. When the jaw is referred to in investigative descriptions, however, it is as a general rule the lower jaw, and any prominent features it might display.

Chin characteristics are directly related to those of the lower jaw. The chin or jaw may be heavy, square, round, protruding, receding, light, lean, delicate, large, small, long, short, pointed, and so on. The chin may be dimpled or cleft, or it may be double. The words medium and normal best describe the chin and lower jaw when they have a symmetrical and well-proportioned appearance in relation to the rest of the face, and lack any distinguishing identifying characteristic.

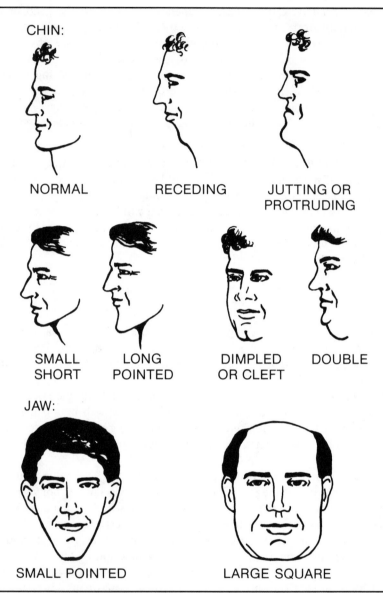

Figure 8-16. The nine sketches illustrate identification clues of the chin and lower jaw. At top, the receding and forward-jutting chins (or protruding lower jaw) are immediate attention factors, and therefore identity clues. The identification potential of short, long, dimpled, and double chins is indicated in the middle row. The bottom two facial views emphasize the contrast between the small jaw, pointed chin, and the large square jaw with corresponding chin size. Both are quite obvious identity factors.

BEARDS. Beards may or may not be an identification factor since they, too, can be removed, giving the overall facial appearance a distinctly different look. If, however, the subject is not aware of any reason to shave off his beard, or does not know he is the subject of an investigation, there is more likelihood that the beard will remain. Beards may be generally categorized as chin whiskers, goatees, and full beards (Figure 8-17).

Goatees tend to be pointed, or somewhat so, but sometimes they are squared or rounded. Full beards, which are considerably larger, may also be rounded, square-cut, or somewhat pointed. They may in some instances be double-pointed. Like special styles of mustaches, they have their different designs, such as the Vandyke and Henry VIII beards. Side whiskers are sometimes worn without the base of the chin itself being covered.

Does the color of the beard match the color of the hair or do the colors differ? When there is a marked difference in the color it may indicate that the subject is wearing a wig or that the hair has been dyed. The condition should be noted. Is the beard well groomed, neat, smart, and tidy? Is it large and bushy but well trimmed? Is it just bushy? Does it have a ruffled appearance? Is it uncombed, unwashed, unkempt?

Does the beard have any striking or unusual features? Is it very long? Is it short and stubby? Is it so extreme that it gives the appearance that the owner is hiding in the brush behind it? Anything unusual about the beard gives it identification value, assuming it is not shaved off or altered in any significant manner.

In face-to-face contact, private investigators should also note the length and condition of facial hair other than the mustache or beard. Is the subject clean-shaven or unshaven? Does he have a few day's growth, or apparently only one day's growth? Does the subject have sideburns? Are they close-cut and short, long, or mutton-chop? Is the quantity of the facial hair thin, sparse, thick, or bushy? Including the mustache and the beard, is the face pretty well covered by hair? Is it neat and well-trimmed or shaggy and unkempt?

Overall Facial Appearance

The total impact of the face on the observer includes both its features and qualities. The impression of the type of person the face reveals may be as strong as or stronger than the impression of individual features or of the overall facial appearance.

The impression the total facial view leaves will vary according to (1) the perceptive, cognitive, and memory retention capabilities of the observer; (2) the situation in which the viewing takes place; (3) the viewer's personal reaction to the observed face; (4) the situation under which the viewer is asked to recall, describe, and identify the face; and (5) the length of time elapsing between the

BEARS:

A. CHIN WHISKERS (GOATEES)

POINTED   SQUARED   ROUNDED

B. FULL BEARDS

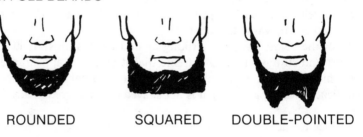

ROUNDED   SQUARED   DOUBLE-POINTED

C. SPECIAL STYLES

VANDYKE   HENRY VIII   SIDE WHISKERS

Figure 8-17. The nine styles of goatees (chin whiskers) and full beards indicate the variations of appearance created by facial hair and its identification value. The descriptive terms are helpful when making oral or written reports. The length or shortness of the beard is also an identification factor. Some beards are obviously far more bushy, untrimmed, and unkempt than those illustrated here.

initial observation and the attempted recall. The first three items have to do with the impression made at the time of the initial viewing, and the last two with the impression that remains at the time of recall.

Memory recall of a face once seen is considerably more difficult than memory recognition of a face that reappears and refreshes the memory as to its features and qualities. There are a number of factors that affect the accuracy or fallibility of recall. To begin with, how strong and accurate were the initial impressions? By what features or qualities or combination thereof was the face at least partially etched on the viewer's mind?

Three types of potential impressions should be noted: (1) the physical impression of the total appearance of the face; (2) the impression made by qualities or attributes registered on the face; and (3) the character impression indicated by the face.

TOTAL APPEARANCE. This is the impression left by the combined features—the face as an entity. Are the features well formed, balanced, and proportioned or not? Are there any extreme variations in facial interrelationships? Do one or more features stand out from the rest of the face? Is the face healthy and alive, or pale, ashen, pallid, wan, dull, or sickly? Is it wanting in tone quality or color intensity? Is it scarred or marked in any way?

With some faces it is the features in combination that make the impression. In others it may be the salience of certain features that are best remembered, although the majority of faces do not have outstanding single features. In such cases it is the total impact of the overall appearance that leaves the strongest impression on the viewer. Then the general shape of the face stands out as a primary clue.

FACIAL QUALITIES AND ATTRIBUTES. By quality we refer to any distinctive capacity or characteristic, including pleasantness or unpleasantness, attractiveness or unattractiveness, indifference or interest, or any aspect of facial appearance that impresses the viewer with a quality of appearance or character. By attributes we mean any distinctive trait, inherent characteristic, virtue or vice, revealed by the face such as kindness or cruelty, or honesty or deceit.

Expression is a quality to be noted, however, emotional expressions are temporary, and to recall one created by a past situation may be of little value. It may even be misleading. The face may not be wearing the same expression when confronted by an investigator as it did when it was formerly seen by a witness. Expressions that are present under pressure are not likely to be present under normal circumstances.

Only expressions of a more permanent nature that tend to be regularly seen on the subject's face have identification significance. Some faces maintain a more or less typical expression, such as a habitual tendency to smile or an almost permanent expression of a hateful attitude. Facial qualities or attributes may also lead to personality assessments.

   CHARACTER IMPRESSIONS. Witnesses sometimes have strong inner reactions to a subject's face. That reaction obviously will be affected by the attitude of the witness and the situation under which the face was seen. Sometimes personality and character traits are too readily, and even wrongly, attributed to facial appearance. On the other hand, faces that register strong character impressions with the witness may thereby provide some recognition value for the investigator. This identification is more subtle, however, than the physical description of features because it is more subjective.

   Some faces reveal little or nothing of importance. Others convey a great deal. A sinister face cannot be ignored, neither can an open, honest face. Some witnesses are able to recall certain identifiable facial qualities and character clues. Others have very fallible memories in this respect.

MEMORY FALLIBILITY

   Memory fallibility is a persistent investigative problem. Most private investigators find that a considerable amount of eyewitness testimony is not truly reliable as pertains either to what happened or how it happened. The memory is selective. Between what it remembers and what it does not remember there is a temptation on the part of some witnesses to attempt logically to fill in the missing elements, especially when they are questioned in detail.

   A good visual memory obviously provides a more accurate description than a poor visual memory. There are usually more witnesses with poor memories than there are witnesses with good memories. The ability of persons accurately to remember the basic facts about what they have seen varies a great deal. This applies also to descriptions of the face and general appearance.

   Many investigators believe that more accurate recall is more likely to be forthcoming in a narrative recital than in response to probing interrogations. The primary reason for this belief appears to be that the witness may be more likely to try to find answers in his memory that will comply with what the investigators want to know as indicated by their questions. This does not mean, however, that private investigators should not question the interviewee on the details of potential identification clues. Quite the contrary, such questions are essential for clarification of information and for searching for significant relevant details. The manner of questioning, however, is very important.

   Initial questions should be based upon the specific identification clues the witness referred to in his narrative descriptions. All questions should be so worded as not to influence the answers. Above all, it is most important studiously to avoid asking leading questions that might prompt corresponding answers.

We have already noted that interviewers often must jog the interviewee's memory by asking for information about potential identification clues. Capable interviewers will know how to do this without influencing the interviewee's answers. While the more accurate accounts may often be presented in the free narrative account of the witness, private investigators should always build on this foundation in moving into the question portion of the interview.

It is not always true, however, that the narrative account provides the most accurate recall. Some witnesses have great difficulty in narrating any adequate description of what they have seen. They need the help of the investigator's questions to help them provide significant clues or leads. They may know certain facts but have great difficulty in describing them clearly. In such cases the art of precise information-seeking questions that do not suggest their answers comes into full play.

NOTES

1. Bacon, F. From "Of friendship." *The Oxford dictionary of quotations.* 2nd ed. (London: Oxford University Press, 1964), 26.

2. Browne, T. From *Religio Medici. Dictionary of quotations.* (New York: Avenel Books, 1978), 217.

3. Montapert, A.A. *Distilled wisdom.* (Englewood Cliffs, N.J.: Prentice-Hall, 1964), 145.

4. Clifford, B.R., and Bull, R. *The psychology of person identification.* (Boston: Routledge & Kegan Paul, 1978), xii.

5. Ibid., 71.

6. Ibid., 12.

7. Ibid., 74.

8. Ibid., 8l.

Chapter 9

Nonfacial Identification Clues

"His identity presses upon me."

—John Keats[1]

"An identification of the defendant made by the victim prior to trial is admissible to corroborate a witness' testimony relative to identity. However, an extrajudicial identification cannot sustain a conviction in the absence of other evidence tending to connect the defendant with the offense."

—Charles W. Fricke and Arthur L. Alarcon[2]

Correct identification is a primary problem of investigation. In the last three chapters we have stressed the observation, description, and correct identification of persons and of related facts pertaining to happenings or situations that make them subjects of investigation. We have also discussed the abilities of private investigators, and witnesses in general, correctly to observe, describe, and identify.

Correct identification is not only essential for suspects or defendants involved in legal proceedings, but for persons placed under surveillance, missing persons who need to be found, and various other investigation situations involving people. Correct identification is also needed when properties are involved such as lost or stolen goods, vehicles, jewelry, and so on. Photographs and documents introduced into evidence must be identified and authenticated. To be able correctly to identify persons, vehicles, objects of evidence, manuscripts, photographs, and other items of substance, liquid, or gas, or any thing submitted in evidence is an essential requirement of investigation. Some of these needs will become more obvious in subsequent volumes. In this chapter we return to the problem of accurate observation, description, and identification of persons, with emphasis on the nonfacial identification clues.

Parts of the human body other than the face such as overall appearance and characteristics of bodily movements may also provide visual identification clues. Included in these categories are height, weight, build, posture, gait, gestures, mannerisms, unique movements, and physical incapacity. All of these combine in a significant number of variables within the populace. Some of them are of a general nature such as weight and height, which may be similar for a number of persons and therefore of themselves may not have strong identification value. In combination with other visual appearances, however, they may add to certainty of identification. Some variables are personal and unique, such as a peculiar manner of walking or other bodily mannerism or movement. We will begin our evaluation of nonfacial identification clues where we left off in the last chapter, with the neck.

BODILY FEATURES

The Neck

Unusually long or unusually short necks have identification value. So do very thick and heavy and very slender necks. The key descriptive features to look for are length and thickness and the prominence of the Adam's apple, the projection in front of the neck formed by the largest cartilage of the larynx. Some subjects have a very large Adam's apple.

The length of human necks ranges all the way from very short to very long. For people with a short neck, the head appears to be sitting almost on the shoulders. The very long neck is also noticeable, but varying in-between lengths have less identification value.

The size of the neck is primarily a matter of its thickness or thinness, indicated by the width across, or diameter. Both the diameter—the length of an imaginary straight line through the center of the neck—and the circumference—the distance around the neck—are important. A neck may be thin or very thin, of average or proportionate size, or thick or very thick.

One should also make note of any scars, birthmarks, moles or other skin colorations, injuries, or marks on the neck.

Shoulders

Very broad, narrow, or rounded shoulders are the most easily remembered and provide an identification clue. Shoulders may be broad, medium, or narrow; they may be round or square. In many cases one shoulder is lower than the other.

Carriage characteristics include straight, square, round, stooped, flat, and drooping shoulders, and hump-back, which condition rolls the shoulders forward and tends to bend the body forward to a greater or lesser degree.

Description of a subject's shoulders will usually combine both size and shape, such as broad square shoulders, narrow round shoulders, narrow stooped shoulders.

The Male Chest

The chest will resemble the shoulders in breadth. In other words, a broad chest and broad shoulders usually go together and a narrow chest accompanies narrow shoulders. The size of the male chest has the same three general classifications: broad, medium, and narrow. What may be more important is the shape of the chest. A man may be deep-chested, indicated by large expansion of the chest, the depth being measured from the front of the chest through to the backbone. Or a subject may be flat-chested with no visible expansion of the chest. Chest shapes usually fall within the general range of deep, flat, or medium. The medium chest is normal, being neither flat nor deep.

The phrase pigeon-chested (or pigeon-breasted if referring to a woman) is used to denote a deformity marked by a sharp projection of the sternum (the breastbone, or more specifically, the compound bone or cartilage connecting the ribs). A person who has had ricketts is usually pigeon-chested. The presence of hair should be noted if the chest is exposed.

Female Breasts

Female breasts are usually described as flat, medium, or heavy, also large or small. Sometimes the adjective "very" should be added to indicate unusual largeness or smallness. Female breasts may also appear to be well-formed and firm, or sagging and somewhat shapeless.

Arms

As always, extreme or unusual features carry identification value, such as arms that are extremely long or very short. The size of the arms is indicated by the measurement around them. Do they appear weak or strong? Are they muscular, fairly large, or fat? Or are they medium or thin?

If either arm is crippled or has been injured in any way that is obviously apparent, such condition is a key identification factor. When the skin of the arm is unclothed to any considerable length, one must be on the alert for needle marks, implying possible drug addiction, and any other scars or tattoos. Amputees, unless provided with a mechanical arm, have that unfortunate identification characteristic.

Wrists, Hands, and Fingers

The thickness and size of the wrist sometimes may be significant, but the hands and fingers are more important. Does the subject have powerful or weak hands? Are they large, even huge, or small or unusually small? Are the palms long and slender, or short and stubby? Are the hands fleshy or bony? Are they freckled or hairy, or both? Are they marked with the brown spots that come with age? Are there any markings or scars on the hands?

Are the fingers long and slender or short and stubby? Fingers are usually long or short, thick or thin, blunt or tapered. Are there any deformities? What is the condition of the fingernails? Are they quite normal, clean, and trimmed? Or are they dirty and uncared for? If lady's fingers, are they polished and colored (what shade)?

Are there abnormal finger characteristics, such as extra fingers (a rarity), or badly scarred or damaged fingers (more common)? Are any fingers or fingernails missing or partly missing? Are the fingers affected by arthritis? Are they gnarled or twisted, or apparently strong and straight? Are there heavy tobacco stains, or other markings or scars on the fingers? All these questions are asked with respect to the different features to indicate clues that can help in describing and identifying a subject.

Shape of the Abdomen

The abdomen lies between the thorax and the pelvis. The thorax refers to that part of the body between the neck and the abdomen in which are located the heart, lungs, and esophagus. The abdomen is located just below the lungs and contains the stomach, intestines, and liver.

The abdomen may be flat or protruding. It may be somewhat sunken or bulging. It may bulge up under the ribs, or lower down at the waist. It may appear rounded or sagging. The basic categories of abdomens are flat, medium (normal), or protruding (bulging). Descriptions, however, often need to be more detailed as well as more descriptive.

In everyday language the abdomen is sometimes erroneously called the stomach. Men with large abdomens are frequently said to have big stomachs. A typical description of a man with a large abdomen should run something like this: the subject had an unusually large abdomen, bulging high up under the ribs and protruding far out from the waistline.

Hips and Waist

The waist is the small part of the body (at least it should be) around which a person wears a belt. It comes just above the hips. Waist descriptions are usually small, medium, or large. The waist length is designated as long, normal, or short.

The hips project from each side of the body just below the waist. They may be large or small, broad or narrow. Extremely large hips provide a strong identification clue.

Legs

There are four general categories of leg length: long, short, medium (normal), or unequal (one leg shorter than the other). Again, it is the extremely long legs and the extremely short legs that are the most readily noticeable.

With respect to size and general appearance, legs may be muscular, thick, fat, medium, slender, or extremely thin. Legs may be reasonably normal in shape, they may be knock-kneed or bowed. Women's legs are often designated as heavy or slender. They may also be described as shapely or skinny.

Leg movements often provide identification clues. Characteristic gaits are noted later, but a minor or major crippled condition may be noticeable. Does the subject limp in any way? Amputations are usually very evident. Any unusual appearance or movement of the legs should be noted.

Feet

Big or small feet are usually readily detectable in personal contacts or in the examination of complete footprints. There are times when the size of the foot enters into the overall identification description. Length as well as its bigness is a factor and is often related to a person's overall size. Sometimes, however, a foot may be very narrow and still quite long. A foot is designated as short, medium, or long; thin, medium, or wide. Some people are pigeon-toed (the toes turn in), or flat-footed (arch is flattened and entire sole tends to rest on the ground). Occasionally, a subject may be wearing a platform shoe on one foot to equalize the length of an injured or deformed leg with the normal one. If the subject is wearing open-front sandals, are any toes fully or partially missing? Foot deformities should be indicated, such as a club foot (somewhat twisted out of position from birth).

BODILY CHARACTERISTICS

Posture and Bearing

In describing the general bearing and posture of the subject one should note if he stands straight and erect or if his posture is stooped or slumped.

Is there anything striking or unusual about the subject's carriage or bearing? Bearing, deportment, demeanor, mien, and carriage all carry somewhat similar connotations with varying emphasis. They describe qualities or characteristics of a person's appearance and in some cases, personality. Bearing is the most general term, referring to how one holds or carries oneself. Deportment deals more with actions and behavior, and demeanor with the attitude of the individual. Mien embraces both bearing and demeanor.

Carriage more specifically refers to posture in standing and walking. Is the subject's head held high and erect, or to the side or forward? Are the arms held tight or loose at the sides? Is the general posture erect, or nearly so, or is it slouched or stooped over?

Body Build and Physical Structure

The overall physical appearance of the subject is often a matter of significance. One may be stocky, another stout, and still another obese. Physical form may be large and heavy or small and slim. Obviously, there are many variations within generalized classifications. A subject's health may strikingly affect the general appearance of the body. Between a slight build and a large or even huge build there is a great range of physical size and strength.

The male build falls under six basic classifications (Figure 9-1), ranging from the very small to the very large, from the very short to the very tall, and from the very slim to the very fat or obese. Any extreme in the size and shape of the human body is an important identification factor. Variations in height are not indicated in the six basic physical structures or body builds. There are three possible extremes with respect to the human figure: in height (tall or short), in size (huge or tiny), and in shape (obese or slim). All private investigators should be able to differentiate among builds as indicated in Figure 9-1.

CHANGEABLE ITEMS

Clothing, footwear, and jewelry are changeable items. They are not part of the physical person, do not represent permanent features, and cannot be relied on to provide continuous identification value. Such items, however,

THE MALE BUILD:

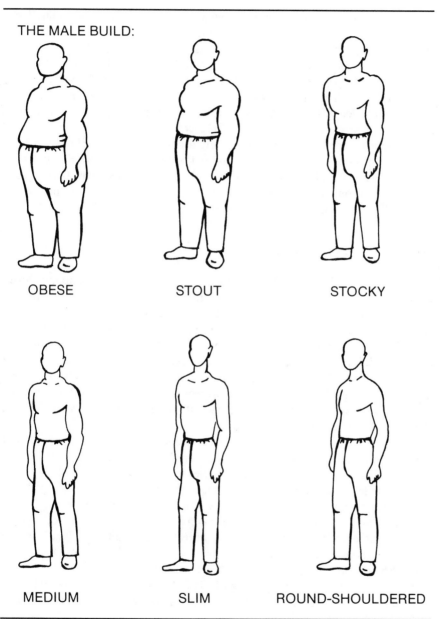

OBESE   STOUT   STOCKY

MEDIUM   SLIM   ROUND-SHOULDERED

Figure 9-1.   Any extreme or readily noticeable variations of the male build are helpful identity clues. Six basic types of builds are illustrated. Numerous other variations occur depending on the subject's height, weight, health, posture, and largeness or smallness of bone structure. A subject's posture may be erect, stooped, slumping, or bent over.

should not be ignored, as they may have a bearing in cases of immediate identification. They may also suggest the subject's preferred style and quality of
clothing and jewelry. In some cases the jewelry might be stolen.

If the investigation is to cover any significant period of time, the most
important factor is the type of clothes the subject usually wears—their style,
color, and care. If the investigation begins soon after a subject has been seen
wearing specified garments, and the subject is not aware of the investigation,
clothing can prove to be a helpful identification factor.

When torn bits of clothing are left at the scene of a crime, the later
matching of those scraps with the torn area of the suspect's clothing is a very
valuable piece of evidence. Consequently, clothes may play a role both in subject identification and in finding evidence that links a suspect's clothing to the
victim. This is a form of transfer evidence.

Type and Style of Clothing

The type and style of clothing may indicate the subject's economic level,
employment, or professional or business status. It may also reveal the subject's
taste, that is, personal preference regarding his clothing. Does he wear business
suits, sportswear, casual clothes, uniforms, or odd garments? Does he wear
high fashion clothing, or is he poorly or slovenly dressed? Is the style of
clothing modern, conservative, trend-setting, flashy, rag-bag, or old-fashioned?
Is he scantily clad? If the subject is a woman, is she wearing a dress, slacks,
suit, blouse and skirt, or jeans? Such information would be helpful to private
investigators searching for a missing person if friends or relatives could describe
the type of clothing the subject prefers.

Another point of possible importance concerns favorite or predominant
colors indicated in the subject's dress pattern. What care does the subject apparently take of his clothes? Are the clothes pressed, clean, and well kept? Or
are they soiled, messy, or even dirty? Does the subject appear prim and well
groomed, or sloppy and indifferent toward personal appearance?

Are there any oddities about the manner of dress? Does the clothing appear too large or too small? Does the subject wear bright, subdued, or odd
colors? Is there patchwork at the elbows, knees, or elsewhere? Observable
details should be noted, for there is no way of knowing what item of clothing
may prove significant as the investigation progresses. The styles and colors of
ties, shirts, skirts, blouses, trousers, jackets, suits, and even socks or stock-
ings might become significant.

Headgear and Footwear

If headgear is worn, it should be described. What color is it? If a man's
hat, what style is it—fedora, stetson, derby, straw hat, or what? Are there or-

naments or feathers on it? If it is a cap, beret, or other form of flexible covering, does it have special marks, decorations, or other characteristics? If it is
a woman's hat, what is its size, shape, decoration, and color?

What type of footwear is the subject wearing? Are the shoes or boots
expensive, well polished, and dressy, or are they cheaper shoes, oxfords,
loafers, tennis shoes, or other types? Are the shoes well worn, with heels worn
down, and other signs of wear or tear? Colors as well as types of shoes should
be noted.

Jewelry

Jewelry can be an important identification clue, especially if it is conspicuous or apparently very costly. People who love jewelry often persist in
wearing it. Although it is a changeable item, sometimes a certain piece is worn
quite regularly. What is the nature and style of the jewelry worn? Where is
it worn? Is it real or costume? Is it flashy or in excellent taste? Is there an
overabundance of many kinds of jewelry—rings, bracelets, necklaces, brooches,
and chains?

MULTIPLICITY OF IDENTIFICATION CLUES

It is certainly obvious by now that there are many potential identification clues that can help in locating and identifying a person. No individual
description would begin to encompass all the facial and body appearance clues
noted in this chapter. One can never predetermine which of them may stand
out in a given individual and under what circumstances they might do so. But
the knowledge of facial and body features that might provide identification
can greatly assist in the perceptive observation of identifiable characteristics.
This knowledge is an advantage that most private investigators have over the
lay witness.

It is easy to see why many potential identification factors are never
noticed or considered by lay witnesses to an event, injury, accident, or crime.
Fortunately, there are some who are observant enough to detect the more outstanding peculiarities of the subject's facial or bodily appearance, provided
they were close enough to have observed him clearly. The greater the number
of identification clues private investigators are able to obtain, the greater the
likelihood of recognizing the subject when and if he is found. In face-to-face
conversation or in a close-up observation of a subject's face through a telephoto
or zoom lens, private investigators will surely be aware of a greater number
of significant identification clues than the ordinary witness would recognize.

Whenever private investigators are hired to search for a missing person,
heir, victim of a kidnapping or other crime, person who has skipped town,

one whose present whereabouts is unknown, long-lost relative, or wanted person, they should first obtain as complete a description as possible, including every known identification feature or characteristic.

Identification by Photograph

Photographs are probably the most effective means of obtaining a visual description, provided they are comparatively recent and give a close-up view of the subject's face. They are the best evidence of personal appearance next to seeing the subject himself. Whenever possible, private investigators should arm themselves with at least one good photograph, especially when the subject is an individual they have never personally seen. Sometimes private investigators may be fortunate enough to examine several photos of the subject, including action snapshots or even moving pictures. This gives them the decided advantage of actually viewing basic identification characteristics. These, together with a reasonably accurate verbal description, provide the best basis for identification.

In criminal cases when a suspect has been seen, an initial brief verbal description, including clothing worn, is flashed over police radios and later through the news media. This is followed by gathering all possible descriptive data and potential identification clues. Police identification experts compile all known information, including photographs when available, or a police artist's drawing of the face as described by witnesses or victim. An alternative of such a drawing is to create a mock-up of the face selected from commercial composites of facial features.

There are several different types of photo-kits available for the construction of facial resemblances. The kits provide a significant variety of photographs, usually of the six principal facial features—eyes, mouth, nose, chin, forehead, and forehead hair. To construct a resemblance, parts are picked out that appear to be like the features of the face they wish to construct. Glasses, mustache, and beard can be added as necessary. Victims and witnesses are also called in to look at the police department's catalogue of mug shots, or to identify a suspect from a police lineup.

BODY MOVEMENTS

Body movements include style of walking and running, arm and hand movements, gestures, and mannerisms or peculiarities of movement or action. The body "talks" by the manner in which it moves.

Gait

Gait may be defined as the manner of walking, running, or moving on foot. It includes the subject's walking style, the measure of his stride, the angle of his footsteps, the speed or slowness of his walk, and other features that could be identifiable. Among the gait characteristics to be noted are:

1. Pattern of feet movements on the ground or sidewalk. Do the feet turn outward at a noticeable angle as the subject walks, or do they move fairly straight forward?
2. Movement of the legs. This pattern involves the length of the subject's stride, the tempo or speed with which he walks — swiftly, slowly, or at an average pace — and the steadiness of his walk. Does he take long steps or short steps? Are his leg movements rapid or slow? Is he steady on his feet? Does he walk at an even or uneven pace? Is his walking tempo regular or irregular? Is his overall gait aggressive and vigorous, sturdy and resolute, slow but sure, or shaky and hesitant?
3. Movement of the arms. What is the arc or degree of the arm swing as he walks? Is there considerable arm movement or very little? Do the arms move with strength and vigor or are they listless or noticeably inactive?
4. Position of head and body while walking. Is the head bent forward or held erect or at some recognizable tilt or angle? Is the trunk of the body bent forward, or does the subject walk upright? The tendency to tilt the body somewhat forward increases for many subjects as the tempo of the walk increases. Some people waddle as they walk, swaying from side to side.
5. Grace or rhythm. Some people walk with considerable grace and rhythm. If a subject walks with smooth movement, that should be noted.
6. Irregularities of walk pattern. Irregularities may be due to physical problems or defects, or to poor health or advanced age. Does the subject limp or use a cane or crutches? Is there erratic physical movement accompanying his walk? Does the subject in any way favor one leg over the other?

Going by a verbal description of the subject's gait is sometimes more difficult for private investigators than observing its peculiarities firsthand. The observer can, however, use precise descriptive words as indicative of the subject's movements. It is accuracy of description, not flowery language that counts. A subject's gait that is described as either rapid, hesitant, erratic, or slow is clearly understood. It should not be difficult to indicate whether the subject took long or short strides, or to state that he walked rapidly with a keen sense of direction, or slowly with frequent stops. In fact, word pictures can create a vision of the subject in another's mind. For example: "The subject strode vigorously down the street with ample lusty strides, arms swinging and breathing deeply, resolute and unyielding"; or the subject "labored as he walked slowly and feebly, shuffling along with his arms hanging listlessly at his sides."

The manner of a subject's walk can play an important role in his identification. It is clearly a recognition factor when shadowing or tailing a subject. Some subjects have a peculiarity about their gait that quickly identifies them. A description of this feature can help others identify the person.

Most people are very consistent in their gait, which shows itself in their walking speed, length of stride, and angle of steps or footprints. Such consistency makes identification more likely.

Gestures

Gestures are primarily motions of the body, hands, or limbs made as means of expression. They accompany an idea, an emotion, or opinion and are used to support an argument or assertion. One of their most frequent uses is to emphasize a fact or point of view. Gestures can be identification clues in close-up situations such as interviews and interrogations, or in public appearances. For example, public speakers and clergymen are noted for their frequent use of gestures to drive home or to illustrate their points. Gestures are also used as means to describe. Most people gesture in their conversations along with their comments, discussions, and particularly in descriptions.

The identification value of a gesture is found in its individuality. It is native to the personality of the subject. Some people have peculiar, frequently used, natural gestures that are quite distinctive and spontaneously expressed. These could involve the hands, head, shoulders, or whole body. Anyone knowing such an individual could well include such gestures as a reliable identification clue.

Any bodily movement that is a spontaneous expression of personality tends to remain fairly constant and stable regardless of changing conditions or situations in which the subject might find himself.

Personal Habits Expressed in a Physical Way

Some mannerisms, body movements, and actions are inherent in the individual's daily life and activities. They may be revealed in the way one eats, sits, stands, relaxes, laughs, or smiles. They may involve the manner in which one goes places — openly, secretly, stealthily.

The subject's health, or lack of it, is also frequently accompanied by related physical actions. Some diseases cause trembling, shaking, or jerking. Others affect a person's ability to maneuver, or partially incapacitate a person in one way or another. Disease also affects the muscular movements of the body. Both physical appearance and physical action are visual indications of the general health or illness of the subject. Drug addiction and alcoholism ravage the human body, often with significant physical signs.

Voice Recognition

Every human voice is different. Even voices that are similar have their distinguishing, recognizable characteristics. Most of us quickly recognize relatives and friends who call us over the telephone. Their voices have been heard frequently and have indelibly impressed themselves on our minds. Many believe that voiceprint identification can rival fingerprint identification for investigative purposes.

In many situations a voice may be heard only once, or several times in a disguised form, before a victim or witness attempts to identify it. When there is very little previous familiarity with the subject's voice, or when the only contact has been when it was disguised, identification from human memory becomes difficult.

There are, however, many voice characteristics that have recognition value. The tonal quality created by interplay of speech components—the mouth cavity, vocal cords, nasal and pharyngeal cavities, soft palate, and so on—and the manner in which the articulators are used—tongue, lips, teeth, and jaw—is different for each person. These vocal cords and cavities produce a combination of sound-wave frequencies resulting in the strikingly individualistic sound of each person's voice. There is very little chance that two individuals would have identical vocal cords and cavities, and that their voice articulators would function in identically the same way.

VOICE IDENTIFICATION PROBLEMS. The recognition of a voice by a victim or other witness is a matter of evidential information. The credibility of that recognition in a court of law will be determined by the factfinding jury or judge, as the case may be. Some people appear able to recognize a voice they have heard before under threatening circumstances. The ability of a victim or witnesses to detect a suspect's voice characteristics, independent of spectrographic analysis, can prove helpful in identification, but such ability is not exact, and may or may not be correct. If it is corroborated by other evidence its probability is strengthened.

Voice disguise often becomes a major identification problem in criminal cases. Most criminals when making voice contact with the victim or threatened victim—such as kidnappers making their ransom demands, or strange voices issuing a bomb threat — will disguise, or attempt to disguise, their voices to avoid detection. Thus a natural voice may not be so easily recognized at a later time. A disguised voice that would not fool a spectrograph machine might avoid detection by a person who has never heard it before.

Laboratory tests have shown that when a voice that originally speaks in its normal pitch is subsequently disguised, recognition is reduced by nearly twenty percent. But in real life situations the disguised voice is usually heard first. In other words, the victim or intended victim never hears the suspect's normal voice, hearing it only in its disguised form. When the victim is asked to identify it undisguised, the normal tones and pitch of the voice may not be recognizable.

A second factor affecting the ability to identify a specific voice relates to the number of voices initially heard. It is far more difficult to pick one voice out of a group of strange voices and recognize it at a later time than it is to identify a solitary voice that was previously heard. The greater the number of voices heard at the scene of an accident, crime, or other injury or event, the more difficult it is specifically to identify any one of them.

There are also two factors that affect voice identification capability: the length of time during which one hears the voice and the time interval elapsing between initial and subsequent hearings. The longer the original speech is heard, the better the chances that voice characteristics are mentally recognized and recorded. Consequently, later voice recognition capability is improved, all other factors being equal. The briefer the period of the initial hearing, the less likelihood there is of subsequent voice recognition unless there was something very unusual about the brief vocal impact. Whispered speech has far less identification potential than normal speech.

As the time interval between the initial hearing and the subsequent hearing lengthens, the fading memory tends to reduce one's ability to identify the voice. The shorter the time between the initial and subsequent hearings of the same voice, the easier it is to recognize it.

SPECTROGRAPHIC ANALYSIS.   The spectrographic analysis of voices is a modern technique used in matching and detecting identical voices. It can be used whenever there is a recording of the suspect's voice while making a ransom demand, threat, obscene call, or whatever, which can later be compared with the voices of apprehended suspects in custody to match and identify the real suspect. The spectrograph considers the frequency, volume, and timing of the suspect's speech, and can penetrate any disguise.

Spectrographic voice analysis is an electronic scaning of speech samples that produces voiceprints that visibly display speech characteristics. Computer technology is now being employed in an effort to establish automatic procedures for voice identification. The possibility of perfecting effective equipment to the point where voiceprint becomes a recognized forensic tool implies a potential new weapon in the war against crime.

VOICEPRINTS. Spectrograms or voiceprints are visible printouts of voice-identifying characteristics. Voices like fingerprints are personally identifiable, and like individual fingerprints, are not duplicated by other persons.

Some experts question the claim that voiceprint identification is as reliable as fingerprint identification. Others are equally certain of its reliability. Still others contend that the aural detections of the human ear are still more effective and reliable than the visual prints of the spectrograph. The courts, at this writing, are not yet all agreed. Meanwhile, the voiceprint process continues to undergo research and development.

When admissible in court, voiceprints can be used by either the prosecution or the defense. They are not generally accepted as proof of guilt, but only as establishing a likelihood of guilt. Voiceprints are often more acceptable as means of removing a suspect from suspicion than of making positive identification. They can be used in the pretrial investigative stage of criminal cases provided there is an intelligible recorded speech sample to be compared with the suspect's speech.

VOICE RECOGNITION CAPABILITIES OF THE HUMAN EAR. Actually the human ear is the only perfected detector of speech characteristics. When the aural input is not impaired by defective hearing, the ear has remarkable voice-detection capabilities.

The individual characteristics of a person's voice are recognition clues. These characteristics include: tonal quality, resonance, pitch, energy, enunciation, pronunciation, loudness or softness, presence or absence of breathy sounds, accent, and other personal peculiarities.

Typical recognizable voice characteristics are highlighted in the following series of questions. Is it high-pitched or low-pitched? Is it shrill, squeaky, nasal, raspy, tense, relaxed, loud, soft, mellow, or deep? Is the subject's speech slurred, obscuring his pronounciation, or does he enunciate clearly? Does he stutter or lisp? Is his speech hesitant, or does he speak freely, even fluently? Are there any words or phrases that he repeats so frequently that they become a characteristic of his conversation?

Private investigators who seek to remember a subject's voice concentrate on any and all individual identifying qualities of his speech. They note its quality. Is the voice clear, resonant and warm, or cold, harsh, grating, or piercing? When the subject speaks, is he pleasant to listen to or irritating to the ear? If a man, does he speak in a deep base voice, in a baritone or tenor range, or in a very high, even falsetto range? Does the lady speak in a soprano or alto range? Is the voice intense or casual? What peculiarities can be detected in the subject's manner of speaking? Does he speak in a staccato manner, with words cut short and even disconnected? Does he mumble, slur, or mouth his words? How effectively does he use his articulators? What expression is repeated frequently?

The subject's speech characteristics go beyond its physical qualities. Does the subject speak like an educated or uneducated person? What kind of a social environment does his speech reflect? Does he have a foreign accent? If so, what is the subject's original language? Is his speech accompanied by few or many gestures? Is there any gesture that continually persists? Do any of his words identify his background, ethnic origin, area of residence, or associates? Does he use any peculiar or provincial expressions? Is he profane?

Voice identification is more difficult than mere voice recognition. How dependable is the identification of persons by the manner in which they speak? The answer varies according to the problem circumstances noted above and the ability of the individual witness or victim to describe a voice previously heard.

OBSERVATION, DESCRIPTION, AND IDENTIFICATION

The interrelationship of observation, description, and identification becomes apparent in the investigative process. All three capabilities are vital to the investigator's success. There are many investigative connotations of observation: to watch, perceive, notice, take note of facts, ascertain, discern, heed, be attentive to, inspect, see and listen to, and in any other way to develop the faculties of a keen observer of persons, information, occurrences, and all forms of evidence. Observation is the investigator's life in surveillance and undercover activities, and in personal interviews and interrogations.

Description provides a mental image of a scene, person, emotion, situation, object, impression, document, or event, and its characteristic features. The ability to describe is vitally important to private investigators. What they see and hear they mentally record, but only what they describe do they communicate to others. Thus private investigators are both observers and describers. To describe is to represent or picture by words, or to give an account of what has been observed. Private investigators describe when they relate, recount, picture, identify, or narrate, and when they write investigative reports or give testimony in a court of law.

Description is an important element in establishing the identity of persons, vehicles, properties, objects of evidence, documents, and stolen goods. By the very nature of the profession, private investigators are often required to identify a person, place, object, or other item that needs to be authenticated or verified as being the same as claimed. To do so they must be able to describe what they have observed.

Powers of Description

Description is the companion ability of observation. Other people can never understand what we have seen unless we are able to describe it to them clearly and accurately. Able description is the acid test of observation. All successful private investigators become adept at describing their observations.

Investigative descriptions should be as realistic and accurate as possible, with no flowery additions. It is the real and accurate view that private investigators are to describe and hearers are to receive.

Description is a means of identifying. For example, if a victim accurately describes his attacker, that description is of great value to the police or private investigators as they search for the culprit. While private investigators frequently describe people and things, they are constantly asking witnesses to describe to them what and who they saw.

Vague descriptions are of no value. Generalizations include too many people in the same category to be of any specific help. Such descriptions as "tall," "short," "average build," "medium size" have no real identification value until they have added to them specific clues that help single a subject out from the crowd. Lay persons tend to describe in more or less obscure generalities, and to overwork words like average, medium, and normal. Only descriptions that provide significant, specific, identifiable characteristics or features are helpful to investigators.

Two basic descriptive problems confront private investigators. They are (1) how does the private investigator describe a subject to someone who has never seen that subject, so effectively that he will be able to identify the subject when he actually sees him? and (2) how can the private investigator get another person — witness, victim, associate, friend, or relative — to describe a specific individual so accurately that the private investigator can identify that individual when he sees him or her? These same questions can be asked about the descriptions of scenes, vehicles, objects, or other items of evidence.

The ability to describe and the ability to help others describe without suggesting any foreign elements of description to them are extremely valuable private investigation capabilities. In helping others in their descriptions the private investigator searches for specific descriptive answers without asking leading or suggestive questions. The "how" of this kind of questioning is considered in the volume that deals with the art of interviewing.

Successful private investigators continually seek to improve their powers of observation and description. Persistence in training, practice, and experience can develop their perception until they are quite capable of encompassing an astonishing amount of significant detail within a brief span of observation. It can also increase the capabilities of memory and recall, which provide the basis for subsequent reasonably clear and accurate descriptions.

NOTES

1. Keats, J. From *Letters,* "To Benjamin Bailey." *The Oxford dictionary of quotations.* 2nd ed. (London: Oxford University Press, 1964), 290.

2. Fricke, C.W. *California criminal law.* Revised by A.L. Alarcon (Los Angeles: Legal Book Corp., 1977), 298.

Chapter 10

Report Writing

"The report should be clear, brief accurate, complete, and have continuity. It should be sequentially organized and objective."
—Kevin P. O'Brien and Robert C. Sullivan[1]

"Ability to prepare a clear, factual, accurate and impartial report is one of the investigator's most important professional tools. The report is the merchandise the investigator sells. It is therefore up to him to package it attractively, and to prepare it in a competent and professional manner."
—Arthur Liebers and Carl Vollmer[2]

The ability to write a clear, factual, accurate, and complete report is one of the investigator's most important skills. Reports contain the results of the investigator's efforts, and make known to the client or employer what the investigator found out regarding the facts of the matter under investigation. Field notes are the report's original source materials, and include notebook, photographic, documentary, and any other records of information or findings.

Investigative reports should be both accurate and complete. Weston and Wells indicate, "An investigative report is complete when it contains all the pertinent information available to the investigator after a diligent performance of the assigned task. It is accurate when the facts are reported as found, observed, or measured, or exactly as told to the investigator."[3]

Every investigator is largely judged by the quality of the report he writes. A report is the finished product that advertises his efficiency or inefficiency to clients, supervisors, and employers, not to mention attorneys and courts. Anthony Golec notes that as the final product of the investigation, the report "reflects back to a great extent on the manner in which that final product was obtained. A sloppy or incoherent investigation report will indicate that the investigation was conducted in a shoddy or haphazard manner."[4] Obviously, a satisfactory report can only be based on a satisfactory investigation. Unfortunately, a very satisfactory investigation can be completely ruined by a totally unacceptable report.

A memorandum from the instructional material of the U.S. Army Military Police School refers to the importance of "the ability to report accurately and completely the relevant facts developed during an investigation." The memorandum further states, "No investigation is properly completed until it has been adequately reported. No investigation, no matter how well done, can be any better than the written report. The report, as the end product of every investigation, tells the reader the manner in which the investigation was conducted; the report is the basis for the evaluation of the quality of the investigation. A poor report gives a poor indication of the investigation, no matter how thorough the investigation."[5]

Reports vary in length and number according to the scope of the investigation. Some may involve only a single activity such as interviewing a witness. Others may involve a series of activities and findings. Extensive investigations generally have a series of reports—the initial or preliminary report, followed by a series of progressive or status reports throughout the investigation, ending with a final summarizing and closing report.

In some complex assignments more than one investigator is involved. Each operative submits a report pertaining to his phase of the investigation; the reports of all investigators are coordinated by the one writing the complete, final summary for the client.

To cover all the aspects and principles of good report writing would require an entire volume, but the importance of this subject creates the necessity at least to outline certain essential guidelines. The principles outlined here should stimulate the private investigator who needs further help in developing report writing capabilities to research more definitive information on a matter so vital to his career.

PURPOSE OF REPORT

The investigative report has one primary purpose—to inform. It should be written with such clarity and accuracy that the one for whom it is intended will understand all the facts presented, including interviews conducted, records obtained, relevant statements made by interviewees, photographs, personal observations, and every other bit of material evidence obtained from any person, document, record, impression, object, or other item of evidence.

PREPARATION FOR WRITING THE REPORT

Prior preparation is essential to good report writing. This calls for careful study and logical organization of field notes. Notes should be analyzed, selected, and arranged according to the chronological order of investigative events and the importance of the information.

All of the evidential facts a report will contain should be thought through with emphasis on the principal findings. Notes can then be organized so that each important fact is presented with its supporting data listed below it. It is advisable to do this in outline form, to ensure logical organization and completeness of the report.

In short, preparation to write a report includes:

1. Planning
2. Reviewing and arranging field notes
3. Gathering together all the evidence
   a. Information received from others
   b. Facts established
   c. Supporting and verifying data
4. Organizing material in logical order
5. Determining the format
6. Outlining the report
   a. Order of presentation
   b. Major facts to be emphasized
   c. Subdivisions such as supporting materials and descriptions
   d. Details to be included
7. Arranging field notes according to outline

The main body of the report should seek to answer the following questions:

- What happened? — nature and results of the occurrence
- Where did it happen? — location of the occurrence
- When did it happen? — time of the occurrence
- Who made it happen? — persons involved.
- How did it happen? — modus operandi
- Why did it happen? — intent, negligence, or chance of the occurrence

The answers to the above questions should be specific, clear, precise, factual, and accurate.

Factual evidence obtained should be verified whenever possible with relevant photographs, documents, casts, molds, sketches, maps, diagrams, blueprints, slides, and moving pictures, depending on which of these the investigation requires. All such demonstrative evidence should be referenced in the report. The report should reveal both the investigator's activities and the total factual results obtained from his investigation.

Seven Essential Qualities of a Good Report

Every written investigative report should have the following qualities.

ACCURACY.   Reported information should be accurate. All data should conform to the facts as exactly as possible. When the private investigator has taken the trouble to verify his facts, he establishes the accuracy of his report. Inaccuracies and careless errors are inexcusable, and can render a report useless.

CLARITY.   The use of simple direct language is the heart of clarity. Reports should be easily understood, distinct, lucid, and free from ambiguity, obscurity, and confusion.

BREVITY.   Reports should be concise and to the point without leaving out relevant details. The writer should stick to the facts without rambling. There should be no conflict, however, between the completeness of the report and its brevity. Shorter explanations usually tend to be more accurate because they have less verbiage.

COMPLETENESS.   No item of importance should be left out, no relevant fact should be left to the imagination. The private investigator should not expect the reader to fill in any of the details. He should assume that the reader's only knowledge of the investigation will come from his report. All sources of reported information should be shown. Only complete reports inform completely.

FACTUALITY.   A factual report is objective, based on evidence rather than conjectures and conclusions. It states the facts of the investigation and its findings, without fancy, assumption, opinion, or sentiment, as they have been found, observed, or disclosed to the investigator.

IMPARTIALITY.   A report should be free from all bias. Everything relevant should be included regardless of which side it favors, or what it proves or disproves. A report is an unprejudiced summation of the facts.

SPECIFICITY.   Reports should be precisely formulated so that they explicitly present the evidential information. They should state the facts and describe the situations with careful exactness, never varying from the truth, resorting to generalities, or bogging down in vagueness and wordiness. Specific reports are exact, explicit, plain, clearly developed without disguised or hidden meanings.

Some Fundamentals of Report Writing

Keeping the above seven qualities in mind, every report should take into consideration the following fundamentals.

LOGIC. Logical sequence is fundamental to good report writing. The facts should be presented in chronological order as they occurred, in narrative form, or in the order of their importance to the investigation, with the most important finding first, together with its supporting data. The logical order should be so clearly evident that the reader can follow the report step by step without having constantly to refer to other sections to piece the information together.

TREATMENT OF NAMES. The full name of each person mentioned in the report should be typed or hand printed in capital letters in full. If a person has no middle name but only a middle initial, the word "only" should be written in parentheses following the initial: JOHN W.(ONLY) MARCUS, or the letters IO can be used to indicate initial only. If a person has no middle name, the initials NMN indicate no middle name: SUSAN (NMN) KELLY. When an individual has an alias or a nickname this is indicated by the use of the letters AKA, meaning also known as, for example, WILLIAM BARNES MOSS (AKA) WILD BILL MOOSE. Whenever it is necessary to write about a person whose name or identity is not yet known, the term "unidentified person" is used.

There are some variations among private investigation agencies relative to the manner in which proper names are treated in reports. Some agencies want the last name first, followed by the first name and middle initial. The last name is usually the only name typed in capital letters, with the other names and initials appearing in lower case letters. Women's names are often designated as Mrs. or Miss. Use of this format would result in: ATKINSON, Miss Susana.

IDENTIFICATION DATA. Identification data should be accurate and complete. Personal names should be spelled correctly; addresses should be specific, including street number, apartment or suite number, the name of the town, city, or subdivision in which the street is located, and the ZIP code. Both business and residential addresses should be recorded. If the current address is temporary, the private investigator should determine if there is a permanent address at which the party can be reached. All telephone numbers, area codes, and extension numbers should be listed.

Dates should be specific. Many agencies prefer listing the day of the month first, followed by the first three letters of the month, and the last two numbers of the year: 15 Jan. 83. Whenever several days are involved, the beginning and ending day of the period should be listed with a dash between them: 10-15 Jan. 83.

Sex of the person can be indicated by the letter M for male, and F for female. Race can be designated by the use of letters as follows: W for white (Caucasian, including Latin and Mexican); B for black, C for Chinese; J for Japanese; I for American Indian; and x for unknown. Agencies often provide a further breakdown of racial designations, using additional capital letters for that purpose.

Age should be based on the nearest birthday. When age has to be estimated, a spread of a few years should be indicated since it is just an estimate. Occupation should be given, or indicate if person is unemployed.

LEGIBILITY.   Reports should be neat, legible, and easily read as well as easily understood. A report that is not readable is useless. If the private investigator cannot write or handprint clearly, he should learn to type his reports. If numerous corrections have been made, the report should be rewritten or retyped. Once it has been submitted the private investigator does not have a second chance to correct bad impressions it might make. It is far better to make it professional and legibile the first time.

CONFIDENTIALITY.   The report belongs to the client (or the private investigator's employer). It is confidential, not open to the public, and only the client has the legal right to determine who will have access to it.

JUDGMENT.   Writing formulas are helpful, but they are no substitute for sound judgment. Good judgment and common sense are fundamental to all investigative activities, including report writing. A memorandum of the U.S. Army Military Police School suggests the four-S formula: shortness, simplicity, strength, and sincerity. Shortness is achieved by avoiding "needless words and needless information"; simplicity is a matter of using "short words, short sentences, and short paragraphs"; strength is found in "concrete specific words" and in "active verbs"; sincerity is achieved by being human.[6]

FORMAT

Reports differ in many ways—in type, simplicity or complexity, the number of items to be included, the extent of the investigation to be covered, and its nature and purpose.

Law-enforcement agencies have reports for different purposes such as arrests, accidents, complaints, and criminal offenses such as theft and homicide. Some agencies have specific forms they want their investigators to use in writing up reports. In such cases, the private investigator is restricted to an established outline. Usually these forms are departmentalized or categorized with preestablished areas for specific kinds of information. There may be blocked out spaces for some information, a section for listing or checking off descriptive characteristics, and always an area in which to write the narrative or chronological outline of events. Forms tend toward uniformity in reporting procedures; and ensure that the necessary items of information will be noted and not overlooked. They also tend to encourage brief and specific reporting.

Some forms, however, are too limited to allow for complete descriptions as well as associated information. If they do not request some items of pertinent information, evidential facts may be omitted. Some suggest that the report writer use additional pages to complete the report. Standardized forms in some cases increase the number of handwritten reports that would ordinarily have been typewritten. For these and other reasons, some agencies do not use detailed forms. Instead, they provide guidelines and then allow their agents leeway in the preparation of reports. The format that appears below is primarily for the benefit of private investigators who have no preprinted agency forms to use for reporting the results of their investigations.

Obviously, the nature and extent of the investigation determine the content and length of the report. Reporting a statement from a single witness or preparing a log of a one-day surveillance is quite a different matter from writing a comprehensive report describing several interviews, investigative procedures, and findings.

Comprehensive Chronological or Narrative Reports

The following is not the only acceptable format, but it indicates suggested organization and contents of a comprehensive report. This outline can be adapted to shorter forms as needed, and also to the needs of an extensive investigation. The main division of the report and its supplements are identified first. This is followed by a more detailed discussion of the basic data that should appear in each section. Most comprehensive reports, with some agency variations, include the following parts:

1. Title page (the face sheet)
2. Body of the report
3. Summary of key findings
4. Lists of evidential data
   a. Names of witnesses and all other persons interviewed
   b. Written or recorded statements made by witnesses and others

    c. Relevant photographs taken, and their subject matter
    d. Items of evidence
    e. Documents and/or exhibits

TITLE PAGE. This is the first page that identifies the investigation and the investigator(s), and provides a nutshell synopsis of the findings as an introduction. Specific items that should appear on this title page include:

1. Case identification or file number, or name of the assignment
2. Date of the report and the time period covered by it
3. Status of the investigative report: initial, progress, final, and so on (reports are usually chronologically numbered and tied in with the case number)
4. Subject persons or subject matter of the report (identification of person, company, or event being investigated)
5. Type of case: civil tort; criminal offense, specific statement of precise wrong or crime, or other purpose of the report
6. Names, aliases, addresses, and telephone numbers of principal persons named in the report (if there is a long list of such persons, only the principal parties are listed on the first page)
7. A synopsis paragraph summarizing the essence of the investigation results
8. Name(s) and signature(s) of the investigator(s) submitting the report, and the city or place where the report was prepared.

The title page identifies the report for quick orientation and contains a capsule statement that is completely detailed in the body of the report.

BODY OF THE REPORT. This main section details all relevant evidential information obtained during the investigation. It is totally factual and contains no subjective material. It is set forth in logical sequence with a separate paragraph detailing and describing each person, fact, object, or point of significance.

1. Introductory paragraph states the reason and authority for the investigation, and information on which the investigation was based
2. Details are presented in sentences and paragraphs arranged in logical sequence (usually chronological, or in narrative)
    a. Full but concise account of all evidential facts
    b. All available answers to the six key questions: What? Where? When? Who? Why? and How?
    c. What the investigator did and found, who he interviewed, what information he obtained, how he obtained it

The primary objective of the body of the report is to inform completely and accurately regarding the precise findings of the investigation. The secondary objective is to inform so clearly and factually that the reader will readily understand all evidential information disclosed.

The report should be written with the basic assumption that the reader knows nothing about the investigation and its findings other than what is presented in the report. It should be further assumed that after reading the report the reader will know the facts of the investigation and its results as surely as the investigator knows them. Any report that attains these objectives is well written.

SUMMARY. The summary should list and reference the relevant and material verified findings of the investigation, including all evidence obtained and uncovered and all written statements made by witnesses and others. Opinions, recommendations, or conclusions of the investigator should be kept separate from the list of items of evidence.

Different policies exist among investigative agencies: some do not solicit the opinions of the investigator, others want his evaluation and impressions relative to the persons he interviewed and his observations. Obviously, the more experienced the investigator, the more valuable are his conclusions and evaluations.

The investigator's observations can be included after the summary and with a proper identifying subheading. They are mainly concerned with such matters as:

1. Firsthand observations and experience with respect to persons interviewed and circumstances, facts, or evidence encountered
2. Opinions as to the credibility and reliability of the statements made by witnesses and others interviewed
3. Suggestions relative to additional investigative procedures or follow-up activities that might prove helpful, including leads and clues that have not yet been investigated

The investigator must show a factual basis and reasons for his evaluations, opinions, and recommendations. There is no assurance, of course, that his conclusions will be accepted by his employer, supervisor, or client. A statement as to what remains to be done in following up other leads or clues can either be included here or under an additional subheading.

LISTS OF EVIDENTIAL DATA. It is very valuable for reference to have lists in one section of the report to bring together evidential data that are scattered throughout the body of the report.

1. The list of names should include all persons investigated, interviewed, contacted, shadowed, tailed, or otherwise involved in the investigation, with identification as to their relationship to the assignment. In addition, full names, home and business addresses, ZIP codes, and telephone numbers should be given.

2. The list of written or recorded statements should indicate who made the statement, where, when, and how. Reference can be made to the paragraph in the body of the report that contains the verbatim statement, or all statements can be repeated here grouped together. This depends on the preference of the private investigator or the agency to which he is reporting. It should be recognized that the more numerous the persons or statements involved, the more need there is for the supplemental list.

3. A list of photographs related to the investigation and submitted with the report quickly identifies the private investigator's visual documentation of evidence. When photographs are numerous, a separate listing should be included together with identification of their subject matter. If there are only one or two pictures they can be included at the head of the list of documentation exhibits. All items in the documentation and photograph lists should be attached to or included in the envelope along with the report. The separate subheading should include photographs, color slides, and moving pictures if they apply.

4. The list of items of evidence includes tangible objects of physical evidence, impressions, liquids, debris, or anything else found at a scene, on a person, in a vehicle, or in the premises of a suspect or a victim.

5. A list of documentation exhibits, when applicable, includes the identification of papers, letters, business or private documents, public documents, or certified copies thereof that are submitted along with the report, together with illustrative documents such as maps, diagrams, and sketches.

STATEMENT OF WHAT REMAINS TO BE DONE. Periodic progress reports should indicate what remains to be done to complete the investigation. Even in a final report it may be that the investigator has uncovered some clues that have not yet been investigated, and these should be indicated. This type of statement would come at the end of the report after the completed divisions as outlined above. It will not be needed in all reports, but when appropriate it should be included, unless the private investigator's agency has another way in which they prefer this sort of information to be handled.

This statement may include names of persons who have not previously been referred to because they have not been involved in the investigations to date. Their addresses and telephone numbers should be given here (not with the list of names with which the body of the report deals) so that other investigators can follow up these additional leads. Only the names of persons not yet interviewed or investigated should be listed. If the information is complete and the firm so desires, some other investigator could start with the data provided in this section. It could also prove a starting point for subsequent investigations should the case be reopened at a later time.

THE PROCESS OF REPORT WRITING

Report writing transforms the private investigator's field notes into an organized, logical presentation of the facts of evidence obtained and recorded during the investigation. Having completed the seven-step preparation for report writing described earlier, the private investigator with his materials organized, his outline before him, and his notes arranged in the proper sequence is ready to begin writing.

Selecting the Right Words

The art of report writing begins with the use of the right words to express meaning clearly. The private investigator is not expected to be a professional writer, but he is expected to become a professional report writer. As such he will need to consider the meaning of words and their correct use in accurately presenting his information.

Familiar words are quickly understood by the reader. Clear, short words are the easiest to understand, and they are the best to use in report writing. To choke a reader's comprehension with long, unfamiliar words makes no sense when the aim is for him to understand the facts of the report.

The private investigator should say as much as is necessary to state the facts and convey the information, but he must try not to use even one unnecessary word. Unnecessary words only help to hide the facts. When one word is sufficient to convey meaning, there is no point in adding a number of extra ones along with it. Information completely communicated in a few words is the most quickly received and easily remembered.

Verbs are the most important words in the report. They are the action words that describe what actually happened. Verbs in their right place make a sentence come alive and help to make meanings crystal clear.

The report writer should never use a word the meaning of which he does not know. He may think it means something that it does not mean. Whenever in doubt, he should use the dictionary to find the precise meaning and proper spelling. A good dictionary is a writer's most effective aid. *Roget's Thesaurus of English Words and Phrases* can also be helpful in the selection and understanding of the most appropriate words for a specific need. Reference books on grammar and English made simple can also prove helpful to those who have problems with construction of sentences.

Sentences Convey Thoughts

Plain words and short sentences are the most effective in keeping communication clear and to the point. Every sentence should convey a complete thought.

The longer the sentence the more difficult it is to make it clear. Confusing sentences are the primary problems in most confusing reports. The private investigator should always keep in mind that he is writing to convey information, not to create a literary gem. On the other hand, he will want his report to show unity, coherence, and effective use of English.

Sentences should vary in length. Longer sentences can be interspersed between a number of shorter ones. Variation is more interesting than sameness. The part of the sentence that is to be emphasized should appear at the beginning or end of the sentence rather than in the middle. What is important in each sentence should stand out.

Reports generally are written in the third person and usually in the past tense, that is, they talk about other persons and events already past. The important exception is when the private investigator takes down other persons' statements. These are recorded and reported verbatim in the first person as direct quotations of the individuals making them. Personal observations are also recorded in the first person.

Even when writing in the third person, it is best to use the active voice rather than the passive voice. It is better to write: "The evidence shows that JAMES (NMN) MONROE wrote the document," than: "According to the evidence the document was written by JAMES (NMN) MONROE." The active verb "wrote" is stronger than the passive "was written by."

Direct phrasing is always forceful. Compare the following:

1. There are four elements necessary to establish the crime of embezzlement that every investigator ought to know.
2. Every investigator ought to know the four elements of the crime of embezzlement.

Note the greater strength of the second sentence. The more direct the route of a sentence, the greater its impact.

Paragraphs Focus Attention

Paragraphs are composed of sentences on the same subject, fact of evidence, or matter of information. As a general rule, each separate fact or item should have its own paragraph. This makes points of evidence stand out more clearly.

Paragraphs make a report more readable; no one likes to read a page of solid unbroken writing. Paragraphs provide mental rest periods for the reader at the end of which he can pause before considering another item of information.

Paragraphs too, will vary in length, and while it is best to keep them short, paragraphs of only one sentence should be avoided. It is easier to think step by step than to try to encompass everything in one grand sweep. Thus each paragraph should be a distinct and complete unit, factual and reasonably short and to the point. When explanations are necessary, they sometimes follow in another paragraph if their addition to the factual paragraph would make it too lengthy.

Paragraphs should be arranged in logical order so that each one prepares the reader for the next. The reader should be able to sense this progression. The general trend is to write reports in chronological order, but sometimes they are written according to how the information was developed. They should always be written so that the reader will not have to try to piece events together. All good reports have introductory and summary paragraphs.

Some private investigators follow the practice of numbering paragraphs and lettering subdivisions. Thus by merely citing the paragraph number they can refer the reader to the item they wish to discuss. This also makes for easier reference when a report is being considered in the courtroom.

Paragraphs have unity when every sentence deals with the relevant subject matter, with possibly a transition sentence when needed. They are coherent when each sentence logically leads to the next. They have emphasis when the fact or information they are meant to record stands out prominently.

EDITING THE REPORT

No report is complete without editing. When it has been completely written, it should be read and even reread to make sure that it says what it is meant to say in a manner that can be clearly understood. The careful editing of the complete draft of the report is important to (1) check on factual accuracy, correctness, and clarity of contents; (2) the logical organization and presentation of the information; and (3) composition, spelling, and grammar. We believe it is better if the private investigator does not attempt to check on all three of these categories in one reading.

We recommend instead that the private investigator read his report aloud the first time to listen to how it sounds, and to concentrate on the correctness and accuracy of its contents. He should then rewrite as necessary to restate more accurately, add omitted items of information, or to delete incorrect or nonfactual statements. When the private investigator is satisfied with the accuracy, clarity, and completeness of the report's contents, he is ready for the second stage of editing.

The report is reread with a critical look at its organization and its logical, or illogical, sequence. The order can be rearranged as necessary to conform to the chronology or narrative account. Subsidiary supporting data should immediately follow the major facts and information they support. The private investigator should make sure the report is so put together that a reader will not have to jump back and forth to piece together the sequence of events.

A third reading should follow to concentrate on mechanical construction. This means making certain that sentences and paragraphs are put together correctly, that grammar is acceptable, and that names and words are spelled correctly. The three-reading editing process is not as complicated as it sounds. In fact, it is quite simple, as it enables the private investigator to concentrate on one basic objective at a time. Although some are able to make all three adjustments in one reading, the inexperienced private investigator will find the triple reading helpful in developing expertise in the art of report writing.

Having completed editing, the report should be accurate and clear; well organized, and easily read and understood; grammatically correct and free of misspelled words or other structural inaccuracies.

REPORT WRITING SKILL COMES WITH PRACTICE

Good report writing is not a mysterious talent hidden away in a few exceptional minds. Its principles can be learned by anyone; its skills can be developed through practice and experience. During the first year of their career, private investigators should concentrate their improvement efforts in two aspects of investigation: the art of interviewing and report writing. Expertise in these two vital areas will go a long way toward creating an expert investigator.

Most private investigators have found that rewriting is the key to learning to write clearly and concisely. The more proficient they become, the less rewriting becomes necessary.

Space does not permit consideration of the different types of reports used by security or police officers. In addition, each type of investigative agency, government or private, will conform to its own reporting responsibilities and procedures. The basic principles set forth in this chapter should provide practical guidelines for all types of report writing. Fuqua and Wilson state, "Learning to write a good report is probably the most valuable thing an investigator can do. When an investigation is completed, the only visible result is the report."[7] All this adds up to the fact that good investigations plus good reports make a person a capable investigator who will always be in demand.

NOTES

1. O'Brien, K.P., and Sullivan, R.C. *Criminalistics: theory and practice.* 3rd ed. (Boston: Allyn & Bacon, 1980), 285.

2. Liebers, A., and Vollmer, C. *The investigator's handbook.* (New York: Arco Publishing Co., 1954), 16.

3. Weston, P.B., and Wells, K.M. *Criminal investigation. Basic perspectives.* (Englewood Cliffs, N.J.: Prentice-Hall, 1980), 263.

4. Golec, A.M. *Techniques of legal investigation.* (Springfield, Ill.: Charles C Thomas, Publisher, 1976), 33.

5. U.S. Army Military Police School. *Criminal investigation methods.* Subcourse MP 92, lesson 4.

6. Ibid.

7. Fuqua, P., and Wilson, J.V. *Security investigator's handbook.* (Houston: Gulf Publishing Co., 1979), 76.

Bibliography

Akin, R.H. *The Private Investigator's Basic Manual.* Springfield, Ill.: Charles
C Thomas Publisher, 1976.

Bentham, J. *The Theory of Legislation.* Dobbs Ferry, N.Y.: Oceana Publications, 1975.

Blackwell, G. *The Private Investigator.* Woburn, Mass.: Butterworth Publishers,
1979.

Blalock, J. *Civil Liability of Law Enforcement Officers.* Springfield, Ill.: Charles
C Thomas Publisher, 1974.

Bouza, A.V. *Police Intelligence: The Operations of an Investigative Unit.* New
York: AMS Press, 1976.

Caesar, G. *Incredible Detective: The Biography of William J. Burns.* Englewood
Cliffs, N.J.: Prentice-Hall, 1968.

Clifford, B.R., and Bull, R. *The Psychology of Person Identification.* Boston:
Routledge & Kegan Paul, 1978.

Conway, J.V.P. *Evidential Documents.* Springfield, Ill.: Charles C Thomas
Publisher, 1959.

Dulles, A. *The Craft of Intelligence.* Westport, Conn.: Greenwood Press, 1977.

Equity. *CBRC Law Summaries.* 5th ed. Gardena, Calif.: Law Distributors, Inc.,
1972.

Fricke, C.W. *California Criminal Law.* 11th ed. Los Angeles: Legal Book Corp.,
1977.

Fuqua, P., and Wilson, J.V. *Security Investigator's Handbook.* Houston: Gulf
Publishing Co., 1979.

Golec, A.M. *Techniques of Legal Investigation*. Springfield, Ill.: Charles C Thomas Publisher, 1976.

Gribble, L. *Stories of Famous Detectives*. London: Arthur Baker, 1963.

Hall, J.W., Jr. *Search and Seizure*. Rochester, N.Y.: Lawyers Co-operative Publishing Co., 1982.

Henderson, J.A., Jr., and Pearson, R.N. *The Torts Process*. Boston: Little, Brown & Co., 1975.

Hormachea, C.R. *Sourcebook in Criminalistics*. Reston, Va.: Reston Publishing Co., 1974.

Johannsen, H. *The International Dictionary of Business*. Englewood Cliffs, N.J.: Prentice-Hall 1981.

Jones, D.A. *Crime and Criminal Responsibility*. Chicago: Nelson-Hall, 1978.

Kenny, J.P., and More, H.W., Jr. *Principles of Investigation*. St. Paul: West Publishing Co., 1979.

Lavine, S.A. *Allan Pinkerton, America's First Private Eye*. New York: Dodd, Mead & Co., 1963.

Leonard, V.A. *The Police Detective Function*. Springfield, Ill.: Charles C Thomas Publisher, 1970.

Lotz, W. *A Handbook for Spies*. New York: Harper & Row, 1980.

McCaghy, C.H. *Crime in American Society*. New York: Macmillian Publishing Co., 1980.

Mettler, G.B. *Criminal Investigation*. Boston: Holbrook Press, 1977.

Miller, A.R. *The Assault on Privacy: Computers, Data Banks, and Dossiers*. Ann Arbor: University of Michigan Press, 1971.

National Automobile Dealers Association. *Summary of Motor Vehicle Laws and Regulations*. Covina, Calif.: Don Christy, Publisher, 1982.

Nolan, F. *Jay, J. Armes, Investigator*. New York: Macmillan Publishing Co., 1976.

Nordland, R. *Names and Numbers: A Journalist's Guide to the most needful Information Sources and Contacts*. New York: John Wiley & Sons, 1978.

O'Hara, C.E. *Fundamentals of Criminal Investigation*. Springfield, Ill.: Charles C Thomas Publisher, 1973.

O'Reilly, J.T. *Federal Information Disclosure: Procedures, Forms and the Law*. 2 vols. Colorado Springs: Shepard's/McGraw-Hill, 1982.

O'Toole, G. *The private sector: Private Spies, Rent-a-Cops, and the Police-Industrial Complex*. New York: W.W. Norton & Co., 1978.

Pinkerton, A. *Criminal Reminiscences and Detective Sketches*. 1879. Reprint. New York: Garret Press, 1969.

Ransom, H.R. *The Intelligence Establishment*. Cambridge: Harvard University Press, 1970.

Sulnick, RH. *Civil Litigation and the Police*. Springfield, Ill.: Charles C Thomas Publisher, 1976.

von Block, B.W. *Super-Detective: The Many Lives of Tom Ponzi, Europe's Master Investigator,* Chicago: Playboy Press, 1972.

Wasserman, P. *Encyclopedia of Business Information Sources.* 4th ed. Detroit: Gale Research Co., 1980.

Weston, P.B., and Wells, K.M. *Criminal Investigation: Basic Perspectives.* 3rd ed. Englewood Cliffs, N.J.: Prentice-Hall, 1980.

Wilson, J.Q. *The Investigators: Managing FBI and Narcotics Agents.* New York: Basic Books, 1978.

Witkin, B.E. *Summary of California Law.* 4 vols. San Francisco: Bancroft-Whitney Co., 1974.

Index

Teeth, 176
Telephone company records, 120–121
Telex directory, 132
Theory of Legislation, The (Bentham), 10
Thomas Grocery Register, 126
Thomas Register of American Manufacturers, 126
Tort, as violation of legal duty, 14–15
Tort, defined, 12
Tort feaser, 14, 16
Tort law, 12–14
Torts and crimes, 15–17
Trade associations, 128
Traffic safety information, 125
Training Key, The, 51
Trespass, 14
Truman, Harry S, 57–58
TRW Credit Data, 121

Uniform Commercial Code, 128, 133
United States: Americans employed
    abroad, 111; American companies
    abroad, 128
U.S. Army Military Police School,
    206, 210
U.S. Attorney General, 117
U.S. Border Patrol, 113
U.S. Bureau of Alcohol, Tobacco and
    Firearms, 112, 117
U.S. Bureau of Customs, 111–112
U.S. Bureau of Narcotics, 117
U.S. Bureau of Prisons, 117
U.S. Central Intelligence Agency
    (CIA), 57, 111
U.S. Civil Service Commission, 116
U.S. Coast Guard, 116, 117
U.S. Constitution, 18, 26
U.S. Drug Enforcement Administration, 8, 117
U.S. Federal Bureau of Investigation
    (FBI), 8, 31, 112, 117
U.S. Federal Information Center
    (FIC), 130

U.S. Federal Records Center, 116
U.S. Federal Reserve System, 127
U.S. Food and Drug Administration, 113
U.S. Government Organization Manual,
    118–119
U.S. Health and Human Services Department, 113–115
U.S. Immigration and Naturalization Service, 112–113, 117
U.S. Internal Revenue Service (IRS), 112
U.S. Justice Department, 31, 112–113
U.S. Labor Department, 113
U.S. Post Office, 4, 113
U.S. president, threats to, 112
U.S. Public Health Service, 113–114
U.S. Secret Service, 57, 112
U.S. Selective Service System, 116
U.S. Social Security Administration,
    114–115
U.S. State Department, 111
U.S. Supreme Court, 61
U.S. Transportation Department,
    115–116
U.S. Treasury Department, 111–112
Uniworld, 128

Vanderbilt, Cornelius, Jr., 77
Vital statistics bureaus, 103–104
Vocational rehabilitation agencies, 107
Voice identification, 199–202
Voiceprints, 201

Weston, P. B., and K. M. Wells, 25,
    205
Whitkin, B. E., 17, 28
Who Knows What, 132
Who Owns Whom (Dun and
    Bradstreet), 127
Who's Who, 132
Wills, 22–23
Wilson, James Q., 90, 91, 92, 93
Workers' compensation, federal, 113
World Guide to Trade Associations, 128